The Lear Diaries

By the same author

Salem to Moscow –
An Actor's Odyssey

The Lear Diaries

The story of the Royal National
Theatre's productions of Shakespeare's
Richard III and *King Lear*

BRIAN COX

*Online,
July 2021*

Methuen

Dedicated to the cast and crew of the Royal National Theatre's
world tour of *Richard III* and *King Lear*

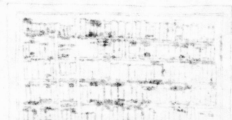

For her invaluable help in taming and editing these diaries,
to Georgina Allen, much thanks

First published in Great Britain in 1992
by Methuen London
an imprint of Reed Consumer Books Ltd
Michelin House, 81 Fulham Road, London SW3 6RB
and Auckland, Melbourne, Singapore and Toronto

A CIP catalogue record for this book is available from the British Library

ISBN 0 413 64970 9

Set in 11½/13½ pt Ehrhardt by CentraCet
Printed by Clays Ltd, St Ives plc

CONTENTS

v

List of Illustrations

King Lear

1. Brian Cox in rehearsal with director Deborah Warner.
   (Photo: Neil Libbert)
2. Susan Engel as Goneril, Richard Bremmer as Albany (left) and Ian
   McKellen as the Earl of Kent (centre). Act 1, scene 1. Brian Cox as
   Lear: 'To thine and Albany's issues be this perpetual.'
   (Photo: Neil Libbert)
3. Eve Matheson as Cordelia (left), Susan Engel as Goneril (top), Clare
   Higgins as Regan (right). Act 1, scene 1. Brian Cox as Lear: 'Know
   that we have divided in three our kingdom.' (Photo: Neil Libbert)
4. Brian Cox as Lear to David Bradley as his Fool (right): 'Blow, winds,
   and crack your cheeks!' Act 3, scene 2 (Photo: Neil Libbert)
5. Brian Cox as Lear to Eve Matheson as Cordelia: 'We two alone will
   sing like birds i'th'cage.' Act 5, scene 3. (Photo: Neil Libbert)
6. Hakeem Kae-Kazim as Edmund (left) to Derek Hutchinson as Edgar:
   'Parted you in good terms? Found you no displeasure in him by word
   nor countenance?' Act 1, scene 2. (Photo: Neil Libbert)
7. Ian McKellen as the Earl of Kent (left) to Brian Cox as Lear: 'Your
   son and daughter found this trespass worth the shame which here it
   suffers.' Act 2, scene 4. (Photo: Neil Libbert)
8. David Bradley as the Fool: 'Then shall the realm of Albion come to
   great confusion.' Act 3, scene 2. (Photo: Neil Libbert)
9. Ian McKellen as Kent (kneeling), David Bradley as Fool (back right).
   Brian Cox as Lear: 'Let the great Gods, that keep this dreadful
   pudder o'er our heads, find out their enemies now.' Act 3, scene 2.
   (Photo: Neil Libbert)
10. Brian Cox as Lear to Peter Jeffrey as Gloucester (front): 'When we
    are born, we cry that we are come to this great stage of fools.' Act 4,
    scene 6. (Photo: Neil Libbert)

11. Joyce Redman as Duchess of York (background left), Richard Eyre (Director) and Clare Higgins as Queen Elizabeth rehearsing the 'Greenham Common' scene where the queens confront Richard. Act 4, scene 4. (Photo: John Haynes)
12. Richard O'Callaghan as Ratcliffe (left), Phil McKee as a soldier (right). Ian McKellen as Richard: 'Come, bustle, bustle; caparison my horse.' Act 5, scene 3. (Photo: John Haynes)
13. Ian McKellen as Richard: 'I do the wrong, and first begin to brawl.' Act 1, scene 3. (Photo: John Haynes)
14. Sam Beazley as the body of King Henry VI (foreground). Eve Matheson as Lady Anne: 'Set down, set down your honorable load.' Act 1, scene 2. (Photo: John Haynes)
15. Ian McKellen as Richard (right) to Brian Cox as Buckingham: 'My other self, my counsel's consistory, my oracle, my prophet! my dear cousin.' Act 2, scene 2. (Photo: John Haynes)
16. Brian Cox as Buckingham in Act 1, scene 3. (Photo: John Haynes)
17. The army. (Photo: John Haynes)

On the road:
18. Brian Cox as Lear with David Bradley as the Fool in the background.
19. Eating sushi in Tokyo.
20. As Lawrence of Arabia in Egypt. (Photo: Helene Kvale)
21. Leading a masterclass in Paris. (Photo: Caroline Rose)
22. Members of the company for *King Lear* and *Richard III*:
    Back row (left to right): Richard Simpson, Sam Beazley, Jane Suffling, Nicholas Blane, Hakeem Kae-Kazim, Fiona Bardsley, Ian McKellen, John Caulfield
    Third row: David Collings, Bruce Purchase, Peter Sullivan, Susan Engel, Peter Jeffrey, Deborah Warner, David Bradley, Mark Strong, Richard Bremmer, David Milling
    Second row: Richard O'Callaghan, Phil McKee, Joyce Redman, Clare Higgins, Brian Cox, Richard Eyre, Eve Matheson, Hildegard Bechtler
    Front row: Colin Hurley, Helene Kvale, Derek Hutchinson, Cordelia Monsey, Stephen Marchant, Bob Crowley, Wendy Fitt
    (Photo: John Haynes)

The cast-list for the London opening of KING LEAR

In order of speaking		*Understudy*
The Earl of Kent	**Ian McKellen**	*Richard Simpson*
The Earl of Gloucester	**Peter Jeffrey**	*Bruce Purchase*
Edmund, *bastard son to Gloucester*	**Hakeem Kae-Kazim**	*Mark Strong*
Lear, King of Britain	**Brian Cox**	*David Bradley*
Goneril, *eldest daughter to Lear*	**Susan Engel**	*Clare Higgins*
Regan, *second daughter to Lear*	**Clare Higgins**	*Eve Matheson*
Cordelia, *youngest daughter to Lear*	**Eve Matheson**	*Helene Kvale*
The Duke of Albany, *Goneril's husband*	**Richard Bremmer**	*David Collings*
The Duke of Cornwall, *Regan's husband*	**Richard O'Callaghan**	*Peter Sullivan*
The Duke of Burgundy	**Mark Strong**	*Stephen Marchant*
The King of France	**David Collings**	*Nicholas Blane*
Edgar, *elder son to Gloucester*	**Derek Hutchinson**	*Colin Hurley*
Oswald, *steward to Goneril*	**Nicholas Blane**	*Stephen Marchant*
Third Knight	**Peter Sullivan**	*Phil McKee*
Lear's Fool	**David Bradley**	*Richard O'Callaghan*
Curan, *of Gloucester's household*	**Stephen Marchant**	*Phil McKee*
Gentleman	**Colin Hurley**	*Phil McKee*
First Servant	**Mark Strong**	*Members*
Second Servant	**Stephen Marchant**	*of the*
Third Servant	**Richard Simpson**	*company*
Old Man	**Sam Beazley**	*Joyce Redman*
Messenger	**Phil McKee**	*Stephen Marchant*
Doctor	**Bruce Purchase**	*Sam Beazley*
Captain	**Mark Strong**	*Phil McKee*
Herald	**Richard Simpson**	*Ian McKellen*

Knights, officers, servants, attendants, messengers, played by members of the company
Musicians: **Martin Allen** (*percussion*), **Sandy Burnett** (*keyboards*), **Colin Rae** (*trumpet/drums*)

viii

Director	**Deborah Warner**
Designer	**Hildegard Bechtler**
Lighting	**Jean Kalman**
Music	**Dominic Muldowney**
Fights	**John Waller**
Voice	**Patsy Rodenburg**
Assistant Director	**Cordelia Monsey**

Production Manager	Stage Manager
Rodger Hulley	**John Caulfield**
Deputy Stage Managers	Assistant Stage Managers
David Milling, Jane Suffling	**Fiona Bardsley, Wendy Fitt**
Sound	Assistant to the Lighting Designer
Freya Edwards	**Paul McLeish**
Design Assistant	Costume Supervisor
Bill Rasmussen	**Jane Moisley**

The cast-list for the London opening of
THE TRAGEDY OF RICHARD III

		Understudy
THE HOUSE OF YORK		
King Edward IV	**Bruce Purchase**	*Peter Jeffrey*
George, Duke of Clarence,		
brother to King Edward	**Peter Jeffrey**	*Bruce Purchase*
Richard, Duke of Gloucester,		
younger brother to King Edward	**Ian McKellen**	*Richard Bremmer*
Edward, Prince of Wales,		
son to King Edward	**Theo Cronin/Nicholas Gordon/**	
	Simon Blake	
Richard, Duke of York,		
son to King Edward	**Matthew Hearne/Ross Monro/**	
	Alex Scott	
Duchess of York,		
mother to King Edward and his		
brothers	**Joyce Redman**	*Susan Engel*
THE HOUSE OF LANCASTER		
Queen Margaret,		
widow of King Henry VI	**Susan Engel**	*Clare Higgins*
Lady Anne, *widow of Edward,*		
Prince of Wales, son of King Henry VI	**Eve Matheson**	*Helene Kvale*
Ghost of Henry VI	**Sam Beazley**	*Richard Simpson*
THE WOODVILLES		
Queen Elizabeth,		
wife to King Edward	**Clare Higgins**	*Eve Matheson*
Anthony Woodville, Earl Rivers,		
brother to Queen Elizabeth	**Peter Sullivan**	*Hakeem Kae-Kazim*
Marquess of Dorset, *son to Queen*		
Elizabeth by her former marriage	**Stephen Marchant**	*Hakeem Kae-Kazim*
Lord Grey, *son to Queen Elizabeth*	**Colin Hurley**	*Stephen Marchant*
POLITICIANS		
Lord Hastings, *Lord Chamberlain*	**David Bradley**	*Mark Strong*
Duke of Buckingham	**Brian Cox**	*Derek Hutchinson*

Lord Stanley	**David Collings**	*Nicholas Blane*
Bishop of Ely	**Richard Simpson**	*Nicholas Blane*
Lord Mayor of London	**Sam Beazley**	*Peter Sullivan*
FOLLOWERS OF RICHARD		
Sir William Catesby	**Derek Hutchinson**	*Hakeem Kae-Kazim*
Sir Richard Ratcliffe	**Richard O'Callaghan**	*Phil McKee*
James Tyrrel – Earl of Surrey	**Hakeem Kae-Kazim**	*Stephen Marchant/*
		Peter Sullivan
First Murderer – Lord Lovel –		
Duke of Norfolk	**Mark Strong**	*Derek Hutchinson/*
		Phil McKee/Peter Sullivan
Second Murderer	**Phil McKee**	*Colin Hurley*
OFFICIALS		
Sir Robert Brakenbury,		
Lieutenant of the Tower	**Richard Bremmer**	*Sam Beazley*
Keeper in the Tower	**Nicholas Blane**	*Sam Beazley*
Scrivener – Second Citizen	**Richard Bremmer**	*David Collings/*
		Phil McKee
First Citizen	**Nicholas Blane**	*David Collings*
Page	**Theo Cronin/Nicholas Gordon/**	
	Simon Blake	*Phil McKee*
THE TUDORS		
Henry, Earl of Richmond	**Colin Hurley**	*Stephen Marchant*
Sir James Blunt	**Richard Simpson**	*Sam Beazley*
Sir Walter Herbert	**David Bradley**	*Brian Cox*
Earl of Oxford	**Bruce Purchase**	*Brian Cox*

Citizens, messengers, soldiers, played by members of the company

Musicians: **Martin Allen** (*percussion*), **Sandy Burnett** (*keyboards*), **Colin Rae** (*trumpet/drums*)

Director	**Richard Eyre**
Designer	**Bob Crowley**
Lighting	**Jean Kalman**
Music	**Dominic Muldowney**
Movement	**Jane Gibson**
Fight	**John Waller**
Voice	**Patsy Rodenburg**
Assistant Director	**Cordelia Monsey**

Production Manager	Stage Manager
Rodger Hulley	**John Caulfield**
Deputy Stage Managers	Assistant Stage Managers
David Milling, Jane Suffling	**Fiona Bardsley, Wendy Fitt**
Sound	Assistant to the Lighting Designer
Scott Myers	**Laurence Clayton**
Design Assistant	Costume Supervisor
Bill Rasmussen	**Christine Rowland** assisted by **Alistair McArthur**

xi

RICHARD III/KING LEAR
TOUR DATES 1990–91

1990	*Performances*
TOKYO, Globe Theatre	September 13–23
NOTTINGHAM, Theatre Royal	October 1–6
CARDIFF, New Theatre	October 7–13
LEEDS, Grand Theatre	October 15–20
BELFAST, Grand Opera House	October 23–27
HAMBURG, Deutsches Schauspielhaus	October 31–November 4
MILAN, Teatro Lirico	November 7–11
MADRID, Centro Dramatico Nacional	(November 14–18)
PARIS, Odéon Theatre	November 21–December 1
CORK, Opera House	December 4–8
CAIRO, Opera House	December 13–16
1991	
LONDON, Lyttleton Theatre	January 5–February 2
PRAGUE, Historic National Theatre	February 7–10
BUCHAREST, National Theatre	February 15–18
LEIPZIG, Schauspielhaus	February 25–26
DRESDEN, Schauspielhaus	February 28–March 1
EDINBURGH, King's Theatre	March 5–9

Preface

This is a diary of a year's work at the Royal National Theatre, in rehearsal, performance, and finally on tour. But a diary is a work of fiction, a version of the truth perceived through the bias, the prejudice, the bile of the diarist. Reviewing this diary, I observe my inconsistencies, swings of emotion and allegiance and downright self-indulgence. The fiction became apparent when, in clarifying events, I rang some of my colleagues who I thought had been through the same experiences – only to discover that their version of events was quite different from mine. I therefore acknowledge that out of the fifty people who took part in the world tour of *King Lear* and *Richard III* forty-nine of them may be completely baffled by this account.

Introduction

I got confused and thought they said we were going to Broadway. I said, 'I haven't made any decision to go to Broadway,' and they said 'But you did.' I said, 'No, I didn't, I did nothing of the sort, I am against the idea, I don't particularly want to go and I never agreed.' Then I realised that they had said Broadmoor, not Broadway.

After performing *King Lear* in national theatres from Tokyo to Paris, that one afternoon at Broadmoor playing to ninety criminally insane people in a bare assembly room clarified not only my views on why I was playing Lear and on the whole business of touring but also on what an audience – mad or sane – can experience.

It was the middle of January 1991, the tour was two-thirds completed and we were back at the National Theatre with a heavy schedule of performances. By this time *Lear* had drained my resources; my private life and the rejection Lear experiences during the course of the play had become intertwined: four or five nights a week of it was too much for any mortal. The Broadmoor experience came when the life of the production was at a particularly low ebb. That afternoon revitalised all our spirits.

The language of the mad can be terrifyingly direct, the truth is presented unadorned, stripped of the codes and signals we build into conversation in normal life, our consciousness of the other person's status or lack of it, our sense of their feelings. Shakespeare uses madness in *Lear*, as in *Titus Andronicus* and *Hamlet*, to devastating effect. In the scene at Dover when the mad Lear talks to Gloucester, his vision of the world is of a place corrupt and painful, pitiless. And he has no pity for Gloucester's blindness because he does not believe blindness exempts anyone from their responsibility for the world's corruption. To Shakespeare, physical blindness is a metaphor for spiritual and moral blindness: 'Get thee glass eyes, and, like a scurvy

3

politician, seem to see things thou dost not. Now, now, now, now!'
Lear is mercilessly direct.

This directness thrilled the Broadmoor audience; they could revel
in Lear's bluntness and respond with unrestrained laughter and total
involvement. Shakespeare's jokes had an extra poignancy; they
specially loved the relationship between the Fool and Lear, the
companionability of the two men, the Fool's comic undermining of
authority which expressed their own battle with authority, both
within and without institutional life. They delighted in the vocabulary
of the Fool, savage, brutal, and off the wall.

The difference between playing in this institution and playing at
the institution of the National Theatre was marked by the whole-
hearted spontaneity of their response. At the NT the collective
enthusiasm, sense of wonder and ritual was deflected, dissipated,
bent out of shape by the very disparate nature of the audience. At
Broadmoor there was a common sense of purpose in being at that
event on that afternoon.

In my fatigue during the early part of the year's tour, I had
forgotten for whom I was doing the play – the audience – and why.
Clearly, if you are doing a play by Shakespeare the audience must
comprise people who are interested in the plays of Shakespeare . . .
but how interested? At the NT there are schoolchildren dragged
there unwillingly for the sake of their GCSEs, husbands who would
rather be asleep in front of the television, socialites who go because
it is the place to be seen, sponsors whose product is patronising the
event, tourists there in error. Ian McKellen says that only nice
people go to the theatre; they do, but sometimes on automatic pilot.

The Broadmoor experience was an example of what is possible in
the actor/audience relationship. The effect of Broadmoor was to
make me appreciate an audience of an open sensibility and to re-
examine why people go to the theatre. Entertainment, of course, is
the prime motive, but there are many elements to entertainment: to
be moved to laughter and tears, to recognise oneself in the performance, to divert the day's worries by recognising greater worries; the
play may debate a conflict of ideas or emotions, purge a personal
painful experience, expiate a guilt. The theatre monitors our behaviour, who we are and what we do, summed up by Hamlet in his

4

speech to the players: 'The purpose of playing . . . was and is, to hold, as 'twere, the mirror up to nature.'

The demands of a dramatist like Shakespeare are huge but the mixture is rich: the audience can extract what it wants to extract. It may be that the majority of London institutional theatregoers want reassurance from their drama, a confirmation of lyricism, poetry and a general aesthetic or anaesthetic; the harder elements of human behaviour can be too painful to deal with. The audience at Broadmoor were more in harmony with the audience in Bucharest, out from under the shadow of Ceauşescu, both very much receptive to the harder dealings of Shakespeare. Each culture, if one can call a group of the criminally insane a culture, recognises truths and jokes in Shakespeare's plays which correspond to their experience. I had a similar experience playing *Macbeth* to an audience in Calcutta: the idea of 'Tomorrow and tomorrow and tomorrow' rang a comic cultural bell with the thought of endless reincarnation.

Acting before an audience of mad men and women in a play where the hero himself has become mad, the ritual of performance was indeed a ritual of primitive expiation. When I said the line 'Is there any cause in nature that make these hard hearts?' one young woman in the front row shook her head slowly from side to side in a very painful manner. Here was an audience that clearly recognised Lear's pain and the very depths of his mental dis-ease. There was a mutual recognition between performer and audience, an energy created from spontaneous laughter, a poignancy to lines such as 'Oh let me not be mad!' The impetus became a helterskelter which carried the performance: I was safe, I wouldn't be thrown off, though I felt at any moment I could, and it was exhilarating.

We were playing to perpetrators of violence, violence linked with mental disorder. The weight of sin and wrongdoing is immense, an enormous burden of pain and suffering. Here we were part of an experiment, possibly a dangerous experiment: something might trigger one of them off. A clinician there said:

We're the people who are supposed to understand madness and all we know is how much we don't know. Shakespeare understands it much better than any of us. Each time we put on a play here there is a risk, but we think that it's worth it because the ultimate effect seems to be purging and healing. What interests me is that we often fail to help these patients develop an insight into their acts of violence but paradoxically they have the artistic and theatrical sense to appreciate a play and its message with remarkable clarity and intelligence. What strikes me is the power of the theatre, the performance, to grab them, to communicate with them, when often the conventional means of talking rationally with them about what they have done may go on for years without any benefit; in a single afternoon I can feel the power of a performance like *Lear* to reach them, and their capacity to respond.

A play like *Lear* essentially affirms life, saying that it is amazing, wonderful, extraordinary, full of the most incredible fuck-ups; a critique and celebration in one. These things go hand in hand. Perhaps the damaged mind can see and accept these paradoxes for what they are, recognise them in some way. Just as a child in a sight test can recognise numbers within coloured cards: you throw them down and you can see in the middle of the roses a four or five; perhaps for the disordered mind the theatre or theatrical experience helps to recognise the numbers within the roses, the power of things which have a positive and healing nature amidst the havoc.

PART ONE

Laying the Ground

March–July 1989

Deborah Warner and I had just finished a production of *Titus Andronicus* with the Royal Shakespeare Company. It was extremely well received and a number of critics suggested we follow it with *Lear* but, quite suddenly, after a very patchy production record, *Lear* is the play everyone wants to do.

On the telephone, Brian Cox and Deborah Warner:
'So we're in a queue, are we?' I asked.
'Yes. Barry Kyle and Bob Peck, then it looks like Nick Hytner and John Wood.'
'All that hype about me following *Titus* with *Lear* – somebody ought to tell Michael Billington there's a queue for Lear – I'm not even sure if I want to play it.'
'Of course you should. You're just at the right age, you have to be fit, though I'm not sure if I want to direct it at the RSC.'

'Bob Peck doesn't want to do it. So Barry Kyle's out of the running. It looks as if it will be Nick and John.'
'Mm.'

'I've had a phone call from Ian McKellen. Richard Eyre wants him to lead a world tour of two plays from the National Theatre. Ian's asked me to direct. I've told him I'd like to do *King Lear* – with you.'

A meeting with Ian McKellen, August 1989:
Ian: 'Deborah wants to do, um, *King Lear*. I think it's a very good idea.'

'I'm amazed. What will the other play be?'

'Haven't the foggiest idea, but I'm very open to suggestions.'

'Another Shakespeare?'

'Mm.'

'Another Shakespeare.'

'I think so. Probably.'

'What about *Coriolanus* again, directed by Deborah? It's a play you both know.'

'God, I'm too old.'

'Olivier played him when he was your age.'

'Mm. It's an idea.'

On the telephone, Deborah Warner and Brian Cox:

Deborah: 'It's *Coriolanus* and *King Lear*.'

'What do you want me to play in *Coriolanus*?'

'Don't know. I think Ian should play Kent in *Lear*.'

Deborah: 'I'm not doing *Coriolanus* – it's too much. I can't concentrate on two at once.'

'Isn't Ian furious?'

'No.'

'Well, I would be. I'd be fucking furious – setting up a double project and you piss off and only do one half.'

'*He* doesn't seem to mind.'

'Richard Eyre's going to direct Ian as Richard III.'

'That lets you off the hook.'

Ian McKellen, September 1989:

'We've asked Richard to direct *Richard III* and he's very pleased. I think it's a good idea to have the Director of the National Theatre directing on the world tour.'

Meeting with Richard Eyre, October 1989:

'Buckingham would be the obvious choice, but I'd like to read the play again.'

'I think Buckingham.'

*

8

Thus I was committed to a year's tour, nationally and internationally, of *King Lear* directed by Deborah Warner and *Richard III* directed by Richard Eyre in a National Theatre company led by Ian McKellen.

Monday, January 22, 1990

Back in London after three weeks of paradise in the Caribbean and a hectic fortnight in New York seeing friends. First meeting at the NT with Ian McKellen, Deborah Warner, Roger Chapman (Head of Touring), Caroline Wilson (Repertoire Manager), Serena Hill (Casting Director), old Uncle Tom Cobbley and all. My heart and my soul are still in the West Indies, my head in New York. I am greeted by the news that the Stratford production of *King Lear* will open on July 11, four days before ours. Apparently John Wood would only agree to doing it if it opened first. I don't mind so long as there is a decent interval between their opening and ours. There is also a general consensus that we should open *Lear* and *Richard* on the same day. I don't quite take this in and sit there for ten minutes before the penny drops – all right, I'm game.

My head, heart and soul being elsewhere, at the moment the idea of *Lear* weighs me down somewhat and as the meeting goes on I become less and less excited at the prospect. After long stints at Stratford and in the West End, the idea of another full year's commitment is daunting. I agreed to do this production when my love of the theatre was at its height, fanned by the frantic activity of work breeding work. Now I am less enamoured. I also have hanging over me a 60,000-word commission from Methuen on my involvement with the Moscow Art Theatre – of which only 5,000 words have been written, all of them extremely badly. This has to be completed before rehearsals begin in seven weeks' time. I'm guilt-ridden.

The discussion returns to the problem of the two *Lear*s. I try to persuade them that it would be better if we delay opening by at least two weeks so we don't have the critics Learified out of their minds. Also, in truth I don't want the productions to be compared: comparisons are always odious and this one particularly odious to

9

me. Of course this is ridiculous, of course they will be compared. Deborah, being Deborah and supremely confident, doesn't care one way or the other. She has the courage of a Sherman tank.

Then comes a discussion about precedents being set, productions being in preview for too long, a schedule is looked at and it is agreed that we should open at the end of July/beginning of August, three weeks after the Stratford *Lear*. I feel much easier about this and retire from the meeting.

Later, at home, on reflection I realise that it is a crazy idea to open *Lear* and *Richard* on the same day; either production must suffer and who would want to sit through a production of *Lear* followed by a production of *Richard III* or vice versa? The history plays and *Nicholas Nickleby* set a fashion for marathons, but, in those, themes and characters are developed throughout the day of the performance; *Lear* and *Richard* couldn't be more different.

Wednesday, January 24

We reconvene. I put my fears to Ian. Richard Eyre is not present as he is opening David Hare's play *Racing Demon*. Stephen Wood, Head of Publicity, is not keen on an all-day opening either. A compromise is reached: there will be four openings over two days, giving the critics a choice. Perhaps this is sensible – though somewhat protracted. Ian is not fazed by anything at the moment; he is a bit like Superman, the sort of state I was in two years ago at Stratford. His performance in the revival of *Bent* has been highly acclaimed and the play will transfer to the West End for eleven weeks; this will be during our rehearsal period. Deborah is a little anxious about it. I am too, but people in glass houses shouldn't throw stones: I directed *Mrs Warren's Profession* and made a film for Ken Loach, *Hidden Agenda*, while playing *Frankie and Johnny* at the Comedy Theatre in the evening, so I'm in no position to complain.

The rehearsals will begin on March 12: a priority system, four weeks priority on *Lear*, followed by four weeks priority on *Richard*; then alternating mornings and afternoons between both productions for a further four weeks; the thirteenth and fourteenth weeks will be

Lear technicals and previews, the fifteenth *Richard* technicals and first preview. (Events overtook this plan – like many others. The reader must bear with the timetable's constant inconsistency.)

We discuss tour dates for the UK: Nottingham, Cardiff, Belfast, Leeds or Bradford, Glasgow; there is a question mark over Glasgow, which is a pity as it is the European City of Culture this year. Our dates abroad will be: Hamburg, Milan, Madrid, Paris, Dublin, ending in Cairo. But the first international port of call will be Tokyo. In 1991 we hope to go to Moscow, Prague, Bucharest, East Berlin; now that the wall has come down Germany has suddenly become a priority. I am particularly looking forward to returning to Russia, as, ironically, I am only known there as a director.

At the moment only a few of the European dates are in place, the rest are speculative. Roger Chapman has a huge job on his hands. He asked me about Moscow. I said the only theatre to play in, the only theatre technically on a par with the Lyttleton, is MXAT, the Moscow Art Theatre founded by Konstantin Stanislavski.

Wednesday, January 31

A telephone call from Ian to say he feels the Tram Shed in Glasgow is unsuitable and we shouldn't go there. I am disappointed by this as I feel it would be a perfect space: Peter Brook's production of the *Mahabharata* was an astounding success there. In our meetings before Christmas I had asked that we should perform at least once in a rough setting in each city and stressed that Scotland was an important place for me, being my country of origin. I haven't appeared on the Scottish stage for over twenty years. Ian thinks our production of *Richard* cannot be served by the Tram Shed as there are no flying facilities: Richard Eyre, Ian and the designer Bob Crowley envisage a great deal of flying material. The Glasgow date is to be at the end of the year, we will have been on the road for ten or twelve weeks and it would be a perfect opportunity to revitalise our work by performing without sets or costumes. Production values can often blur the text for the actor and create a barrier between player and play. By performing in a rough setting the barrier is removed and the actors are brought back to a basic relationship with the text – physically, rhythmically, emotionally. I know that Deborah is keen on this idea but Ian feels we might have grown attached to elements of the productions that it would be hard to let go of. I suspect that Ian will win but it seems a shame to miss such a challenge – perhaps I'm just an old radical at heart.

Friday, February 2

Richard Eyre's office. Richard reassures me that we will go to Scotland. He is particularly keen. Aberdeen is being looked at, the MacRobert Centre in Stirling, or Edinburgh where both Richard and I spent our formative years. My first job after drama school in the early sixties was at the Lyceum Theatre in Edinburgh of which Richard became Artistic Director some years later. The trouble with Glasgow, apart from the venue, is that the date proposed is December and by then Glasgow as the City of Culture will have swollen with an artistic glut.

The meeting turns to the problem of Christmas: whether or not we should play over that period. I would like Christmas out: I had intended to get married in September when there was supposed to be a break in our performing which has since been cancelled. Wedding plans were postponed – I had hoped till Christmas. Oh dear, oh dear.

On Monday I start my book, *Salem to Moscow*, six weeks to get 60,000 words under my belt. It's all there, I have scraps of paper all over the place and they've got to be mashed into some kind of shape. Lyn Haill, who is in charge of National Theatre publications, suggested that I might like to keep a diary of *King Lear* – this was in December – and of course I said yes, I didn't think of saying no, I never think of saying no. Since then I have been keeping very rough notes – mainly in my head and on scraps of toilet paper. I must be crazy, I haven't even started one book and I'm thinking of starting another.

Monday, February 5

Began *Salem to Moscow*. Had lunch with prospective publisher. Told him the only way I could keep notes on *King Lear* was by speaking into this wretched tape machine. No mention of money for this new book and I have got to get myself a new literary agent as Valerie Hoskins at Jeremy Conway has left Jeremy Conway. My kitchen – which is another story, work begun on December 18 – is still not finished and is going to need a little extra cash to complete. It looks as though the *King Lear* book is a must. Life is like painting the Forth Railway Bridge. Anyway upwards and onwards.

Wednesday evening, February 7

Spoke to Deborah on the phone. Casting is beginning to shape up. David Bradley, whom I had suggested when the possibility of *Lear* was first mooted, is set to play the Fool. I am really excited by this: he is one of the best actors around, with a terrific sense of humour and great naturalistic flair. He has that wonderful ability to give the lines completely new meaning. Emaciated, spider-like, he reminds you of those great northern comics of the thirties. During the time I was with him at Stratford there wasn't a performance he gave that wasn't flawless.

Derek Hutchinson, who played my son Lucius in *Titus*, will play Edgar, which particularly pleases me. Derek has worked with Deborah since the Kick Theatre Company days and was Kent in the Kick production of *King Lear*. I'd love to see Jim Norton or Richard Wilson play Gloucester; the part at the moment is on tender to various actors – Nigel Hawthorne, Ronald Pickup. Deborah and I have a disagreement about the daughters: I feel there shouldn't be any great disparity in their ages and as women they should be fecund so that Lear's curse on Goneril makes some sense. Deborah has offered the part of Goneril to Susan Engel; I adore Susan as an actress and would love to work with her but she is in fact older than me. Mind you, she was in Peter Brook's film of *King Lear*, playing Regan, and does have great knowledge of the play.

13

Clare Higgins will play Regan, which is very exciting. She will also play Queen Elizabeth in *Richard III*. Clare is a truly 'female' actor, she has tremendous sexuality and will bring enormous dynamism to the part. The question of Cordelia has not been solved: I suggested last year that Irina Brook, my girlfriend, should be considered for the role, but Irina has decided she would rather not be involved. These situations are always difficult and nepotism is not very attractive but I do feel that Irina has many of the qualities that are absolutely correct for the part.

Monday, February 12

Oh dear, oh dear. My editor at Methuen, Pamela Edwardes, is none too pleased with me: I thought I'd better inform her about the *Lear* diary idea and she reminded me that she had already suggested it last September. I, fearing I would never even get the first book written, had wiped it from my brain. I now find myself in a very awkward predicament with two publishers vying for the book.

The good news is that I've got a new literary agent: Jenne Casarotto. Needless to say, she's thrilled that there are two publishers after my book and says, 'Well, Brian, it'll just have to go to the highest bidder' – so maybe I'll get my kitchen finished after all.

At the weekend I saw Deborah's production of *The Good Person of Sichuan*, with which I was duly impressed. Fiona Shaw was excellent but the surprise was Sue Engel, playing a toothless Chinese woman in the first half who transforms into a glamorous shopkeeper. For a minute I didn't recognise her, a dolly bird had come on stage, so I'm reassured about the age problem. And she will double perfectly for Queen Margaret in *Richard III*.

Deborah rang me. I congratulated her on *Sichuan*. She had just been interviewed for an hour by Peter Jeffrey about playing Glouces-ter. The other news is that Bob Crowley, who is designing *Richard*, has declined to do *Lear* which he has already done for Adrian Noble at Stratford. The new plan is that Bob and Sue Blane, who designed *King John* for Deborah, might work on *Lear* together, sharing the costumes and set. This could be an excellent compromise.

The only image I have of Lear at the moment is of an old man in a wheelchair. The wheelchair could denote helplessness and also perhaps cunning. I got this idea from the amount of time I have spent in air terminals noticing the way the old are manoeuvred through passport queues or security checks: they arrive at the airport with loads of baggage, hale and hearty, and are transferred to a waiting wheelchair, which causes them to age twenty years. As soon as they arrive on board they are sprightly young things again.

Tuesday, February 13

Apparently the Blane/Crowley combination is off and Hildegard Bechtler will design *Lear*. Hildegard designed Deborah's production of *Electra*. She first came to my notice as a student at the Central School of Art and Design where I was teaching. For her final exam she designed a set for Brecht's *Trumpets and Drums* of an abattoir covered in white tiles with sawdust on the floor.

I whisk into the NT to have my photograph taken for the advance schedule brochure. I am greeted by Ian on his return from lunch with Mr Tamura, the gentleman who runs the Globe Theatre in Tokyo. The photograph for the brochure is to be one of Ian and me looking longingly at one another – except we have to be taken separately. I was requested to wear a black sweater which I duly did. After my session Ian arrives, whips off his shirt, and says, 'I think it would be better if we were topless.' 'Too late,' I cry, 'I'm done.'

He then informs me that David Aukin, Executive Director of the NT, is worried about our opening so late. Apparently there will be a total of thirty-eight performances of *Lear* and *Richard* before the opening nights so he would like to bring them forward a week. Once again I say, 'I don't mind so long as there's a reasonable gap. And as the NT will have its own way in the end, quite frankly, I couldn't give a toss.'

On my return home, I receive a call from my theatrical agent, Jeremy Conway, to say that the rehearsals for *King Lear* and *Richard III* have been postponed by a week.

On Friday – very thankful for the extra week – I finally finished *Salem to Moscow* and got it to the photocopier's, a huge weight off my mind. I have been panicking that I haven't done enough work on *Lear*. There has been a script lying in every room of the house and in between strenuous bouts with the word processor I have been snatching the odd glance. I keep a copy of Granville Barker's *Prefaces to Shakespeare* by my bed: when I was at drama school nearly thirty years ago the principal, Michael McCowan, insisted that every student had a copy. An actor as well as a playwright, Barker has a great simplicity and actor's commonsense in approaching the heavy tragedies, *Lear* in particular. Reading Barker has rekindled my enthusiasm. His picture of Lear, the character and play, is so vivid that I can't wait to get at them both.

It has been lovely this weekend to switch off for a few hours and be with Irina. She has a wonderful calming effect; her serenity has taught me a great deal. I don't think I've ever known how to be quiet before. I suppose this is what must be known as domestic bliss, a state I'm not used to. Perhaps it has contributed to my reluctance about the tour: for the first time I have a settled home life so I'm unwilling to venture onto the stormy heath.

PART TWO

The Rehearsals

Week 1: Monday, March 19

The first rehearsal of *Lear*. I wake up early and start the day with a visit to Dreas Reyneke's body-conditioning studio in Notting Hill Gate. I return at 9.15 for some breakfast and await the arrival of sprightly Sam Beazley, who is playing Gloucester's servant in *Lear* and the Lord Mayor of London in *Richard*. After more than forty years as an antique dealer Sam has returned to the theatre with the enthusiasm of a novice. He has the bearing of a retired major, which he combines with the wistful gentleness of a country schoolmaster. I first met him at a Chekhov workshop I conducted at the Actors' Centre and when Deborah and Richard were looking for an older actor prepared to understudy and tour for a year he came to mind instantly. I couldn't remember his name but Irina recommended someone she was working with at the Gate in Camus' *Malentendu*. There was Sam.

With my copy of *Lear* and my son Alan's *Shakespeare Made Easy*, an aid to A-level, like a couple of boys on their first day at a new school we bid farewell to Irina and drive in Sam's car to the NT.

'The last time I was in a major classical production,' he says, 'was fifty-five years ago – with Olivier, Gielgud, Ashcroft and Dame Edith Evans in Gielgud's famous production of *Romeo and Juliet*. I played Paris. I was eighteen and I'm as nervous now as I was then.'

I hope this augurs well for us.

To mark the occasion Ian McKellen has laid on champagne and orange juice. Richard Eyre makes a welcoming speech, remembering everyone's names and telling us that this is the biggest venture the National Theatre has ever taken on, adding that we shouldn't feel overawed by the NT. It's been interesting to see Richard develop in stature over the years. This is the first time I have actually worked with him though I first met him in 1966 when I was a young actor at Birmingham Rep and he was Assistant Director at Leicester. Then, as now, Richard had an enigmatic air, keeping his cards very close to his chest – more out of shyness than guile. In the early seventies he was quite clearly a front-runner to take over the Royal Court Theatre but was blocked by the Royal Court old guard; as a result, he developed a new-writing policy at Nottingham Playhouse, which included Trevor Griffiths, David Hare, Howard Brenton, writers ignored by the Court, though Hare and Brenton had debuted there. His nursery also encouraged the acting talents of Jonathan Pryce, Tony Sher and many others. He looks much younger than his forty-eight years, in spite of the demands of running the NT. He has obviously won a great deal of loyalty, particularly from the stage management team. He said, touchingly, that as Director of the National he has never actually been asked to direct a play, so he was delighted to be asked to do *Richard III*.

We ran through the rehearsal schedule for the next thirteen weeks, as well as the itinerary of the tour, and Roger Chapman filled in some of the details. Then he handed over to Deborah who explained that the first week of the *Lear* rehearsal will be mainly concerned with getting to know one another.

We set to work: first a voice class with Patsy Rodenburg. We did a lot of work on breath support, on the principle that a Shakespeare line requires a gathering on the one breath, something that demands considerable breath reserve. We start with stretching exercises, a development of basic yoga, to get the lower back working. Then, picking a point in the room and directing our voices towards it, we speak a sequence of numbers from one to ten: we count '1', '1,2', '1,2,3', '1,2,3,4', '1,2,3,4,5', etc., and have to control it from the diaphragm in order to maintain intensity and prevent strain in the throat. Then we take a line from the play, mouth it in an exaggerated way, without vocalising, then say only the vowels, and then the whole line, noting the difference in intensity. She wears us out by lunchtime.

In the canteen at the National there are a lot of familiar faces, still here after seven years. It's strange to come back after all this time away. For some unknown reason they've just changed the doors

18

between the stage-door foyer and the backstage; they've been moved and today the new ones were tried out. New doors – like a new beginning.

In the afternoon we start the first read-through of *Lear*. Deborah's method, the method she has always used, is for everyone to read someone else's part; this lessens the burden of having to give some kind of performance. Peter Jeffrey, who is playing Gloucester, read Lear, and Ian McKellen read the Fool, David Bradley read Edgar and I read Cordelia – which I thought was apt. Tomorrow we will read it again. Though I've had reservations about some of the casting, the company seems strong: Deborah has a very clear idea of what she wants and I have to trust her; she is very strong-willed and always gets her own way in the end anyway.

We will see Hildegard Bechtler's set, I hope, on Wednesday or Thursday. A good day. I re-met friends I hadn't seen for a while, Clare Higgins, Susan Engel, Richard O'Callaghan (Cornwall); and met new people: Eve Matheson who is playing Cordelia and Richard Bremmer who plays Albany, among others. I think I'm beginning to look forward to it all.

Tuesday, March 20

I went for a run, trying to build up my stamina for the role, then Sam collected me. We read the play again in the morning. I read Goneril and it has to be said that my Goneril was not nearly as good as my Cordelia.

In the afternoon Deborah made us do some exercises with a tambourine: Richard O'Callaghan and I started, which brought back memories of our antics as students together twenty-six years ago, touring one-night stands in Holland. The object of the game was to beat your opponent's tambourine, while keeping up a rhythm on your own. One hit on theirs and the game is over. After a little time two or three people are introduced to the circle, all trying to beat each other's tambourines. The result of the game is a manic dance. The most impressive was David Bradley, who played it very much

19

on the back foot, sly and cunning. I found it all a bit competitive – which I'm not sure is a good thing.

We then did some mirror exercises, which were more constructive. A and B sit on chairs facing each other. A starts to mirror B's movements; on either side of A are C and D; C asks simple mathematical questions which A must answer, D asks A personal questions, which again A must answer – all the time continuing to mirror B's movements. Ian mirrored me while Bruce Purchase and Colin Hurley asked the questions; then we all swopped round. It was quite comic. These games are designed to break down inhibitions and knit the company together in as short a time as possible. They will go on for three days or so.

We also did some more work with Patsy Rodenburg. I think she's a very good teacher though I'm not convinced about speaking on the one breath. My old voice teacher Lizzie Wilmer believed in using as much breath as you wanted, saying that breath is thought, the more breath you put in, the more thought you put in.

Observation on Lear: surprisingly, it's not a huge part; the play is very bitty, with a lot of strands – one reason why I think productions are difficult; it really is an ensemble piece.

Wednesday, March 21

Day 3. Read *Lear* again. This time I read Gloucester and Ian read Lear, Peter Jeffrey Edmund, David Bradley Cordelia, Clare Higgins and Susan Engel their husbands and the gentlemen their wives. It went well; Ian was very impressive: he can say lines about kings with a sense of authority which I envy.

In the afternoon we saw Hildegard's set which is a large, empty white space on a slight rake, fractured by a series of cloths lowered to change locale and climate – a leaden sky, the white cliffs of Dover – and a white floorcloth which can be torn up at the beginning of the storm, leaving a vast muddy underlay. All this will be dominated by a long catwalk that will divide the floorspace. The catwalk is to be built by aircraft manufacturers for maximum lightness and flexibility. Throughout the design she has tried to simulate natural materials

20

though she has had to use plastics and paint in order to accommodate the problems of touring. I think it has enormous potential, and I only hope the design will not be compromised to facilitate the tour. Anyway, we must work with it soon, we can't have all these things arrive on the technical rehearsal.

We went through the usual business of electing the Equity Dep: I proposed my old pal Richard O'Callaghan, one of Nature's busy-bodies, and he's going to be helped by young Stevie Marchant. A few things have to be sorted out Equitywise: the iniquitous National Theatre contract has a start date moveable by two weeks; as a result of the postponed rehearsals we're only being paid for half a week – which is pretty shoddy.

It's hard to remember things for this diary, there are bits I keep forgetting that I want to say. Anyway, that's today and we look forward to tomorrow. Meantime I'm off to Richmond to see the new Orange Tree Theatre which I hope will be an exciting new space.

Thursday, March 22

We read again: I read the Fool and my reading has got progressively worse as the week has gone on. There's a certain atmosphere which makes me lose my bottle. This afternoon went slightly better, though, because we worked on the text, breaking it down and paraphrasing it – with fairly comic consequences. Ian proved conclusively that the Earl of Kent was gay and the Fool became a sort of Chick Murray figure (Scots comedian) who explained everything in triplicate. I made an absolute ass of myself paraphrasing badly and saying things like 'Right', 'They gave me a hard time' (the daughters). Eventually I started to crib from my *Shakespeare Made Easy* but was caught in the act which caused a great deal of hilarity. Peter Jeffrey was particularly good but I was the worst.

Old Lear's denseness provoked a few jokes too and one of the things I discovered today was how many questions he asks. 'When were you wont to be so full of songs, sirrah?', 'Does any here know me?', 'Who is it can tell me who I am?' He is aware of his stupidity and his cruelty towards Cordelia; the Fool is a kind of conscience

21

figure who rubs his face in it and he deliberately allows the Fool to do so. The Fool more or less has the upper hand and is very vicious to Lear – which Lear allows.

Tonight old RSC hands were supposed to be going to a reception for Vaclav Havel, the playwright now President of Czechoslovakia, at the Barbican. Ian was a bit miffed because he wasn't invited. I don't blame him; I was invited but couldn't go as I was already going out to dinner. David Bradley went on all our behalves.

Friday, March 23

We struggled on with paraphrasing. I am hopeless at it, absolutely hopeless. I find myself getting anarchic and starting to use swear words and substitute things which are not really there. It's a very good way, though, of working out exactly what you are saying and agreeing on the meaning. There's a lot of arguing about interpretation; how a line is said and how a line can be interpreted are two entirely different things. You can say a line one way and the audience can get an entirely different meaning; the emphasis must convey precisely the actor's interpretation.

We've been going very slowly. Some of the younger members are finding it difficult, but this older member finds it the most difficult. Points in descending order: Peter Jeffrey is best, Ian is quite good and his knowledge of Shakespeare is enormous. The girls are good and so is David, though having to examine the Fool's humour and break it down into little bits is not the best way to convey it. The young people, Hutchinson and Kae-Kazim (Edmund), are having trouble but it's obviously very useful for them and I, as I say, am a disaster.

I watched Paul Scofield's Lear in Brook's production this evening and it was very provocative. Peter's approach is to strip the play to its bones, his Ancient Britain is dour and unwelcoming, a bit short on the laughs. I do think there are a lot of laughs in *Lear*, it's a play with humour; and Lear's a bit of a curmudgeon, a bit of a silly old boy.

The wheelchair idea is getting stronger. Ian got quite excited and thought perhaps it should be taken further – the idea of infirmity.

We've a lot of things to pursue, but I think I'll enjoy playing the old bugger. I may come back tomorrow, Saturday, and think again.

Week 2: Monday, March 26

At the start of the second week, the director, Deborah Warner, is late. Would Miss Warner like to say anything? Dear Diary, Miss Warner has no comment! The clocks went forward this weekend: there are twenty-six people in this room and one of them didn't realise that the clocks went forward. Thank you.

More parrot-phrasing. I'm beginning to feel like a naughty school-boy. It does take for ever, it's very boring, absolutely boring, but necessary, I suppose. Nicholas Blane, who plays Oswald, arrived from Dundee where he was playing in rep – a difficult town to commute from.

In the afternoon, the fruit game exercise: everyone chooses a fruit with not more than two syllables, we sit in a circle and one person walks round on the outside, telling a story, trying to say the name of each fruit and repeat it a second time before the person whose fruit is mentioned can say it three times. For me these games reflect a bourgeois English childhood which means nothing to me and I'm not sure of their value here.

Lear seems to have two or three false endings. All the summaries at the end of the play seem a bit unnecessary. Shakespeare does go in for a lot of exposition, tidying up – it's very much an actor thinking. Actors think like that; they think the story has to be told to every character, endless exposition and reiteration, and then surprising shortcuts.

The Oscars last night: Daniel Day Lewis won one for *My Left Foot*, well deserved, a brilliant performance, a fillip after his break-down during Richard Eyre's RNT production of *Hamlet*. Perhaps there is an intrinsic danger to the actor's health in doing these great roles. The stress certainly told on Dan.

Tuesday, March 27

Everybody read their own parts today for the first time. Forty-five chairs were arranged in a huge circle, and the company sat on one side of it so the other side could be used as a playing area; each of us joined the semi-circle when it came to our turn to read and it automatically developed from a reading into a performance.

Lear's part is distributed very strangely: after the interval I only have three scenes. It is not as physically demanding as Titus, though it's a great deal more difficult mentally and spiritually, and needs a finer touch altogether.

Everybody seemed pleased with the reading. Richard Eyre was extremely complimentary and I thought we did very well.

We had an amusing afternoon playing Grandmother's Footsteps, charades and old Musical Chairs, and then a murder game where I bumped off young Stephen Marchant. It's nice to have so many people in the cast I've worked with before: Bruce Purchase, Stephen Marchant, Sam Beazley, David Collings, Richard Simpson. Tomorrow we start blocking the play from Scene 1.

I had dinner with my daughter, Margaret. Irina is exhausted from filming.

Wednesday, March 28

Today for the first time we put the play on its feet. My first idea of Lear was of a sort of Howard Hughes figure, a recluse, a man who keeps himself away from his family, living in an antiseptic environment, Kleenex boxes on feet, visitors made to wear gloves, attended by various white-coated medics – combining this with a Beckettian influence, *Krapp's Last Tape* etc. Deborah's vision is different. The Beckett influence we certainly agree on but her Lear is an altogether rougher affair: she wants to begin the first scene in a very original way, as though it is some kind of a party, a celebration of the division of the kingdom, Lear bestowing his divided kingdom like Christmas presents, a demented Santa Claus, seeking the reassurance of his daughters' love. It worked surprisingly well: to be swung round the

24

stage on a wheelchair, coming in on a high, laughing and slightly hysterical, it gave the scene a context and did indeed show the instability and lack of dignity and judgement in Lear. I am resistant, I have to confess, I still need to be convinced though for the moment I am prepared to go along with it. It is certainly an original opening for the play, though maybe perverse and there are no doubt more classical and conventional approaches, but the great thing about Deborah is, of course, her unconventionality. What it does is make the scene much more private and domestic, playing down the public aspects, and this, it has to be said, has enormous benefits.

Deborah confessed to having been a bit in awe of me when we first worked together on *Titus* at the RSC but she's got my measure now and knows how to push, how to prod. I am extremely impressed by Ian's work: he is meticulous and his Kent is going to be very fine. The girls took to the scene well too, Clare and Eve and Susie.

One interesting point came up: it is important that I actually rise from the wheelchair more than once, to Cordelia and to Kent. If I don't it looks as though I really can't do without the chair instead of it being a contrivance – I do want to keep the air terminal image. The wheelchair idea is growing, there are a number of ways we could use it: it might be effective at the end of the play to bring on Cordelia in it.

A good day's work, it gave me an idea of where to go. I have got to watch the physical side of the part because it is exhausting and I think that one of the reasons I lose my voice as I did in *Titus* is because of the physical demands of bending into Lear's shape. I've got to get my body back into condition. I am looking forward to the next rehearsal but I must start learning my lines for *Lear* as we will soon be switching over to *Richard* – which I haven't even begun to think about.

Thursday, March 29

The rehearsal was cancelled because Susie Engel is ill: voice, throat – bug. I went in and did a line session and tomorrow we get back to Act 1.

Yesterday was a good day, we had a lot of good results and they've stayed with me overnight. By the detailed work we've done, the paraphrasing and the games, breaking down reserve, approaching the text from a totally fresh standpoint, Deborah has managed to lay a bed of confidence so that when we came to working the scene yesterday, the first scene, we were able to take risks and do things which I think in other circumstances, with other directors, we wouldn't have been able to do. It's been impressive, the work; bored though one might be at times, it has succeeded in bonding the company in a way I hope we will continue when we get to *Richard*.

Week 3: Monday, April 2

A slow start. People were late this morning, illness, whatever; we haven't done anything since last Wednesday because of illness – and there's obviously going to be a lot more of it. The work we've done so far on the first scene has been fairly generalised, now we have to be more specific and attend to the details and shifts and what we know about the scene when it starts. Deborah is very good but demanding, trying to engender an atmosphere which is very difficult to whip up all the time. I think the cast felt a bit disconnected, as though we weren't quite belonging. We've lost a lot of ground over the two days we've missed. It's important for the whole company to feel involved and I told Deborah that I felt everybody should be invited to come to whatever rehearsal they want and not feel left out.

After the morning the work went better, we gathered pace and found ways of handling the scene. The first problem was the map of Britain, how big it should be – the size of the stage or something far smaller – how physically to divide the map up, the right pitch for each of the girls in winning their particular section of the map, Cordelia's unwillingness to degrade herself with avarice. It was

26

decided that the map should be quite small and that the division should be made by simply cutting it with scissors, showing the irony of something so huge as a country being reduced to the size of a school atlas, the irony reinforcing the edgy humour of the scene.

The big discovery of the afternoon was the tremendous advantages of the wheelchair. Unlike a throne fixed in the centre of the stage it is a shifting focal point which allows interesting staging variations.

My problem with the lines is not retention, it's switching from one thought to another. I know the lines but they're a bit like the bar on a trapeze: I can hold onto them but to turn and do somersaults is more tricky.

I'm off to Maria Aitken's house now for a board meeting of IFTA, the International Foundation for Training in the Arts, which we set up, as a result of my work in Russia in 1988–9, to facilitate exchanges between theatre students and practitioners from different countries.

Tuesday, April 3

We started with Act 1, Scene 4, Kent arriving at Goneril's house, Lear and his men returning from the hunt. We wasted a lot of time and really didn't get going until the end of the morning.

The main problem, which Deborah didn't seem to be attending to at all, is to convey the idea of the one hundred knights, what they mean and what precisely their function is in the play. She has this extraordinary habit, Deborah, of sitting there like the school prefect waiting to admonish latecomers but only going into action when the pupils are actually late. The actors do all the work and in a sense she selects and edits but she waits for us to offer it up – most exhausting . . . not really, she's very good once we get going. Once we get the ideas she's very good at saying, 'I don't want this, I do want that', but it can be frustrating if you're asking for impetus and you don't get it. Of course, I should know from experience that this is one of Deborah's tactics.

Ian continues to be as inventive as ever, showing Kent to be the perfect valet. We spent a long time on his entrance into the scene – which was not the priority really, we should have been concentrating

27

on the knights, making five appear like a hundred, and it wasn't until the end of the morning that we started to straighten that out.

The afternoon went much better, as usually happens. We got some ideas going, very simple things. Deborah provided the knights and me with buckets of water to wash from the hunt (I suspect this is a throwback to her previous production – so much for the voyage of discovery); Kent offered Lear a towel and a biscuit, and we established the old man's bemusement about what's going on around him. We came to the sequence with the Fool: David has a very intelligent grasp of the Fool but one of things we have to create is a sense of the physical world in which the Fool takes precedence over the knights. That is something that isn't quite being realised. We did get a sweep on the scene towards the end of the day. Lear's speeches admonishing Goneril have such a strong rhythm they almost play themselves. It's now simply a question of modulation and establishing the space: we have to give the space life, give it meaning, we have to find out the temperature, find out the weather, find out where we are, what we're doing.

A frustrating day which really ended quite successfully.

Wednesday, April 4

We worked on the scene after Lear walks out on Goneril with his knights, when he sends on Kent as his messenger to Regan and he and the Fool are left alone. Again trying to create the personality of the knights and the geography of the play. The scene has a Beckett-like quality, two fools in a desolate landscape, Lear a sort of . . . the image that came was of Jack Benny, in his long-suffering relationship with the Fool.

Thursday, April 5

I had a costume discussion with Hildegard. My original idea of
Howard Hughes etc. isn't going to work. We looked at various
pictures of regality, kings and coats and things like that; we don't
want to be tied into any specific period but the danger of being over-
anachronistic is that you may not create a specific world for the play
to sit in. You look to the practical necessities and in the middle acts,
when Lear is hunting, obviously some kind of hunting garment is
required; the opening of the play needs something quite different.
At the beginning I want to give a sense of faded grandeur combined
with the idea of an old man who spends a lot of time loping around
the corridors of the palace in dressing-gown and slippers. Putting
these two images together is very difficult. I kept thinking of *Titus*
and the faded colours we used in that: eroded statuary, gold and
tarnished metals, the green of copper, marble and the wonderful
colours of worn stone. If we can give that effect in the first part it
would be light and we could go into dark hunting colours later.

I think David's costume is going to help, a simple black suit with
a kind of clown's hat. Ian has lots and lots of ideas – the thing is to
select them. It's very interesting to compare Ian and David, both
northerners: David is very spare and economic – it's almost a
Lancashire/Yorkshire difference.

Friday, April 6

Exhausted, well, tired anyway. We did the stocks scene this morning,
more work on the relationship between the Fool and me, the
development from Act 1, Scene 5, plotting the graph of the journey
and how to manage the wheelchair. We decided that perhaps David
should be pushing it empty. We also want to convey the fact that the
knights are beginning to desert and that at this point the third knight
deserts. The story of the knights is a difficult one to tell and I fear
that Deborah isn't addressing it as well as she might.

We've started to deal with the proxy row with Gloucester, the
reason Lear's denied entry, the fact that neither Regan nor Cornwall

will speak to him and that when Regan and Cornwall finally arrive he makes no reference to them not speaking to him, only wanting to know why his man was put in the stocks. Today's revelation was Lear's relationship with Regan. Apart from his annoyance at Kent being put in the stocks he spends most of the scene placating and reassuring Regan. Regan is obviously Daddy's girl; the tom-boy of the family is probably Cordelia who shows great independence; and Goneril, being the eldest, is in many ways the least loved. Regan, the sort of pretty girl with doe eyes, obviously flirted with her Daddy, a relationship based on teasing, conspiring together, Daddy succumbing to her wishes and having macho appeal for her. Clare Higgins thought that Regan was perhaps sexually abused by her father; I thought this was a somewhat fashionable notion and taking it a bit far. Prior to Goneril's entrance, I got Regan to sit on my knee, desperately trying to re-establish my power over her, playing her off against her husband, reassuring her of my love. To which she impatiently replies, 'Good sir, to the purpose,' and I am left reiterating: 'Who put my man in the stocks?' At that moment what struck me was how Lear loses concentration and that Cornwall and Regan talk over him as if he wasn't present, his brain wanders and is suddenly recalled by the arrival of Goneril – which was as far as we got.

It's been a hell of a week. I've been trying to prepare a surprise party for Irina's birthday, get that organised and get on with the play. Next week we start *Richard III*, which is a big pill. I can't tell Buckingham from Derby from Dorset from Hastings.

Postscript on the first block of *Lear* rehearsals. When Peter Brook did *Lear* at Stratford thirty years ago, according to Peter Jeffrey, who understudied Lear and played Albany, he started the rehearsals by saying *Lear* was so great a play that they could only begin to scrape at the surface, and even with the sum of all their talents they could never reach the heights demanded. That could be true but at the same time the beauty of the play is its simple accessibility: it's about children and parents, fathers and daughters, fathers and sons – within the realm of all our experience. It's a great play because it's true. We have learnt a lot in the past thirty years about relationships and particularly about their absurd and ludicrous aspects: the idea of parenthood – how it is formed from generation to generation; the things we wrongly or rightly try to invest in our children – how we try to collect our investment; the consequences of these actions, which can be both tragic and comic. The greatness of *Lear* is that it reflects the humour and poignancy of our own lives.

Sunday, April 8

Went to the memorial service for Ian Charleson. Ian was one of my first students at LAMDA, the first group I ever taught. An extra-ordinarily talented boy. I hadn't seen him for two or three years and was driving down the street one day towards Shepherd's Bush when suddenly there he was. He had been ill for some time with Aids and I was utterly shocked at how changed he'd become. I met him again at Dreas Reyneke's body conditioning studio when he was debating whether to take over Daniel Day Lewis's Hamlet. He was angry because he hadn't been asked to do it in the first place. We had a long talk and I persuaded him to. I had seen his first *Hamlet* just after he left drama school which was quite remarkable for a young man. He had a great purity of tone and was able to say a line as though you had never heard it before. Unfortunately I was not able to see his last Hamlet but those who did felt it was a most moving performance.

It was a sad afternoon, the church was filled to the brim and at the end of the service, hearing a recording of Ian singing 'Come unto these yellow sands' from *The Tempest*, there was a catch in all our breaths.

When Ian was playing Hamlet he knew he was dying, and with Hamlet's constant meditations on death the sense of that must have been all the more acute. The closeness of death is something of which I have to remind myself in *Lear*.

31

We started rehearsals of *Richard III*. Like Deborah, Richard Eyre had us reading different parts. Basically there's one part, and it's Richard. Clarence is a good role but the others are hard to get hold of. Buckingham is especially evasive; he's a man who seems to talk a lot but say very little, an empty man. My friend Oliver Cotton, who played him at the RSC last year, gave me a tip: the man is godless, has lost his faith. I can well believe it, there is something hollow about Buckingham.

The status games that are played among the leading characters are important and need to be accurately plotted. There is little metaphor, none of the subtleties of writing that are in *Lear*, it rambles on and on and on. It's incredibly long, though Richard has cut it – and obviously it needs cutting. It was nice to get a script that looks like a script and could be by anybody instead of one of those small Shakespeare books which are always so inhibiting.

Jane Gibson, whom I met yesterday at Ian's service, mentioned that she was planning to teach us to foxtrot, which threw me into a tizzy. The idea of foxtrots suggests that we are setting it in the thirties. In preparation for *Lear* I haven't shaved since Christmas and my present appearance is particularly hirsute: my hair is long, my beard is long and I don't want to cut either of them. It's going to be tricky to move into a thirties image: maybe a wig, I can't lose the beard. Perhaps a naval look.

Tuesday, April 10

Continued to read and paraphrase *Richard*. The cuts began to show, though on the whole the cutting is as it should be. One of our problems is that because we can't tour eight children we're going to have to lose some of the scenes with them in. I was very relieved at first that Buckingham had been cut, but on reflection I think that it's to his detriment, the floridity of his language is very important. He talks politics-speak. Richard is encouraging us to experiment with accent and go quite far; I've suggested that we get Joan Washington

32

to come and coach us. David Bradley and I, he a Yorkshireman and me a Scot, are playing aristocrats and it's going to be quite an education – something I've always shied away from, playing pukka and posh – to find a way of speaking that suits the verse and the pulse of the play.

It's clear that we're going to do it in some kind of twentieth-century guise. Ian has obviously been thinking about Richard's image and was doing doodlings (we were sitting next to one another). He drew a face and then suddenly hit on the idea of a birthmark. I said if we visit Moscow and Leningrad, with Gorbachev in power, a birthmark might look a little close to the bone.

Postscript on *Lear*. I've come up with an idea to make the party work: I'm going to try using paper party whistles, and perhaps wearing a paper crown, replacing it with a real one, an idea used by Shakespeare himself in *Henry VI Part Three* when Margaret of Anjou puts a paper crown on the Duke of York's head. In *Richard III*, one of the strangest things about Queen Margaret is how she's allowed to wander round the palace.

Wednesday, April 11

We started by doing some dancing with Jane Gibson. She used to teach at LAMDA – clown work and dancing – and I've known her for several years, someone completely immersed in her subject with a real organic understanding of it. Richard Eyre still isn't revealing anything, but it does look as if the play is going to be set in the thirties and I'm going to look ridiculous with this great shaggy beard and hair – I'll probably look a bit like the Marquess of Bath's son, like an old sixties hippie. We started with the basic dance, the farandole: everybody holds hands, and moves round in a circle; then we went on to the later dances, a very quick study, and we seem to be working up to the foxtrot. I am incapable of putting one foot in front of the other, I have no logic about dancing whatever. It reminded me of how, as a student, I always had to dance with

33

Matthew Guinness because nobody else would dance with us – we were the most graceless young men in the group.

In the afternoon we continued to break down the text and I think began to make more sense: I could see everyone's role and what we were doing. I haven't found Buckingham yet, though I've got a few ideas, namely godlessness, picking up what my pal Oli said. I think he's a man of great fastidiousness, could be slightly decadent, Oscar Wilde.

It's a play I have felt no connection with before, mainly because the historical plays leave me rather cold, but I think as an exercise in political villainy and machination it could be a lot of fun. I still want to know why Queen Margaret is allowed to wander round the palace, I find it quite extraordinary. I had a theory that she might be hidden in a dumb-waiter that goes up and down, there are about three of them, and she's actually hiding in the palace walls.

On Tuesday, after the Easter break, we're going back to *Lear*: this is the first of the wranglings that are going to go on between Richard and Deborah, I can see. It's wonderful how they field their stage managers to take the blows. I overheard Richard saying, 'Oh, I've got four weeks,' and they said, 'No, no, you've got three,' and he said, 'No, no, Deborah had three weeks,' and of course it's true that we originally had another week which we lost and there was the great row about not being paid. I'm sure Deborah's going to be starting on Tuesday morning, even though Richard has priority rehearsal.

Thursday, April 12

Read-through of *Richard*. It's the thirties – as if we didn't know by now. Bob Crowley's design was unveiled. Not sure whether I altogether agree with it, but it could be a way of making the play work. It will be set in a Third Reich environment. I suppose the play is about tyranny but it's also about grief, almost Greek in that way.

The design is fairly simple, using height and groups of lamps hung in rows of diminishing size to create a false perspective, plus a large, black veneered wall that flies in and out. This wall masks a huge mechanical arm that acts as a moving podium, used mainly by

Richard III. Very much a leather-jacketed production, with contemporary army uniforms, evoking a sense of Visconti's *The Damned*, I suppose.

I'm off to France for the weekend chez Peter Brook, Irina's father, which I'm looking forward to. It's now 5.45 and I hope we get there in time. We've got to leave at 7.00.

Week 5: Tuesday, April 17

We spent three days, Irina and I, at Le Mousseau. I didn't really think about the play very much.

Peter Brook told me that when he did the film of *Lear* Paul Scofield had no beard and it had to be laid on hair by hair, quite extraordinary when I think about it because the beard looks so magnificent. Brook said that in many ways it inhibited Paul from making any violent movements and Ken Lintott who used to do the wigs and hair at the RSC went quite berserk.

I also met the painter Edouard Boubat. We were talking about art and he told me a story about a man travelling through Japan looking for the greatest archer in the country. As he passed through a village he saw some targets with arrows right in the bull's-eyes. He went to the chief of the village and said, 'Who shot those arrows?' and the chief replied, 'A madman, a madman.' But after much exchange, the traveller insisting 'I must meet him, I want to know how he did it,' the chief answered, 'Well, it's very simple, he fired the arrows and then he drew the targets.' It reminds me of the shifting timetable of our rehearsals.

We drove to Normandy to look at a house and on the way back ran out of petrol – in true Brook fashion. It was late and nobody would stop for us, the cars would slow down and on seeing this shaggy King Lear accelerate off. We finally went to a house and I had to remain hidden while Father Brook persuaded the owner to lend us some petrol.

Deborah returned from Greece and we went on with *Lear*. We're now doing *Lear* and *Richard* simultaneously, which is going to add up to a lot of confusion. I spent part of the weekend trying to learn

35

the storm scene and, needless to say, we didn't do the storm scene, we did the first two scenes with the Fool.

The audience has high expectations of the Fool and the Fool has an interesting history in the play. There have been so many widely different Fools. I've now seen two films, *Ran* and Brook's *King Lear*. In *Ran* he is played by a curious – I believe – hermaphrodite, who looks like a girl with a man's voice dubbed on, but apparently was a genuine hermaphrodite; he/she is very much the aping Fool, slightly hysterical in that Japanese way. In Brook's film, the Fool was played by Jackie MacGowan, who was an alcoholic, but throughout the filming he was dry: he didn't know what the hell he was doing yet the performance is one of strange intensity, like an implacable shadow. Brook was telling me that when Guinness played it he played it in a series of impressions, he didn't have any real personality, he reflected whoever came into his orbit. At the end when he was left alone he was devoid of all character.

Then there was Tony Sher's Fool for the Royal Shakespeare Company, played as an out-and-out circus clown, a very indulgent Fool. It was a successful performance but I felt that it upset the balance of the play. Either through Lear's (Michael Gambon) lack of involvement with him or the Fool being given too free a rein, they didn't gel as a unit. Also the production ended with the Fool being killed by Lear. I cannot see any rationale or justification for that in the text, it's quite clear that the Fool fades away, the Fool doesn't die; it was a production conceit, which is fine but I don't think it was Shakespeare's intention.

The most successful Fool I have seen to date was that of Frank Middlemass in Jonathan Miller's production with Michael Hordern as Lear. The production had faults but its chief virtue was that Lear and the Fool were almost contemporaries. This Fool had been with Lear all his life, man and boy, and Lear referring to him as 'boy' had a wonderful and touching double-edged irony. It also brought out the friendship between the two men. Friendship is a key note in the Lear/Fool relationship.

I have a very clear image of the Fool as a tired old vaudeville act, a man who is entirely dependent on Lear for his living and without Lear simply has no existence. But he is also a constant reminder to Lear of how things really are, the only man who tells him the truth.

36

At one point the Fool says, 'I would fain learn to lie', and Lear replies, 'An you lie, sirrah, we'll have you whipped'.

We discussed whether Ceauşescu might have had a better understanding of what was going on in Romania if he had had a Fool; and whether if Lear's Fool cries wolf he is listened to; is he there to remind us of doom and gloom but, since his brief is essentially to entertain, alleviate it through humour? Lear and the Fool's relationship is of two people who thoroughly know each other, who have a rapport and a shared sense of humour. The humour, like all humour, is funny to them because it's the badinage of close friends. It isn't necessarily funny to those on the outside or to the audience. And the fact remains that the Fool has to keep within his brief, that whatever criticism is done is done through humour and irony and wit and never oversteps the mark, re-emphasising the order, 'An you lie, sirrah, we'll have you whipped'. My main concern is to get right the precise physical relationship between Lear and the Fool – the precise body language.

Tomorrow morning I start my Duke of Buckingham – the schizophrenic process will begin in earnest.

Wednesday, April 18–Thursday, April 19

I've got two days to catch up on.

Yesterday, Wednesday 18th, *Richard* and *Lear*. No, I didn't do any *Lear* yesterday, I did *Lear* today. I didn't do *Lear* yesterday because I spent yesterday doing the dinner-table scene where Margaret curses the dramatis personae. Richard presented us with the idea – in principle a good one – of treating the scene as a formal dinner. We spent the whole day working it out. At the moment it's a little laboured.

Clare Higgins is beginning to find her stride as Queen Elizabeth. It seems to me that certain questions weren't being asked in the rehearsal: during the dinner what are the precise expectations of the characters other than Richard and Elizabeth waiting for the impending death of Edward?

The thirties thing still worries me a bit though the set will be fine.

Ian is very struck by the religious images in the text – I believe he even suggested playing Richard in a dog collar with army fatigues but someone pointed out that chaplains don't fight.

Ian and I have very different styles but there are certain similarities between us, I think: we're both very spontaneous, both whores to the moment and I recognise that in him. If acting is about anything it's about being alive to the moment. There are areas of pre-planning which are necessary, of course – and I'm never very good at that. Ian is much more of a strategist; my manipulative skills work in an entirely different way, I use what happens.

The text now it has been cut presents difficulties for Buckingham; Buckingham is someone who likes the sound of his own voice and it damages his three-dimensionality if he can't indulge his verbosity, so I found myself having to ask for lines back, something I don't really like doing.

I think the younger members of the company are feeling inhibited. One of them asked me whether he could argue about his status. This creates an ironic situation: he is playing a character of quite high status in the play but he feels that his own status within the company is quite lowly and doesn't know how to protect the status of the character he is playing. I advised him to talk to Richard Eyre quietly.

Today, Thursday, we worked on both *King Lear* and *Richard*. We started with dancing, which I find impossible. I'm very slow and these long numbers remind me of school when you had forty people in a class with the teacher going at a rate not suited to the slower members.

I saw Joan Washington on the horizon and I can't wait for her to get a hand on my vowels.

At mid-day we did some work on the scene in Goneril's house when the Fool riddles about dividing an egg into two crowns. Deborah wants to use a real egg for the scene. I feel the egg doesn't work unless it follows the letter of the text. It just becomes messy and gimmicky. One thing that works well is the whole business of the Fool's coxcomb: he first proffers it to Kent, then places it firmly on Lear's head. The scene has to be sad, Lear knowing the Fool so well, the Fool a deliberate irritant, 'I know . . . you know . . . I know'.

This afternoon we went back to *Richard* and Edward's death scene. We propose to play it as a royal group photograph with the dying king in the centre. The only trouble with that idea is that if you have the chairs set up ready you know what's coming. Watching Antony Sher's Richard, I was always waiting for the moment when he first moved his crutches before springing across the stage. The problem with physical things is that they anticipate the events – egg, or for that matter dining chairs set up. I suggested that, so as not to give the game away, the dramatic happens in a moment, the chairs appear suddenly and we sit down and the photograph takes place; then it's over and we're on to something new.

Great consternation because there was a wheelchair standing by and should we use a wheelchair for Edward when there is already a wheelchair in the other production? I felt there was no reason why not. Ian at one time even thought of playing Richard in a wheelchair. Instead of armchair theatre we could have had wheelchair theatre.

It's a very monomaniacal play, *Richard*, made more so by the cutting, and it's very difficult to make the characters work independently of him. I'm still struggling with Buckingham's physical image. I came up with the idea today of playing him in a kilt, which might seem ludicrous but Ian was telling me that when asked to turn up in civvies Goering used to put on lederhosen, so perhaps the idea isn't as outrageous as all that. I must get on to Bob Crowley as soon as I can, wherever he may be, off designing another hundred and twenty productions.

I find I have to compromise between the two productions. At Stratford in 1987 the great bonus in working on two plays at once – *Fashion* and *Titus* – was how they complemented and fed each other's rehearsal and it was like playing the piano, left and right hands working independently but in harmony. It may be that in the case of *Titus* and *Fashion* both plays dealt with nihilistic themes; the fact that one was modern and one Elizabethan made for greater cross-fertilisation. *Richard* and *Lear* seem to be rubbing each other up the wrong way and there's the difference in directorial styles: Richard Eyre's style is for much more preparation, much more work has gone on beforehand over the physical aspects of the production and how it's going to look, the ideas he wants to follow through, the images he wants to use. Whereas Deborah is far more carefree and

39

her line of production creates itself. You have to work harder with Deborah. With Richard you have to accept an idea and try to fit that idea to your own discoveries. It can be difficult to move into a set pattern, but at the same time I find it a good discipline; I don't mind having a suit of clothes I'm forced to wear.

I had a very strange sense of *déjà vu* today at lunchtime. In the canteen were Tom Wilkinson and Oliver Cotton who were both in *Julius Caesar* with me in 1977, and also Paul Moriarty, who was in *Danton's Death* in 1983. I had an overwhelming feeling of everything as cyclical, no progression, here we are still at the National, caught in a groove. Is it '77, '83 or '90? In 1991 I'll have been in the theatre for thirty years and here we are, still here, still doing it, still flogging away.

I'm not really enjoying things at the moment. I don't think people can tell, I think people think I'm having rather a jolly time. I don't know why it is exactly, but it's to do with the clash of the two plays and to a certain extent with ego, my ego, Richard's ego, Ian's ego, Deborah's ego. Maybe I should start all over again with *Lear*, abandon my ideas. Perhaps it's only in my imagination but I feel there's a sort of race on between the two productions. I know now why Lear needs a Fool, someone to give him a perspective on things, which I'm lacking at the moment.

Friday, April 20

I had a line rehearsal with John Caulfield: they're there, I know them, but I was cheating a lot. I should have made a bigger attempt to get one part under my belt. I admire actors who can learn their lines and come into rehearsals line perfect. I can't do it: so much depends on what is going on in the room at the time.

This afternoon we went on with *Richard*, the scene when the young princes arrive. There is something about children and the way they act that asks for a kind of simplicity from those around and gives an ability to focus one's thinking. I found I could get to grips with Buckingham and we worked on the notion of him as a very rich man, a bored man, who has decided to fix his attention on a cripple in whom he sees possibilities for intrigue, advancement and power. His ego and vanity are ultimately what trip him up. Unlike Buckingham, Richard does have beliefs, does have a certain amount of self-doubt.

Week 6: Tuesday, April 24

Shakespeare's birthday yesterday. I've been a bit down over the last couple of days and felt so low I didn't make an entry last night. Buckingham gives me enormous problems and I'm rapidly losing touch with *King Lear* which is depressing me no end. I can't sustain it somehow. I couldn't remember a single word of the lines today. There is a point, and Ian and I have both reached it at the same time, when we feel we'd rather be off making films – theatre is hard work.

We did the demagogic scene, the Baynard's Castle scene, in which we use microphones to rouse the rabble (Nuremberg rally-style), and I had to have explained to me what was actually happening in the Council scene beforehand when the Mayor is gulled by Richard. I think the text has been overcut, the microphone scene if it's going to work needs full fuel from the text.

I can't think of anything else to say. I feel very negative and one day is fading into another. I long to do some work with Joan Washington, get my RP up to standard.

Friday, April 27

For the past two days I have been working on the death of Buckingham. I felt perhaps Buckingham should go to his death in a state of terror and today I discovered, reading a book about Richard III, that Buckingham was indeed gibbering at the end. As I see Buckingham as a relatively hollow man, I feel such a demise is necessary.

We discussed the battle scenes, which I'll have to be involved in, too, as a soldier to swell the numbers. I don't relish the thought of changing out of Buckingham into full battle fatigues circa Second World War – heavy boots, Sam Browne and all – and running round a slippery stage, helmet and dry ice to impair the vision, before preparing for an evening performance of *King Lear*.

Richard Eyre gave a fascinating talk about making the film *Tumbledown* and his experiences of war filming in Wales as a mock-up for the Falkland Islands. In the Falkland conflict the equipment was all wrong and the soldiers took time to remember their purpose, which is to kill. He wants to capture some of that confusion at the end of *Richard*, the chaos of war, the brutal facts of being trained to kill and killing as a job – something brought home to me during *Titus*. It's a good idea to stress the chaos but there is also quite a clear structure, very precise steps in Richard's downfall, leading towards his ultimate state in the battle – a man stripped of everything, alone, fighting like a cornered animal – and I think the production has to bring that out.

We did some work in the afternoon on the ghosts who appear before Bosworth and it is intriguing that the audience have never seen Henry VI except as a corpse, so he can be presented as an ordinary soldier who you suddenly realise is the ghost of Henry VI, which effortlessly sets in train the series of ghosts, Buckingham the last.

I had a conversation with Clare Higgins yesterday about *Richard* and what I feel, that I am finding it difficult to divide my attention between the two plays. I said perhaps I should look on it like working in a film situation where you slot yourself in, but she argued that that wasn't a good way to view it. I'm not sure that my feelings aren't ones of threatened ego, a restlessness when I'm no longer the star of the show, not necessarily to do with disliking the play but with my own status. These are difficult questions because you do come up against your own ego in these situations and I have to deal with it so that when I am doing *Richard* I understand my responsibilities. There's an element in the actor which is childish and wants to be the centre of attention. It's something which rather tires me about actors, something I don't like about myself as an actor and yet it's part of what fuels the work. It's at moments like this when one comes up against one's own personality that you think, gosh, I wish I were doing something else, something a little bit more productive in the world, something a little bit more ... I don't know ... a doctor, anything.

There are also personal problems and money problems hanging over me at the moment, as there always are, the day-to-day running of life. I suppose it's the mid-term blues.

I've just agreed to write a piece about Arthur Miller, a diversion, which I think I need – not that I need a diversion, I've got enough work on.

Week 7: Monday, April 30

I had a good session on voice with Joan. And then some *Titus*, I mean *Lear*, the thunder scene: David and I went to the drum room and belted a few drums. In the afternoon we continued with *Richard* and the so-called dinner scene.

Tuesday, May 1–Wednesday, May 2

I can't remember what we did on Tuesday morning – oh yes, we went on with the dinner scene which was extremely tedious, and after the rehearsal Richard said that the Buckingham we had come up with didn't seem to be evident in that scene and I realised that, of course, he isn't evident in that scene, he's quite clearly keeping a low profile and only in the scene after the death of Edward IV do we see him showing off a little bit in his reconciliation with Elizabeth. Really he comes to the fore when Richard is bemoaning his brother Clarence's death.

By accident, by backing off the problem and being at the lowest level of depression about the role, I suddenly found a way of taking the part forward and felt at the end of the day that I had established Buckingham as an entity.

My session with Joan Washington was very good but I am quite unable to come to terms with standard English – for deeply

43

psychological reasons as well as the whole caste system of this country.

Anyway the big factor was that we got back to *Lear*. Deborah was sitting there like a great female Buddha nitpicking on what you don't quite understand. I always spend the first ten minutes of a Deborah Warner rehearsal wondering what the fuck she's talking about: sometimes she seems to talk for the sake of talking, but what happens is that by her unhelpfulness and partly because she's such a passive creature in many ways, like an obelisk, passive yet solid, you feel that you have to take the play by the scruff of the neck and do something with it. Whereas Richard is always obliging, in the way he moves, in the way he directs, in the way he has a sort of enthusiasm for the work while it is all preordained. Deborah's kind of tacit boredom, really – oh, be theatrical, entertain me, do something – means one has constantly to be on the alert; it's like doing takes as opposed to rehearsals.

Clare Higgins and I picked up the arrival at Regan's house literally where we stopped for the three-week break. There was a synthesis between actor and character, a moment when I suddenly started thinking on my feet, which I'm supposed to do as an actor, and Lear began to think on his feet out of a similar panic. The scene began to have physical movement, Regan scurrying like an animal, Lear's tactile pursuit of his daughter, holding her, tickling her, pulling her on to his knee, Regan teasingly reciprocating to avoid direct confrontation. Regan always reminds me of my middle sister, Irene, who as a child spent her life avoiding confrontation. Regan is a bit more ditsy than my sister was.

In the afternoon we came to the storm which we haven't really touched yet. The storm is created by Lear, it's his storm. When Deborah produced it before, she had Lear conducting the storm. It can't be quite that detached, I think, but he talks to the storm, gives it advice, encourages it to do its worst and the storm turns against him. I think the image is of creatures coming up out of the ground, scurrying around, man stripped to his nakedness, in his pure state against the elements. So we struggled with how to create the storm percussively and I ended up with a cymbal on a stick and a bull whip – from nowhere – and I have to pause and consider how things do come: the more I work as an actor the more I realise how abstract my work is; it's not realistic and not always logical. There is a hidden logic, which isn't always apparent even to me until I've done more work, more examination, almost until I'm playing and then I can discard, I can throw away. When we started off we had nothing, and this again is an interesting thing about Deborah's rehearsals, we do start with nothing, we start almost from a state of abject panic when we don't know what to do, then things begin to grow, we follow things through, we use materials lying around the room to help. It's always like this and it's exasperating, it's tiring, it's exhausting and again, it's such a God-awful contrast to the work we're doing on *Richard*.

Thursday, May 3

Richard: We worked on the scene with the children, where the young princes arrive in London, the Victoria station scene, and again Buckingham seems to be changing and becoming more serjeant-majorish, more Mr Fix-it, which is what he is. The whole business has to be very English and I must try and work on it.

The problem with doing a classical play in a contemporary setting is that certain compromises have to be made and today we had an example. In the scene with the Lord Mayor the soldiers make a mock attack on the Tower of London and there are phrases such as 'look to the drawbridge' and 'o'erlook the walls', also Richard and Buckingham are described as being in 'rotten armour and marvel-lously ill-favoured'. The basic intention of the scene is to show the Lord Mayor, who has the ear of the common people, the sort of strength that Gloucester (Richard) has behind him. Richard Eyre has chosen to have Richard dressed in a sort of Nazi uniform and the scene set inside the Council Room instead of on the castle walls, the soldiers dressed like stormtroopers. The trouble with the con-temporary aspect is that it creates as many problems as it solves – usually with the motivation of a scene – and we have to solve the difficulty of drawbridges and castle walls. A compromise was reached: the drawbridge and castle walls will be outside the room

45

and a barricade was made by Ian turning over the Council table. Let's hope it works.

Sam came off the book which, he said to me afterwards in the car, was nerve-wracking. He's absolutely right, the first day off the book is nerve-wracking.

At the end of the day we had a session on the battles with Jane Gibson. She made us do some exercises based on inhabitation of the words 'attack', 'retreat', 'victory', striking attitudes in the manner of the words.

Friday, May 4

I finally decided to have a wig for Buckingham and a beard as well, pommaded, with make-up plastered on it to get an image like Edward VII or George V. I think it might look like the present Duke of Gloucester.

We went back to *Lear* and did the heath scene with Derek (Edgar) and David and Ian. Ian had a difficult morning and I had a difficult afternoon. Deborah was being extremely exasperating and not helpful. The whole business of the storm and the noise: I've never heard a storm scene yet, the dialogue, because you are always acting storm instead of acting the lines. Ian is feeling towards a naturalistic effect, people treading through mud; I find all that very stagey and I never quite believe it. I think you have to use the circumstances you've got.

We came to the scene where Lear is taken out of the hovel and into Gloucester's home. Now it seemed to me there were wonderful images we could have pursued which Deborah didn't want to pursue, for no apparent reason, just her stubbornness, and she kept coming up with very general and unspecific notes such as 'You're all in your own worlds' – well, it's quite clear at the end of the previous scene that I have adopted a new Fool, Edgar, and am obsessed with him until the hovel scene; then Lear is indeed in his own world but there's quite a complex journey to this point which has to be charted. It took Ian to solve the hovel scene in terms of the dialogue and he, bless him, came to the fore. I knew what had to be done but I'd had such a spat with Deborah: I wanted us all to be in the same naked state, all in blankets; I feel it is very important that everyone in the storm, not only Lear, should be stripped down, and I also felt that the Fool should disappear at the end of the scene. It was fundamental to me and I didn't think that we were pursuing it properly.

Deborah expects us to behave like performing seals, she doesn't direct, she organises, and sometimes you require the director to have done a little more homework on the inter-relationships of the characters. I think the cast all suffer from the fact that she picks on something that seems to be completely unimportant and dwells on it and people get confused because it seems the wrong priority. Deborah should have started earlier; I think her pace of work is far too slow to be working in tandem with someone like Richard whose pace is faster, though perhaps Richard's work is done ahead; Richard does do his homework, maybe too much homework. I do like Richard, I like him enormously. I think he is an extremely nice man, a very good man, and his intelligence and understanding of the visual aspects of the play are very strong.

Richard III is a simpler play than *Lear*, partly because it is designed as a one-man piece, much more so than *Lear*. The characters in *Lear* are infinitely more interesting; we have got to make the characters in *Richard* interesting, dig them out without over-emphasising or over-scoring them.

I'm worried about Buckingham because I do feel he has to be an aristocrat and at the moment he's too much like a serjeant-major.

I was supposed to meet Bob Crowley at the end of rehearsals because he wanted to do a sketch but we didn't make it. They had a meeting about my wig. They have a great problem about wigs. Deborah yesterday, again, made me very angry. She said, 'Will you please consult with the designer before you get your hair cut,' and I pointed out that it isn't up to the actors to consult with the designer, it's up to the two directors to get together and say what they are going to do about wigs. I solved my problem by saying I would wear a wig as Buckingham and tuck my hair underneath but I was very angry, really angry, at the onus always being put on the actor. Ian came back after a meeting and we agreed that we are all treated like unruly children.

Big disaster. The catwalk we had made which was guaranteed

would be as light as a feather, turns out to be made of the material you use for lightness in aircraft. The bloody thing has arrived and takes four or five men to move.

Having moaned to Irina last night – who, poor girl, has to put up with this heavy load plus the fact that I have a few domestic problems with ex-wife, children, what have you – it looks as though today and the last couple of days have perhaps been a breakthrough.

This weekend I had to do the piece for the book on Arthur Miller, which proved difficult, but I managed to get an 800-word piece off to Chris Bigsby at the Department of American Studies at East Anglia University.

I saw the film of *Richard III* last night, which is so bad, quite appalling. The battle scenes at the end are the best things about it.

Week 8: Monday, May 7

Another bank holiday.

Tuesday, May 8

Richard: In the morning we did our dancing, which I enjoy more and more, and we started to do the foxtrot. I do feel a bit like Matthew Guinness and my dancing skills are not exactly . . . I'm no Fred Astaire, but it is enjoyable and I think in terms of period it does say a lot. I hope we continue with it.

Then we went on to rehearse the Baynard's Castle scene, the scene where the Lord Mayor of London is brought in by Buckingham to persuade Richard to take up the crown. When we sat and read the scene we were able to keep up a kind of contact, but Richard Eyre wants to do it with Ian above – as he needs to be because the text suggests it – and me below; I have to play out in front so I can't see Ian and that's extremely difficult and very, very stagey.

We broke at about 2 o'clock and then came back and worked on the coronation scene. Here again we were trying to do something very stylised – Richard wearing a red cloak the size of the whole stage and we attendant lords carrying his train around the stage in a very complex formation. I felt it didn't work and I think in the end everyone else realised it wasn't working.

The coronation is about Richard's isolation: when he gets the crown he is alone, then he starts addressing the various people participating in the coronation, Buckingham among them, almost in a stream-of-consciousness style. Buckingham realises that Richard wants the princes killed and has a struggle of conscience, which Richard sees as delaying tactics. Buckingham eventually comes back after asking for time to think and accepts the deal that Richard has offered. However, everything goes by the by, Richard reneges on the deal and Buckingham is left with the fact that he is a dead man.

I found the staging so deeply uninteresting: we have this huge cloak and Richard sitting on the throne slap centre-stage. It all goes back to the business of everything being pre-digested, all the discoveries are already made before we get to rehearsal and it's just a question of filling in. I find that way of working frustrating and dead, I can't relate to it in any way, shape or form. It's impossible. You stand around working on technical things which have already been created on the model or whatever: there's a way of playing the scene we did this morning in the style – which is how we're doing it . . . I'm sorry, I can't find any enthusiasm for *Richard III* whatsoever, I'm feeling really low about it, quite frankly it bores the ass off me. There's nothing else I can say at this stage, we trundle on.

Wednesday, May 9

Working so hard I forgot the Board meeting of IFTA.

I felt much happier today. I realised that the production will tend to be camp but we have to go along with it, play the thirties idea for all it is worth, and not try to resist or rationalise or make it difficult. I think the argument for the thirties is that, like Shakespeare, thirties plays have to be done via the text, you can't overweigh them with subtext as the modern actor wants to do. In the thirties Lonsdale

49

comedies, Coward etc. you had to play the line, you couldn't play beside it. The boulevard actors of the thirties had a great sense of naturalism but at the same time they felt a duty to play the text. As in Shakespeare, rhythm and meaning go hand in hand, a difficulty for a lot of people working on this kind of material today. The discipline required in boulevard and classical theatre is the same: the inherent rhythm must be understood and followed for the phrase to have its effect.

I've really come round to believing that it is possible to do it this way. It was out of the thirties, too, that a consciousness of reality came; in the thirties life was held at a distance – poverty, depression, the rise of Fascism in Europe, anti-semitism – particularly among the aristocracy. There are snags. Shakespeare's language is elaborate and the higher up the social scale, the more rich the language – not necessarily true in the thirties, when the higher up the social scale the more monosyllabic and choked the language became. But there may be advantages: the contrast of styles, a sense of unreality, decadence, Kristallnacht, thirties people talking about death in such high-blown ways. I feel now I'm resolved.

We did some good work on the ghost scene using the soldier idea – the orderly delivering Richard's wake-up call, who transforms into the ghost of Henry VI.

Thursday, May 10

In the morning I rehearsed Buckingham's death. He repeats the list of all Margaret's curses and I feel that the thing to do with a list is to treat it quite plainly as a list and not shy away from it.

Then *Lear*, and it was the first time I've touched the mad scene with Gloucester and all the sexual innuendo. Again, playing *Titus* has prepared me for this. So many of the themes have been dealt with in that play. Titus instructing his servants to fire arrows of request to the gods is like Lear addressing his imaginary army at the beginning of the mad scene. I decided that when Lear comes on and he's toiling and moiling and arguing with his imaginary soldiers, these are his hundred men still with him but by this time getting

50

fractious and wanting more money. The scene is interrupted by the entrance of Goneril in a white beard who is in fact Gloucester. Lear then rails against the sexual politics of women, also indirectly attacking Gloucester whose suffering is the result of a sexual peccadillo (Edmund). From rejection of sex, betrayal by children, Lear graduates to the hypocrisy of power, and culminates with the infant coming to the great stage of fools and the roles he or she will play for the duration of his or her life.

Deborah wanted me to carry a potted geranium but in those fantastic scenes you have to be very free physically and use your body and hands for full expression. To have your hands cluttered up by things isn't an advantage.

Ian is tired; he's working very hard, I think probably much harder than I am. I seem to be underworked and he seems to be overworked. It's wonderful to be working with someone like Derek Hutchinson with whom, as with Deborah, I have a shared past and shared tastes and experiences and who understands things immediately as Deborah does.

Friday, May 11

We started with Lear's waking-up scene, when he's back in his wheelchair asleep, rescued by Cordelia's army. Deborah, Eve and Ian decided that when Eve comes on she doesn't recognise Kent still disguised as a servant. I had all sorts of fantasies about breakfast and Lear being given a croissant which is why he says 'Am I in France?' We were trying to diffuse the sentimentality of the scene. Eve is very good and tender-hearted and the scene played itself, partly because of the ground we had covered and partly because of the simplicity and brilliance of the lines. There's no question but that when you have a play like *Lear* you're floating.

In the afternoon I came back to Buckingham and we tackled the dreadfully difficult scene when the head of Hastings is brought in. We decided – which was an enormous help to me – that I didn't know Hastings' head was going to be brought into the cabinet room and, presented as a shock, it worked. We then rehearsed the first big

51

group scene with all the lords, the dinner scene, with Queen Elizabeth, Edward dying offstage and Richard's entrance after his soliloquies and two-handers. The problem is the way characters like Hastings and Derby are introduced: they're not covered for in this scene, so you have to find a way of embroiling them.

It was also Deborah's birthday and we all hid behind a white curtain and surprised her in Rehearsal Room 2. You feel so silly when you've got about ten people standing behind a white sheet pretending to be silent, but it was touching.

Funny situation over Dublin: we can't go to Dublin because the Abbey have done a deal with Murphy's and it's Guinness who are backing our tour. So now we're going to Cork. A perfect example of the whole business of sponsorship.

Irina is back this evening. I'm about to rehearse, in fact I'm on now, I'm going to rehearse the prison scene with Edmund.

Saturday, May 12

We did our first run of the first half of *Richard*, two and a half hours, ridiculously long, but it showed great promise. Ian's concentration, particularly at the beginning of the play, was most impressive. The strength of the play is really in the first two or three scenes, that's what you remember, and Ian's performance is going to be very fine, very inventive, with great simplicity.

Other things: seeing Peter Jeffrey, who is sixty, play Clarence made me realise that with so many parts nowadays cast so young we miss the weight and authority of experience in a part like Clarence. My performance was terrible and I'm in despair, I don't know what I'm doing. I get it, it comes and goes, I can't get a line on the part at all now.

Week 9: Monday, May 14

Fights today. John Waller and Jane Gibson spent the whole day choreographing the fights, dividing the company between Richard's army and Richmond's. We worked it out that the total age of the soldiers involved was about a thousand years, an average age of fifty, the oldest army ever.

Then we were left with time on our hands. Deborah wasn't there so I ran the first scene and was horrified to be prompted by David Bradley, my understudy, who knows the lines better than I do.

Tuesday, May 15

I went through Buckingham with Richard Eyre and we decided that he needs to be played more on the front foot, that really he was much more of a campaign manager. Then I spent a chaotic hour in costume fittings for *Lear*; tried on a sort of green Marks and Sparks coat and Hildegard has found some extraordinary material, rubber embossed on silk.

This afternoon was *Lear* and the death scene. I want to try bringing in Cordelia on the wheelchair. We've now done the whole play, after nine weeks, finally finished the play.

I'm off to Cannes for two days for the launch of Ken Loach's *Hidden Agenda*, in which I play a chief constable sent out from the mainland to investigate the shooting of an Amnesty International lawyer in Northern Ireland. The film steps on a lot of political toes and openly discusses MI5's involvement in disinformation, i.e. the policy of discrediting certain political figures in England during the 1970s. I saw it on Sunday and I feel quietly confident but, who knows, one can never tell in the film business.

Two very extraordinary days in Cannes. The film was received quite well on the whole by the industry but had fairly mixed notices from the critics, particularly from the right-wing elements, the British so-called yellow press. David Robinson gave it a good review in *The Times*, but Alexander Walker – the *Evening Standard* – is an Ulsterman and a patriot and naturally he found the film offensive and accused it, unfairly I think, of being pro-IRA. There was a press conference and I could see him seething with anger as we walked into the room. Eventually he stood up and attacked Ken Loach. Some of the British journalists formed a phalanx behind him and endorsed his aggression. Finally someone from the European ranks weighed in and accused them of bias and being right-wing.

Cannes was strange – a Disneyworld. The whole thing had an air of unreality about it and I felt like a walking exhibit. We really worked very hard. We had a lot of interviews. I was constantly being asked whether it would be possible for me to work in England again after making the film but people were very complimentary about it and I'm proud of it. It's a very good thriller – in the tradition of Costa-Gavras' *Z*.

I got back to England on Thursday night and on Friday we had a full day, from 10.30 to 9 o'clock at night, rehearsing *Lear*. We started off with a run of the second half. I carried the book and it was surprisingly fluid. Clare played Regan as a sort of hysterical banshee, Regan and Albany were like two avaricious ferrets and it worked very well. Susan played Goneril as a rather knocked-off girl, very disturbed and lacking in confidence.

We then turned to the first half and did some good work on the opening scene. There was an hour of really extraordinary direction by Deborah after we'd wasted a lot of time trying to find out how to start the scenes, arrangements, areas – I had to back off, my energy gives out and I allow other people to deal with things, because the amount of input I give to the rehearsals ... She examined a completely different way of playing the bit with Cordelia, keeping the humour up until the last possible moment, the banter which then turns sour, and squeezing every ounce from it.

We looked at the scene with the knights, which I haven't done for ages. There are so many crossings of the stage, ordering one knight to go and look for Oswald, another to find the Fool, another to find Goneril. Ian and I worked on the Lear/Kent relationship, Ian making himself totally indispensable. When I got home I was absolutely exhausted.

Last night I dreamt about *King Lear* – mixed up with *Titus*. I had to kill my son, on horseback, and my son was played by a rather middle-aged bareback lady in spangled clothes which seemed to me very odd. I couldn't work it out. What I do remember was that I'd watched a production with Anthony Hopkins playing Lear and then had to do my production after he'd done his. After I'd finished Hopkins came up and asked me a question, 'Is it emotionalism or the Corsican brothers?' to which I replied, 'Oh, of course not, it's the Karamazov brothers.' What that means, I have no idea.

Week 10: Monday, May 21

We managed to crack the scene at Baynard's Castle. It needs confidence on my part. Richard was very helpful about trying to get the irony out of my voice. I find that in trying to do a frightfully, frightfully English accent irony immediately creeps in, but anyway we stationed it and the idea of the bowler-hatted brigade of aldermen attending the Mayor worked extremely well. It gave me something to play off. I think the scene will look quite bizarre.

We've just heard that *Hidden Agenda* won the Jury Prize at Cannes, which is a smack in the face for the British journalists who asked the President of the Festival why the film was shown. To which he replied 'Pourquoi non?' There is obviously going to be quite a stink when the film comes out here.

55

Very good day on *Lear* and the first scene, which is becoming more and more crazy. My worry is that we may lose the balance of the ritual and the domestic. The domestic is always more attractive but even in his madness Lear holds to certain beliefs and values, the whole notion of kingship etc. So we are going to have a game with a rope which Lear swings round the stage to make the girls leap over. I carry a bag with the crowns in it, like an eccentric bag person, odd as most dictators become, and will bestow the kingdom by producing the crowns from the bag, Father Christmas giving out presents. Suddenly it all goes wrong, the jolly king isn't jolly any more, and with the curse on Cordelia the whole scene turns vicious. The wheelchair is a prop for Lear to hide behind metaphorically and whip up the girls' hysteria.

We have got to watch how we build and change tone and pitch to make sure it doesn't get too loud, too boisterous, too unrelated to the text. Also it is important to keep moving on a stage like the Lyttleton, which is where the wheelchair comes into its own, the moveable throne. It is particularly helpful in creating patterns of movement so the whole thing has fluidity and we can also change the access. If an actor is speaking, though, Lear must be able to move downstage so he, Lear, can still be seen. This is easily contrived and I'm a great believer in the downstage in acting anyway.

The scheduling, with the priority system and the speed the directors are working at, causes constant problems. If I'm not on priority, I'm needed for something else and I never stop doing scenes – though now I'm delighted to be playing Buckingham. The Stage Management are having a rough time because they've become piggies in the middle; we really need someone to liaise the calls but everyone is too busy. Cordelia Monsey, the Assistant Director, is sorting out understudies and Ian has got enough on his plate as producer.

Wednesday, May 23

David Bradley has a grasp of *Lear* like no other I can imagine; I knew I was right to insist on having him as the Fool. The rapport we have sustains so much of the play for me. We worked on Act 1, Scene 4, and made a great joke in ridiculing Lear, putting the red nose on Lear, a bobble from the end of his hat, making Lear look like a fool in the limelight. I've also found a little stool for Lear to sit on.

We worked on Goneril's entrance and the curse on Goneril which echoes the curse on Cordelia. It had a violence about it which I think is necessary, but Lear is both ludicrous and sentimental so there is also an extraordinary humour in the scene, the bathetic sight of the knights in various stages of undress watching Lear berate Goneril, Lear cracking his whip at the Fool, the Fool exiting with the knights, giving Lear a long, hard, quizzical look. In 1/5, the following scene, David came up with the idea of sitting in my lap for the 'Let me not be mad' speech. It made perfect sense.

I want to try and use the red nose for the death of Cordelia.

Thursday, May 24

Last night I had a dream in which I had a bet on a horse called Diction – I don't know if it won or not.

We did some exciting work on *Richard* today and changed a lot of the moves. We went over the dinner scene endlessly; it creates as many problems as it solves – more, because it's imposed. Everybody is feeling under an enormous amount of pressure and I think, like me, Ian is very tired and dislikes some of the moves.

I'm using a monocle for Buckingham and it's working very well. I have to watch that it doesn't dominate, but it seems to suit the character and give him a kind of largeness and juiciness he needs, a sweaty wideness. I think it helps to focus the character; in a way it's a metaphor.

We do need a company masseur, all our bodies are feeling quite wrecked. I'm not as fit as I was. I miss going to the gym – that's the trouble with over-rehearsing.

Dominic Muldowney, Director of Music, came to watch and I sang Buckingham's ghost speech as a lullaby. We did it again and Richard Eyre wanted me to shout it – so I did. But Dominic felt as I do and said I should sing it.

Friday, May 25

Ian's fifty-first birthday.

Saturday, May 26

We did a full day's work on Act 2, Scene 4, 'the reason not the need' scene, Kent in the stocks, sorting out everyone's positions and where they fit in. There is always a problem over getting Kent out of the stocks and we have to find a solution that isn't distracting from the main thrust of the scene, keeps the scene moving. We've got the movement of the scene now but I've got to find ways of varying the tone. I can't always start on the same sort of indignant note, it's boring. There is a lot of variation but I've got to get the measure of it and get it working from scene to scene. There are more traps in *Lear* than *Titus*, just in the musicality of it. In *Titus* you can spring more surprises because the text isn't as well known. The end of the scene, the 'Oh Fool I shall go mad', was given a final cap by David whisking me off in the wheelchair.

Another bank holiday, a weekend – Monday – off. I'm going out with my daughter this evening, being Daddy.

We did some more work on the storm scene and decided that the thunder sheet was too inhibiting but that we would keep the cymbal and the whip. We worked on the hovel scenes and had a long and turgid struggle trying to plot the disintegration of Lear's relationship with the Fool and Lear's growing dependency on Edgar. We finally got a few clues but it was so difficult to recall what we'd done several weeks ago that we had to start almost completely afresh. Derek Hutchinson had a lot of difficulty with some of the language – though he's got the craziness of it – and he's pushing himself too much; when he takes his time it goes well.

I had a costume fitting this morning: the first costume works quite well but the second was too costume-like: it needs to be more practical, more of a coat. I wore a fur coat in rehearsal but it was far too heavy and as I'll be in pyjamas I'm going to need pockets. The Wardrobe seems a bit pushed for time and under pressure and obviously drawings hadn't come in. We tried out various garments on top of each other, building up layers, and this seems to be a solution. It was decided that an outer coat and an inner coat would be made. The costumes feel a little anachronistic, not properly integrated. David is very unhappy about his hat. He's been using a leather airman's hat which looks fabulous but Hildegard wants him to wear this strange headpiece from somewhere like North Africa.

When we got downstairs we struggled again with the catwalk which no one can budge – a pity, because the stage is going to look mighty empty without it.

This evening I had dinner with Katya from the Film-Actors' Theatre in Tbilisi and she asked whether we could take *King Lear* there.

Wednesday, May 30

We started with the hovel scene and what we should have finished yesterday. David and I did some work on the storm scene with good old-fashioned kettledrums, which give a rougher sound than modern tympani, and orchestrated it with Dominic Muldowney. The drums will be on either side of the stage and Martin and Colin, the musicians, will talk to one another on them. We ended up with Act 1, Scene 1, and at the moment I'm like a walking prop basket – buckets, and stools, and whips, crowns, wheelchairs.

Tomorrow we do a run-through of *Lear*, the first half, which is a bit daunting. I start at 10.15. I do *King Lear* in the morning and in the afternoon I go back to *Richard* and do Buckingham scenes till 7.30; Friday, we'll do the same and, Saturday, a run of *Richard*. Ooof.

Thursday, May 31

Well, today was the heavy. The run-through of *Lear* was as expected, fairly chaotic but lots of ideas. Poor Ian obviously couldn't remember any of the moves we'd done and was not feeling too well, so he was out of it. He is suffering as I was from the difficulty of focusing on two roles. David was excellent, so was Derek Hutchinson who had made a breakthrough in the hovel scenes.

The first scene went reasonably well. We had one or two problems with it, trying to remember bits and pieces. I need to run it more and more and more to find a way of modulating the music of the part. I'm on one note at the moment and only just have a nodding acquaintance with the text. I'm still behind the lines, I'm still saying them and I need to be free of them to find things within them. My main concern is to shape Lear, give the part size and humanity, but keep its regality, its danger. The ideas I've put in are there and are working, I think, to a certain extent. I don't know if they'll come off, they're not to everybody's taste; I don't know if my Lear is tragic or kingly enough. People were very nice about it and genuinely touched

60

but I'm nervous about the whole thing as usual. I feel, though, it's the Lear I can do.

In the other *Lear* apparently they're all visiting lunatic asylums and doctors. Clare Higgins wants us to go and play it in Broadmoor. Someone suggested a limited season. The company spirits are very good.

I was curiously affected by a strange programme on rat-catchers on the telly last night. It said a lot to me about low-life and various things like order and tidiness and keeping squalor at bay, things we take for granted in our lives.

This afternoon was *Richard* and we did the endless, most rehearsed scene, the dinner scene – we rehearse it time and time again. Richard Eyre always starts smoking at around 4 o'clock in the afternoon, when he's at his most nervous. He has cut some more of the dialogue; it isn't the greatest writing but it's nonsense to cut it . . . I haven't got the energy to argue.

At the end of a day like today you feel that you never want to act. People were exhausted. I had to keep going, I couldn't rest, I couldn't even sit down for two minutes: if I did I'd fall asleep. We're all tired, we're all knackered, doing the two plays is impossible.

Friday, June 1

My forty-fourth birthday. I'm sitting in the quiet room of the National. It is a wonderful idea, I must say, to have a quiet room and here it is. I haven't used it before.

I've been thinking about Irina's patience and endurance of me at the moment. She really is remarkable. I don't think I would have found the same tolerance and kindness and understanding in my previous relationships.

I've just done a voice class with Patsy Rodenburg and we're about to do some more battles. We did some battles last night. We always seem to do battles at 6 o'clock in the evening when we're at our most tired. Someone like Sam Beazley, the oldest member of the company, thrives on it. Sam was saying yesterday in the car how extraordinary it was – we were talking about a programme on 1940 that we'd seen

61

– when he'd started in the Olivier company he was the youngest man in the company and now he's the oldest. It's curiously moving, I understand what he means – the cycle of theatre life. He was also saying how remarkable Deborah is and she truly is. She exudes calmness and precision, allowing things to come to the boil and then checking them. She's become more ruthless, she's certainly become tougher.

We had a birthday cake. It's almost a weekly ritual now. Then I spent some time looking at wheelchairs. In the photograph of George Bernard Shaw's wheelchair – which I originally saw at Ayot St Lawrence – the wheels are in the wrong place for us and a modification has to be made.

Saturday, June 2

Run-through of *Richard*. It was very promising and the line of the thing, the sense of narrative, began to emerge. In some places – the cabinet scenes – we must move more quickly; Ian has a tendency to take everything at a kind of measured pace when I know for a fact that the narrative will not bear it. Richard Eyre, Ian and I worked out the details of Buckingham and Richard's relationship.

And then we did some good work on *Lear* and I tried out a few ideas with bags of flower petals, hurling flower petals when he says 'Kill, kill, kill', using ears of corn to hide behind like army camouflage, binding his feet in the bags like a tramp for the line 'It were a delicate stratagem to shoe a troop of horse with felt; I'll put it in proof'. These images heighten the humour and the fantastical. Much of the mechanics of *Lear* is in the humour and we need to exploit it to the full to keep up a buoyancy – a reflection of the madness – and suddenly switch and make people cry at the same time.

I couldn't remember the line about 'the rascal beadle', which follows 'the dog obey'd in office'. I suddenly thought 'beagle', the link with the dog. And I want to do hunting cries, I keep meaning to ask Cordelia Monsey if she's done any research into hunting cries.

I also had an elocution lesson with Joan Washington. My vowels are improving.

Week 12: Tuesday, June 5

We did the waking-up scene, then I had to come home and deal with my poor girl who is sick and I wanted to see her. When I got back we did the scene with Cordelia, 'Let's away to prison; we two alone will sing like birds i' the cage'. It was extremely difficult to concentrate and I was tired and couldn't deal with it. David and I want to do some little vignettes, sort of silent film excerpts, David battling the storm, pushing me in the wheelchair, me pushing David, the wheelchair being abandoned, but Deborah feels that it might be too comic and she may be right.

The two boys, Kae-Kazim and Derek – Edmund and Edgar – still haven't done their fight scene and Deborah is hoping they will work it out themselves. It strikes me that she greatly undervalues the fights; she did this before, with *Titus*: we rehearsed and played for a whole year before she finally got an arranger to come and sort out certain movements. I find her lack of respect in that area quite dazzling and quite surprising. She wants them to solve it *à la* Kick, *à la* poor theatre, when in the NT we have experts we can call on. It seems quite crazy. She said she would do something about it, but I discovered later that she had told the assistant director it didn't matter, the boys would sort it out. I then talked to Kae and Derek who were extremely nervous about it and need help. The Richmond fight scene in *Richard* was set three weeks ago. We have two weeks left for *Lear*. I think it shows a blatant disregard for (a) safety and (b) a very crucial part of the play, but Deborah likes to dice with danger.

Wednesday, June 6

We rehearsed the dinner scene yet again. I'd like to go through these tapes and find out how many times we've done the dinner scene but we've done it more times than I care to imagine. We also did the scenes with the children, Victoria station – three sets of children.

It looks as if we're going to have a run-through of *Richard* on Wednesday and another on Saturday. We're having no runs of *Lear* – but I leave that to Herr Doris Waters.

We went through the cursing of Goneril, which I played a few weeks ago in a very physically demonstrative way: somehow I don't know if that will work. It was very good and show-offy but it was me and all my theatrical pyrotechnics. I don't know if it was really what an eighty-year-old man would do. I've got to think how to modify it. My Lear isn't detailed enough yet and I don't feel I'm able to rehearse him enough to find out the details. The previews are going to be the process of actually locating him.

Thursday, June 7

Technical stuff with Richard – the fights – comic cuts to say the least. Dominic came in and changed the music, then Jane Gibson did a version, then poor John Waller had to do another: 'Hold. Say a word. Don't slice, don't cut.' It was a bit like children's kindergarten.

Tonight I ran lines with dear Sam Beazley and I'm still drying all over the place. As we were doing the thunderstorm, suddenly a storm started outside. It was quite uncanny.

Everybody seems to be doing a book about *King Lear* at the moment or various bits and pieces.

64

Friday, June 8

Run-through of the second half of *Lear*. This time without the book and the lines weren't too bad. It required a lot of concentration. In the morning we did the death scene, the Lear/Cordelia entrance. Eve and I worked out how she might have been hanging when I cut her down and I suddenly realised the thing to do would be to turn her round so her head is hanging down in the wheelchair. We had to time the scene properly. I also tried out the idea of finding the red nose from Act I and putting it on myself – when she's dead – to make her laugh, trying to get some response from the body. There's a line of Albany's, 'Oh see, see . . .' which shows something is happening, and Eve suggested the possibility of putting the nose on her, linking the Fool and the daughter, making her my Fool substitute. At first I was wary of it but, of course, when one did it it made the perfect connection. The death does work, it is startling and treads a razor-thin line. Jean Kalman from the Bouffe du Nord who is lighting the show, an absolutely charming man who has summed up the productions – 'It's like having two affairs, two mistresses on the same day' – he and Hildegard, the Europeans, loved the nose. It's a very unEnglish thing to do. David Bradley thought it was dangerous but exciting. The reaction, I think, was quite good.

We had the musicians in for the waking-up scene and the trumpet, a muted trumpet we're using to wake Lear up, went on and on and on, it wouldn't stop and drove the lines, which have barely gone in, straight out of my head.

The main worry that emerged was that Lear and Cordelia going to prison still isn't right. David Bradley who watched it was very unhappy about it and kept saying, 'There's no positive image.' It certainly needs investigating.

This morning I woke up at 4.30 and couldn't go back to sleep until 7.30, there are so many things going round inside my head to do with children, Lear's relationship with his daughters. We must find an image for Cordelia, I think St Joan, armour, perhaps being stripped of armour which would show her vulnerability and Lear taking control of the scene. In a way it's Lear's sanest scene and as such the most difficult one to play. It's a very small and delicate scene and, if I remember rightly, the best scene in the Olivier TV version. In fact I might have a look at the video to see just how they solved it.

We had a bit of a discussion with Deborah: her priorities sometimes are not our priorities and sometimes I feel her priorities are quite wrong. She wanted to work on the hovel scenes and we felt it was more important to work on Act 1, Scene 4, which involved Ian, myself, David and the knights. Ian, who has been very busy with *Richard*, was all over the place when we last did it. The technical demands and timing of the hovel scenes aren't so great, the stuff she wanted to do with him was obviously acting stuff and in the end she did admit she was wrong.

We went on to Goneril's entrance and 'detested kite' and I finally cracked the curse by getting her off balance and throwing her to the ground. I've also been developing another idea I've had of keeping the crown in a bag, carrying it with me throughout the first half of the play, and at 'Thou shalt find that I'll resume the shape which thou dost think I have cast off for ever' suddenly brandishing it in Goneril's face. Throughout the earlier scene with the Fool, 1/4, I am fondling the crown – though you can't see what it is – and maybe giving it a little clean and polish, and then in 1/5 I hold it out and say, 'Take it again perforce'. It seems to work quite well.

I'm just taking this time in the quiet room at the National, which is like a little chapel, free from tannoys and things. They're running a bit late downstairs.

The end of a really dreary day's rehearsal, technical rehearsing for *Richard*. My God, it's boring, I'm so bored, I'm going to go back to the cinema, I've had enough of the theatre. It's a very, very technical production and I don't think it's going to be much fun to tour because being so technically bound we'll have to run-through the play wherever we go, and it will probably be a very boring production to play, too, because it won't change very much.

I tried something in the ghost scene – bringing on the crown and brandishing it over Richard's head. Bob Crowley thought it should be a crown of barbed wire. I'm not happy about my death scene. John Waller, the fights man, quite rightly pointed out that he thought the way I was doing it was very odd and said I seem to be saying one thing and doing another, resisting, when the speech indicates resignation.

Good morning with Deborah, working through costumes, when to put on and when to take off. It's a slightly bigger costume plot than I'd originally imagined. In *Richard* we have the huge *coup de théâtre*, the massive cloak for Richard's coronation which it takes about eighteen of us to move onto the stage – we've been doing it from Day 1; there must be several Indian restaurants minus red velour on their walls as Bob Crowley has bought the whole supply. Deborah and I have been going through *Lear*, talking about the storm scene and going through the odd thing; it's nice to be able to sit down with her. Apart from that the day was tedious and too long.

We had a discussion about the various props as well, like the wheelbarrow Hildegard insists be metal. The one we've been rehearsing with is perfectly good but it's not aesthetically pleasing apparently. I had a session with Jane Gibson on Buckingham's movement, dealing with the fact that I shift from foot to foot – to do with uncertainty – and also trying to reassess the character of Buckingham, to clarify what has been developing.

Wednesday, June 13

The day started off really well: I had to go and get my car out of the car pound – not something which puts you in a frame of mind exactly conducive to work.

We had another run-through of *Richard*, about our third or fourth. The technical stuff we've been doing was to no avail as the sound computer didn't work. So much for productions dependent on the technical. My accent is shot to hell, I haven't done any work on it because of *Lear*.

Thursday, June 14

Back to *Lear* and we introduced the musicians and all the storm sequences into the second storm scene. Deborah wants the scenes to be done with floating lights catching the various characters. Derek has the hardest job, in many ways he's the engine of the second storm scene. He shows the transformation of a man who is not a natural hero and it's very moving. He grows all the time as Edgar and is learning how to take his time, direct his energy.

After lunch we tried to finish the scene but we had trouble with the entrance of Gloucester and Lear's undressing, the precise sequence of what comes off first. Then David and I worked with the musicians on the thunder sequences, punctuating the storm Lear creates with the whip. By whisking it round my head I can make the sound of the wind.

I'm now knackered and sweating and completely exhausted.

Friday, June 15

What a day! In the morning we did more work on the hovel scenes. Ian must feel very frustrated with *Richard* all ready to go, having to break off and go back to *Lear*.

In the afternoon we tried out Act 1, Scenes 1 and 4. They worked quite well, really. I was surprised, I think we all were. We gave a bit of attention to some of the details – the crowns, the paper-cutting, etc. You begin to find out about the scene as you play it. The wheelchair isn't ready yet, one of the wheels nearly fell off in the run, the balance is not correct, it's a bit of a mess. I tried on my costume for the first scene, which is very light but being rubber and silk very hot and doesn't breathe. Poor David's pulled a muscle and for some reason the nurse wouldn't refer him to a hospital. She gave him some cream which then brought him out in a rash – the bureaucracy at the National is unbelievable. The Wardrobe – the budget problems they're having . . . the girl who's come to help finds it very inept. We had a costume fitting at the end of the day for *Richard*, the blackshirt costume.

Saturday, June 16

We did our first full run-through of *Lear*. I woke at about four o'clock this morning, couldn't sleep, and watched Scotland v. the All Blacks on the television – an extraordinary experience at four in the morning – and then got back to sleep after about two hours. Got up and did some lines with Sam Beazley who came early. The run-through went very well until my energy and – really – familiarity gave out. The text, every time, I'm struggling with it, struggling to keep it in my head. We've been rehearsing for thirteen weeks and I still feel I'm under-rehearsed. None of the storm stuff worked, but that was because I was exhausted and fighting a bug. Apparently everybody was quite excited by it all. David Bradley was brilliant and on the whole I must say that things are in quite good nick.

In the afternoon we did some work on the scene which had gone wrong, the big row with the girls. It's mainly a matter of knowing the text. We open next Friday – our first preview. I've got five days to go through it. I'm going to try and go through it tomorrow. I'm going to have a quiet, lazy day. I can't understand how a man of a certain age could play that part.

Sunday, June 17

I'm enjoying a day off. I've been looking intermittently but not a lot at the lines. Ian rang me tonight to talk, the second call from him, the first was about poor Susie Engel's terrible ordeal, being burgled at knife-point. He suggested I should stay in a hotel for a few days. I told Irina about this and she was extremely hurt after she'd taken great efforts to stock the fridge before she went away for the two days. We discussed the various problems.

I'm still a bit worried about the lines but I can't get any more into me at the moment. And I hope no more waking up to watch rugby matches at four o'clock in the morning.

Week 14: Monday, June 18

The second run-through. On the whole it was much better. The first scene wasn't as good as it had been and I still have trouble with the knights in Act 1/4 – they're not concentrating enough, they're not giving enough attention to the scene – but the end of the play worked very well. It still needs to be a bit quicker, but that's quite a good fault. Ian's getting into his stride, so are Derek and Clare. Richard Eyre came to see it and was quite impressed. He feels a little out of it – poor Richard, I feel sorry for him – now that *R.III*'s gone on ice for two weeks. The two bags didn't work, I thought I'd try having some feathers in among the blossoms, but it turned out that Clare Higgins is allergic to feathers, so we couldn't have that. And one of the new crowns got broken.

Tuesday, June 19

Today was the technical, and the usual – the wheelchair broke on the second try round, the wheelchair we've known about for twelve weeks, that we've known would have to be tough, the whole thing disintegrated. I felt rather sorry for the prop guy who has to cope

70

with it but it was just disgraceful. In the afternoon we did a line workthrough of the text – ironing out all the little errors – as though we were doing a radio play, except that people tended to use the microphone as if they were pop-stars. It became quite funny, Bradley doing his songs as though he were a compère in a northern club.

We've got dressing room trouble. Three of the leading actors were put in a dressing room without a window and objected. Obviously the dressing room situation at the National is pretty bleak and it took a bit of sorting out.

The costumes work, the stage is very spare and open, someone said reminiscent of bygone productions, *à la* sixties. One has to fill the space, which is probably a good thing, we're naked; it means that it's up to us to create. John Caulfield didn't like it, he felt it was too bare.

I was watching Kae/Edmund's first major scene and when he comes to the lines 'O, these eclipses do portend these divisions! Fa, sol, la, mi,' suddenly felt he should have played the notes on a saxophone or trumpet or something. We need concrete images which are emblematic of the characters – Edmund the cool dude. Fooling around, trying to keep the spirits up, I suddenly had an idea of the boys in their jackets as Hell's Angels when they come on as the knights. I got them singing a dirty song, 'Roll me over in the clover, roll me over, roll me down and do it again' – we need some kind of bawdy.

Richard O'Callaghan had a video tape of some of the stuff we've done. It looked very good, in fact it looked exceptionally good, so there is hope.

Wednesday, June 20

Everybody is rather tired and exhausted, the Stage Management particularly. I can detect a bit of an atmosphere. Deborah becomes very imperious, trying to get things done as time runs out, but some of her commands are not quite clear.

We went over the first entrance of the Fool again, which took a bit of time to focus. The bare set with the onus on the actors means that the sculptural sense of the actors' bodies has to be clear and well defined. In the big scenes it became more and more apparent that we should be moulded by the lighting. If anybody can achieve this it's Jean Kalman.

We returned to the knights and their exit, then the re-entry to the stocks. I have great difficulty with that moment, the moment of discovering Kent. I've never been happy about how to play it. Ian suggested I come and sit with him, which helps root it, but to be agitated sitting down is also a problem. We had more trouble with the wheelchair, getting it on and off stage. We worked on the scene with the girls, their entrances and exits, and suddenly I felt the space of the stage and the energy it gave.

Apparently Susie Engel and Richard O'C. are not being heard upstairs – partly because they have a very good throw-away technique which is lost on that huge stage. The degree of under- or over-statement – that debate is a key issue in the development of an actor's technique and personality.

We did some work on the storm scenes, some very good effects, curtains which fall from a great height, disrupting the order – it's very elemental, Hildegard's use of white sheets – tearing back the floor cloth at the start of the storm, the use of small lamps held by the actors during the storm and the montage sequence that David and I do at the back of the stage finally reaching the front and whipping up the sound. The bull-whip works very well but my technique sometimes fails me – I think I've mastered it and then I haven't. David must watch that he doesn't get obscured by my bulk. I've also been wondering how we should do the waking-up scene. The image of a corpse being dressed in a funeral parlour – we might try and pursue something along those lines.

We have a dress rehearsal this evening and I've asked David Gryn, a young artist, to do some drawings as first-night presents for Deborah, Richard, Ian, Hildegard and Bob.

Thursday, June 21–Friday, June 29

No entries made. June 22, first preview of *Lear*; June 27, *Richard*, technicals and dress rehearsal. I think it was like living under sand through which light and sound do not filter.

PART THREE

In Performance

Saturday, June 30

First preview, *Richard III*: We've just done the battle scenes, we're all too old for this carry-on. David Collings is a grandfather, Sam Beazley is a pensioner. It's just too much, it's ridiculous, we can't see, the helmets don't fit, there's too much smoke on the stage, Ian McKellen couldn't get up out of the fight because his neck and body got locked in his armour, it's just ridiculous. Oh, the theatre, the theatre!

Well, we're halfway through the first preview of *Richard*. It seems to be going all right. Ian says he's acting badly. I think we are all very nervous. Technically the show isn't finished, the dress rehearsal proved that, especially the last twenty minutes – the weakest part of *Richard* anyway. The problems with Ian's armour – I think it's almost impossible to manoeuvre on that floor, it's too slippery and the armour's too cumbersome – and the dry ice is impossible to see through, in fact visibility was almost nil, we couldn't see the people on the other side of the stage; and the music was all wrong, the sound was so bad Freya Edwards, Head of Sound, came up and apologised afterwards.

It looks well but it really is just a spectacle to make up for the fact that it's not a great play. I think I'll enjoy it, though, because it is a good contrast to Lear; Buckingham in the end isn't a very taxing role.

We've just done the coronation scene and I'm having my little rest. I had a long chat to Derek Hutchinson about Edgar: I'm beginning to see how it works as a role. I think the problem for all Edgars is that in the guise of poor Tom the part is very self-centred, self-obsessed. Derek is not a self-centred actor, anything but, he's extremely generous and he needs to be more selfish.

The children in *Richard* are being particularly good, they're quite a collection of little boys, all very good in the roles. We continue the technical work on Monday, when poor Richard Eyre won't be here. His father died last week. Richard has been waiting for the inevitable since the beginning of the year when his dad had a severe stroke.

Monday, July 2

Just finished our second preview of *Richard* which was very well received. Things are still going wrong: our carefully rehearsed battles were a total shambles again because the music is wrong.

There's a lot of whinging going on in this theatre backstage. I'm amazed at the unprofessionalism. It seems to have deteriorated over the years.

Thursday, July 5

We've had a bit of a week. We nearly didn't have Ian because he did his back in last night. There was an alert for the understudy but Ian went on and we're halfway through the performance now. He's insisting on doing everything; we've tried to persuade him to leave off his armour but he's insisting on wearing it. There's a general feeling of fatigue. The company are very, very tired and unfortunately Richard has a lot on his plate with his dad and all that.

These wretched battle scenes don't work. We've changed them and also the tableau which still looks slightly artificial. I'm longing to have time off, it is driving me mad doing this every day – you go to bed, get up, come to the theatre, one day off a week. Soon there will be eight performances a week – no time at all – one week's holiday is all we will have to recover. I think we've been crazy and over-enthusiastic, Ian and I, to agree to all these performances.

75

Saturday, July 7, 7.00 a.m.

We did our last preview of *Richard* on Thursday night, which was actually quite good, I've begun to get into it. Then we came back to *Lear* for our fifth preview. The problem at the moment is tiredness, we're all fighting it. I'm awake now because Irina is doing a film at the moment and today's her first day. The poor girl wanted to go to sleep early last night because it's very nerve-wracking preparing for the first day of a new film and she was naturally tense. I normally have a lift arranged but that didn't materialise last night and I was a bit late back, just before 12.00. I got back, rushed in thinking I was back on time, got into bed, waking her up, slept, woke up early because she was waking up and now I'll try and get a few more hours' sleep.

It focuses your mind when you wake up this early: you suddenly think, what's the point of all this? You're in the theatre all day, every day – fourteen hours a day, or twelve hours, it's just too much. I now resent it. I didn't in the past; when I was much younger, I thrived on it. I don't any longer. The reasons for being an actor do change, and at this stage I find that (a) my domestic life is more important to me than it ever was and (b) if I'm going to work I want to combine both elements. I was very happy last year directing Irina in *Mrs Warren's Profession*. The feeling you get as an actor sometimes is a sense of aloneness. I see it in someone like Ian. You lose your place, you don't quite know why you're doing it and the reasons seem to be just very selfish, self-aggrandisement, fame, all of that, and they become cancerous, they eat away at you so the slightest thing disturbs you: the fact that there is another *Lear* going on at the moment – you open the paper and people are saying 'Possibly this is the *Lear* of the century', naturally it dents your confidence, it dents your ego; these things are very difficult to live with, one has to have a philosophy to deal with them and when you're tired and exhausted the philosophy runs very thin. My confidence is quite good at times, and my ego, but it's not enough just to have confidence and ego, one needs to be able to say it doesn't matter, it's not important. But, of course, once you say it doesn't matter, the activity becomes pointless; you think, well, why am I doing this if it doesn't matter, why am I battling on, why am I still trying to prove something?

76

I understand the monomaniacal drive of someone like Peter Brook and also of Deborah who really believes she doesn't want to be troubled with anything else, she just wants to get on with her work. I have felt that. When I was at Stratford doing *Titus* it was at the centre of my life; even though I was doing other plays, *Titus* was the key. In a sense *Lear* is too, but I have a responsibility towards *Richard* and it's a battle to keep the balance between the two. It doesn't help when you're battered by things which are not important but do dent the ego, like the fact that in Prague they only want *Richard*. They don't want *Lear* because Barry Kyle is doing *Lear* in Prague and is clearly upset that we're bringing our *Lear* out. I understand that. I embarked on this venture knowing there were going to be at least two other *Lear*s – John Wood's for the RSC and Richard Briers' for the Renaissance Company. I knew there were going to be comparisons and you naturally want your *Lear* to be the best. There's room enough ultimately for all, but it's a test of character, it puts you through all kinds of emotions and I think partly it's a struggle because it's the argument of life in action, ego, all the things that come together, all the things that feed in. For instance, the difference between the sounds of applause for *Richard* and *Lear*: Irina noticed this the other day when she came to see the show. I pooh-poohed it but it has crossed my mind – though it doesn't cross my mind every time – that really they'd rather be watching *Richard* than *Lear*.

These feelings in the end are unproductive. One needs a philosophical base to deal with them, to say it actually isn't important, it's not the priority; the priority is that you do your work to the best of your ability whatever the situation and you cannot allow anything to make you deviate from that. I suppose it's what is dissatisfying about being an actor, it's the thing that nags you: it's subjective work and you really are always coming up against yourself. Sometimes you long not to be pitched against yourself.

The whole notion of the world tour is a nightmare to me at this stage. The fact that I'm going to be away for all this time is driving me demented, it's the last thing in the world I want to be doing, I just want to be with my girl. I want to see the two girls in my life, the one I live with and my daughter. I can't take my daughter to Cairo because my ex-wife won't allow her to come out of school a week early. All these problems impinge and try and deviate you and of

77

course you must take the attempted deviation in your stride. I suppose the real point of living is living and allowing life to present obstacles so that you can deal with them, and deal with them in such a way that you overcome them or you learn from them or you see it as ultimately creating some kind of balance and some road towards a nirvana or a spiritual state, a sense of peace.

But at this stage I am just tired. The point of recording this is that it is the thoughts of someone exhausted, who is being impinged upon, who has a lot of problems, a lot of ego problems he has to recognise and deal with. It's bloody difficult. I want *Lear* to be good, of course I want it to be better than any other *Lear*, but does that imply that I want the other *Lear* to be worse? That is, of course, a thought which is unworthy and wrong. I know ultimately that it is wrong because it gives you a wrong perspective on things. I really have got to come to terms with it, really have got to learn how to deal with it – perhaps the struggle is the dealing with it, perhaps it's the battle that's the point. Now I must try and get some more sleep.

I waited till my sweetheart had gone off to work, made myself some tea and discovered the milk had formed solid cheese so I couldn't even make myself a cup of tea this morning. It's crazy, the whole thing is crazy.

Here is a remark I heard last night when I went upstairs to find Richard O'Callaghan and get my lift home: there was a sponsorship party going on and I was caught by a man who said, 'It must have been exhausting for you: it was exhausting for us. It may be representative of Method for you, but for us, the audience, it's Method,' and another man said, 'Well, you see, since *The Dresser* we're so aware of *King Lear*.' I don't know whether Ronnie Harwood has done a service or disservice to the play. If people know *Lear* through *The Dresser* then I think it's time they knew *Lear* through *Lear*.

5.30 p.m. We've just done the first half of the marathon, *King Lear*, and it was the best performance we've given. Because of tiredness and having been so depressed yesterday, I had a new concentration and somehow I was able to give it a gravitas after all the humour and lightness. The two-hander with David Bradley, 1/5, was on the mark

78

but I still have to get up early and get off before his exit; it's taking too long and I'm screwing up his last little speech. Eve came in afterwards and was a bit alarmed by the way I held her face when I throw her across the stage in the first scene. She thought I was going to break her neck, which I wasn't, because if I was, I would have done. Ian was in good form, having cut a lot of speeches last night. He turned to me and said that he had been thinking over the past week how old he looked and then he saw my face in the first scene and I looked even older. I think we've all aged this week. I asked Ian 'Why do we do it?' and he said, 'It's energy, we provide energy for others, people who are tired and sit and watch and get a boost from our energy.' I think that's probably true. Then he said, 'I'd much rather be doing this than an Alan Ayckbourn – that's harder because it's so boring.' And he's absolutely right, this is being at the sharp end of life.

The audience reaction was wonderful, it went on and on. I was a bit cheeky and turned to them at the end and said, 'Please, ladies and gentlemen, we have to go, we have to do *Richard III* tonight' – thinking about the changeover: it was rumoured that the changeover had taken four hours the other day and this is the first time we've done the two plays together. As I speak, they've just called the half hour so perhaps they're on schedule. I must say, I feel quite rested and quite good, I'm focused now in a way that I haven't been for some time. Longing to get home and see my girl tonight. Just reading Michael MacLiammoir's book about Orson Welles. What a wonderful combination of fanatic and winger he was: a marvellous story about when the costumes didn't arrive so he decided to shoot the scene in which Cassio is maimed and Roderigo is murdered in a Turkish bath – bit of a Shakespeare-obsessive was Welles.

Why we do it, God alone knows: it's the energy, that's what it is, the energy.

I spent the morning explaining to a whole bunch of Americans about *Lear*.

Last night was the opening of *Lear* at Stratford. I've put an embargo on all notices and press and discussion about the other *King Lear*. Just simply don't want to confuse any issues – I've got enough to think about with this one. I did happen to see a notice in the *Mail* and found myself quickly turning over to read some article on an ice skater who is getting married. It's extraordinary, having said I wouldn't read any notices, I get in a taxi and there's a paper and the first thing I open is a review of *Lear*.

On the whole the previews are going well, audiences are being very good and appreciative. I feel much happier about *Richard III*, I think I'm actually enjoying it. Ian's lines in *Richard* – poor Ian, I don't think we've ever had a performance yet where all the lines have come in the right order, or come right. Instead of saying the other night 'my pains are quite forgot', he said 'my planes are quite forgot', to which in the context of this production I felt like saying, 'Oh well, we'll catch the next one.'

Lear is playing well, Deborah has been quite tough with her notes – on the link between his responsibility to his family and his responsibility to his kingdom, his understanding of when he's been slack and when he's been tyrannical. We had some helpful people who make wheelchairs round last week and now the wheelchair is transformed – which should have happened in the first place. It's finally workable.

This afternoon we're going to change something in *R.III*'s coronation scene. Apparently Richard Eyre wants to work on it, which is a pity because I'm behind on these books. I've got to sort out bits of *Salem to Moscow* which is going to drive me demented.

We've had a nibble from BAM, Brooklyn Academy of Music, about going there, but Ian seems to want to hold on and see if we can get a bigger bid from New York – it would be a nice way to finish.

This is halfway through the matinée. *Lear* is shaping up and I'm beginning to wear a little make-up, which I didn't earlier on, simply because I'm beginning to see Lear's face and what he looks like. I've had some good responses from various people, nice letters. My agent came to see it last night and presented me with a portrait Tony Sher did of me as a mournful Titus. He, Jeremy, was pleased with *Lear*, didn't like the plastic bags which I've been worried about lately – I think I'm going to change them to canvas. I dirtied the costume down for the Dover sequence because Deborah thought it wasn't pitiful enough, too pristine – so I tore the sleeve as I had done changing the other day; my clothes must be more urine and shit stained, with much more of a sense of Lear's incontinence.

I'd like to record my own physical journey through the storm scene to the interval: before it, my whole chest opens up and I pump up like a huge balloon; after, I'm left with an acute pain in my stomach. When I get to the interval I gladly, gladly get into a shower and wrap up in towels, and Elaine, my dresser, tucks me up with a cup of tea and I drift into a comatose state until we're ready for the Dover scene. We have the ritual of bedecking me with flowers of the season (interesting to think about the possible blooms of Egypt). By the by, the lights came on too early today in the storm and caught me getting into action with the whip.

I persuaded Bradley to do his last speech in 1/5 to the audience because he felt it wasn't working. I think he needs a direct pay-off to the audience and the audience need it too. Everyone is surprised at the humour in the play. Laughs on 'No, no, no, no! Come, let's away to prison' – rather prison than seeing Regan and Goneril – a comic conceit which makes the moment more poignant. This reawakened a debate I had with Glenda Jackson in *Strange Interlude* about whether humour undercut or underscored the tragic dimensions of a play.

I had a little wind on the John Wood *Lear*. I think reception has been mixed. Apparently the set somewhat overshadows the evening, a revolving cube – must be like riding a fairground Waltzer. I wrote John Wood a note on his first night saying that *Lear* is a mountain with many faces to climb and we can only climb one face at a time;

that I'm sure his approach will be a formidable one and I hope he will wave when he gets to the summit to give luck to the rest of the mountaineers. I feel sure it is the only way one can regard these things. Battling on.

Tuesday, July 17

The shows have been going well. Last night it seemed very Mondayish: I'd been swimming in the afternoon, I was late and when I got to the stage I felt completely tired and felt, oh, resentful of the effort of doing the play. I more or less marked my way through the first scene and then in the second when the Fool came on I began to feel a sort of resentment against the audience. There were a lot of coughers, my resentment turned to anger, and I got more and more angry and started to confuse anger at the audience with anger in the Dover scene at the girls and their shallowness. At the end, Deborah said she thought it was the best performance so far and I rushed home, as is my wont now, to get away.

I had a little session with Richard Eyre in the interval today: he felt that I was being over-deferential to Ian in *Richard III*, not playing it large enough. When I suggested a few physical things he said, 'Oh, no. No, I don't think that's quite right,' so I shall have to work on it. We still haven't cut the battles. Richard is holding on to them determinedly but everybody says they should go, that they're very bad – and they are very bad, they plainly don't work with the costumes – but one has to be sensitive in this kind of thing.

I also went to the doctor yesterday. Something was playing me up last year and I think it's started to give me trouble again: it looks as though I have a gallstone which I'll have to have seen to before we go off on this adventure.

Wednesday, July 18

I showed my face more as Buckingham last night, was less self-effacing, and Richard dutifully rang me up and said it was much better.

We've just done a performance of *Richard III* and I'm having a rest – it's about 6 o'clock – before the evening *Lear*. I think Ian is fairly nervous about the build-up to opening. It seemed to me his concentration was to bits. He talked about the king his father rather than the king his brother – not that that's difficult to do.

I'm getting a little annoyed with people comparing the two productions, complaining about the shabbiness of *Lear* and saying it looks as if it's only had about £5 spent on it.

Friday, July 20

We rehearsed the battle scenes, I think for the last time. Really everything is in much better order now. I think that Richard's realised it was too much and we've simplified considerably.

I've had two letters about *Lear*: one from a lady who enjoyed my performance but thought my legs were too beautiful, and a very touching letter from a teacher who said, 'I've never come to terms with Lear until you created him. Now I'm crazy about him. I can now teach the play with conviction.'

The drum revolve is playing up at the Olivier. The poor people in *School for Scandal* have had to re-rehearse. The drum revolve has never worked, it is now twelve years, thirteen years, since the theatre opened and it still doesn't work – fourteen years, I think.

Thursday, July 26

Day after the first night, the first night of *Richard*. It went well, apart from having a frog in my throat. The company were in very good nick, I don't know how the production was received – people liked it, people didn't, but that's always the case. Ian was in very good form and gave his all. We await the press verdict. I think there are certain elements in what we've done that are valuable and some good ideas, but the over-planning and inorganic nature of the production clearly show. A bit early for post-mortems – *Richard* was just the first, *Lear* is to come.

Friday, July 27

The first night of *Lear*. The reaction at the end was astounding, the audience was standing, I've never known a reaction like it. It was quite overwhelming. The whole evening was very strange in many ways. It turned out to be my best performance so far, but there was a very odd feeling right at the beginning. I was quiet, I didn't have a lot of nerves. I don't get nerves very much nowadays, but what was strange was a feeling of roughness, for the first time a feeling that the play was playing me, that I had to allow myself to go through it. I suppose in the past to a certain extent I've always acted what was demanded. This time, I really felt my emotional centre was open to the play, and the play and the part just took command and drove me. As a result it was a very rough and bumpy ride.

Starting from the beginning, the disinheritance of Cordelia: Eve kept very still, she contained her energy quite brilliantly and really rose to the occasion. Both Clare and Susan were in great form too and in the scene with the knights and the cursing of Goneril, I was able to be quite quiet and precise, just allowing the energy to take me. Derek Hutchinson – he has put himself through it – had a real grasp of Tom. Ian was very moving, his Kent had great dignity and humanity. In the simplicity of his playing you could see some of his own extraordinary goodness which is clear to anybody who meets him but which isn't always apparent on stage. As for Bradley, well,

K I N G   L E A R

1. Brian Cox in rehearsal with director Deborah Warner.
(Photo: Neil Libbert)

2. Susan Engel as Goneril, Richard Bremmer as Albany (left) and Ian McKellen
as the Earl of Kent (centre). Act 1, scene 1. Brian Cox as Lear:
'To thine and Albany's issues be this perpetual.' (Photo: Neil Libbert)

3. Eve Matheson as Cordelia (left), Susan Engel as Goneril (top),
Clare Higgins as Regan (right). Act 1, scene 1. Brian Cox as Lear:
'Know that we have divided in three our kingdom.' (Photo: Neil Libbert)

4. Brian Cox as Lear to David Bradley as his Fool (right):
'Blow, winds, and crack your cheeks!'
Act 3, scene 2 (Photo: Neil Libbert)

5. Brian Cox as Lear to Eve Matheson as Cordelia:
'We two alone will sing like birds i'th'cage.'
Act 5, scene 3. (Photo: Neil Libbert)

6. Hakeem Kae-Kazim as Edmund (left) to Derek Hutchinson as Edgar:
'Parted you in good terms? Found you no displeasure in him by word
nor countenance?' Act 1, scene 2. (Photo: Neil Libbert)

7. Ian McKellen as the Earl of Kent (left) to Brian Cox as Lear:
'Your son and daughter found this trespass worth the shame
which here it suffers.' Act 2, scene 4. (Photo: Neil Libbert)

8. David Bradley as the Fool: 'Then shall the realm of Albion come to great confusion.' Act 3, scene 2. (Photo: Neil Libbert)

9. Ian McKellen as Kent (kneeling), David Bradley as Fool (back right).
Brian Cox as Lear: 'Let the great Gods, that keep this dreadful pudder o'er
our heads, find out their enemies now.' Act 3, scene 2. (Photo: Neil Libbert)

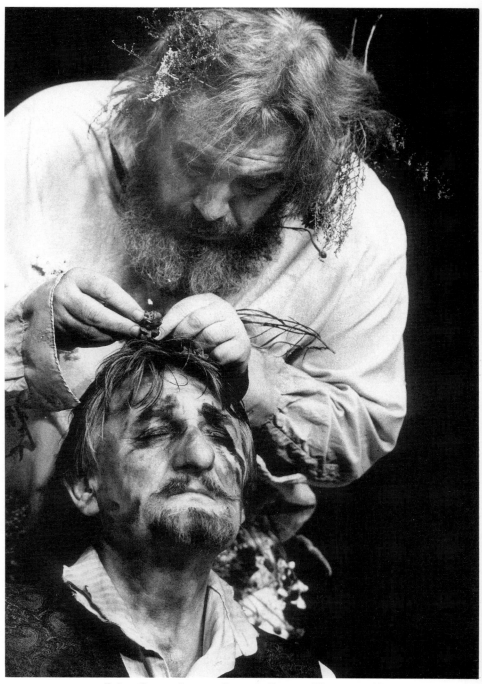

10. Brian Cox as Lear to Peter Jeffrey as Gloucester (front):
'When we are born, we cry that we are come to this great stage of fools.'
Act 4, scene 6. (Photo: Neil Libbert)

he is simply the Fool . . . And people said he and I played as one and I think it was true.

By the interval I was, as usual, wrecked. Went and had a shower and wrapped in my swaddling clothes and got ready for the Dover scene, in which I now wear a pair of long-johns because of the letter about my beautiful legs. I suspected it, I saw a photograph in the papers a week ago, a preview photograph, and they quite clearly didn't look right. The concentration of the younger actors in that scene – Colin Hurley, young Stephen Marchant and Peter Sullivan – was complete. I think Peter Jeffrey is showing more pain now as Gloucester because Deborah has accused him of being too English. In the last few days I've noticed a great anger he produces and a sigh which is very disarming. Then we came to the waking-up scene, the way-to-prison scene and the last scene of all, the entrance with the body of Cordelia: I just had a sensation of absolute spareness, no forcing and literally allowing the scene to play me in a way that I've never ever done as an actor. Finally the end.

The reaction, as I say, was astonishing, the audience stood and clapped – I've never known that on a first night. Deborah came round, bursting into my dressing room with incredible energy and just grabbed me and hugged me and said, 'That's it, that's it, the best ever.' I thanked her again; she is the one person who I feel I can work with. She spoils me because she and I have the same sense of what a play is and how a thing opens like a flower and you must allow it breathing space. Richard Eyre came in and was quite clearly moved by the evening and I thanked him for allowing us to do it at the National. A couple of friends came and finally after about twenty minutes Irina arrived. I wondered where she'd gone, it's very important to be with people you love on a night like this. My son was there, the only sadness was that my daughter wasn't. But all in all quite a remarkable night.

We've had a curious mixed reception from the press. Some understand the production and like it but others find it lacking in regality or intellectual rigour. I think the strangest notice is from Michael Billington who shot himself in the foot as far as I'm concerned by his headline which said: 'The trouble with the Lyttleton's production of *Lear* is that it makes too much sense,' and he ended his notice, after being very charming about me, 'Ms Warner's production makes sense in that it shows Brian Cox's Lear earning grace through love. But sense is exactly what Shakespeare's play does not make.' The one thing that is true of *Lear* is that it makes absolute sense, searing sense – spiritual sense, emotional sense and even political sense – and what Deborah has done has been deceptively simple and this is what has flummoxed people.

I'm described as being 'wonderful' and 'dull' by Michael Coveney. Coveney seems to require a lot of signposting from the actors which I'm never prepared to do. He's a sucker for the tradition of English acting which involves disguise matched with a kind of insistent pyrotechnics, topped off with an intellectual fervour, whatever that may mean. They keep talking about a lack of intellect – it would sound like a negative reaction, but there have been other notices which have talked about the emotional impact, and certainly the impact on the audience on the first night was astonishing. Never in all my years have I experienced such an impact, apart, maybe, from the first night of *The Crucible* in Russia. (This was covered in *Salem to Moscow*, a chronicle of my experiences directing students of the Moscow Arts Theatre School Studio in a production of Arthur Miller's *The Crucible*.)

Ian, on the whole, has come off extremely well with his Richard and deservedly so. I suppose the main differences between Ian and me come from the fact that he acts from a different source. I don't quite know what that source is, I don't quite agree with a lot of what he does, but he acts the way he acts and it is obviously effective. He is part of one tradition and I'm from another.

The reception of art is subjective but in dramatic art you hope to achieve a shared consciousness. I think the actor wants to have

86

everybody in the audience feeling the same, which is clearly impossible – though maybe one should keep on trying.

Deborah has gone off for a few days' holiday; I was hoping to
speak with her but she's incommunicado. Richard, I think, is feeling
a little bruised, I don't know why: the notices of *Richard III* on the
whole have been good; the criticism has been for his absolute pursuit
of the fascist analogy.

Wednesday, August 1

Just about to do two performances on the trot. Most of the press
have been now and notices are very favourable. One or two quibbles
about the productions, one or two quibbles about the casting. The
company are pretty exhausted because they're still doing understudy
rehearsals which will go on for the next two weeks. We continue to
make nonsense of the lines. I said, 'Oh let me think of Brecknock
and be gone to Hastings while my fearful head is on,' instead of the
other way round. I stopped. We were in the middle of the matinée.
Tonight I was off before 'Howl, howl, howl' which caused a great
deal of hilarity to all and sundry.

Things are actually going quite well, we can't really complain, the
audiences are coming in. I just feel that I could quite gladly give
anything to have some time off because we are really tired. These
eight performances a week are just too many. Ian and I were crazy
to agree to them – *folie de grandeur*.

Saturday, August 4

I did a question and answer session with some students from Oxford.
They asked all kinds of things about *Lear* and *Richard*, including how
I deal with a director's concept. It was a very difficult question to
answer – one just has to go along with a concept and in honesty I
had to point out that I didn't agree with the fascist interpretation.

We are still waiting to hear about the second half of the tour.

Frank Rich from the *New York Times* came yesterday and will come again tonight. Ian isn't very keen on the BAM idea, which I think is a mistake. He would like to go to Washington.

I finally laid the ghost of my *Richard* understudy today: it is impossible as I'm going off as Buckingham just as the character I'm understudying is coming on.

I made no recordings for a month after this and continued the exhausting schedule at the Lyttleton, plus re-writes on *Salem to Moscow*.

One incident marred the London run. In the first scene there are three coronets to be given to the three daughters. In frustration I fling Cordelia's into the wings. As I was throwing the crown it got caught in the folds of my costume and went straight into the face of a young woman sitting in the front row. I felt sick. I could observe a slight commotion out of the corner of my eye, but had to finish the scene. As soon as the scene was done I rushed to the theatre nurse's station. The young woman was sitting in a state of shock, comforted by her boyfriend. She had a gash in her forehead. Little did she expect on her way to the theatre that she would be attacked by King Lear. The image of her bleeding face stayed with me throughout the performance.

Meanwhile my domestic life was coming under severe strain. The first leg of the *Lear/Richard* experience drew to an end and we embarked on the tour.

PART FOUR

The World Tour, I

Tokyo

Tuesday, September 11

Just arrived in Tokyo. It's now 5.30 a.m. I left home at about 9 a.m. yesterday. We were supposed to be at the National at 8 o'clock to catch a coach. I decided against it and went from Clapham Junction, getting an extra hour in bed. In fact I arrived at Gatwick before the others. It was a long, long flight. We went via Moscow and seemed to stay there for ever. I thought we were going to try and seek asylum. It's ironic: I used to catch the return part of this flight sometimes, from Moscow to London, and it seemed a luxury after two weeks of Moscow because of the Japanese food. I bought *Bonfire of the Vanities* for the flight to keep me company.

Most people are fairly cheesed off. We've had a week off and it's not really been enough to recover from ten weeks of eighty performances. Irritation came to a head one day when Richard Eyre called a note session for *Richard* immediately after the afternoon performance of *Lear*. I found myself wandering down to it only to discover that Ian, who is much better at conserving his energy than I am, was – quite rightly – tucked up in his dressing room.

We had a good week off, Irina and I, strained but quite good, at Deauville. We went to Paris and saw her father's production of *The Tempest* which put everything else to shame. The detail of his work made me think about what I had to do and how inadequate it all felt. *Lear* underwent a lot of change during the ten weeks. The storm scene changed completely: I decided that what we were doing was too clever by half and we have now made it bolder and, I think, more true to the text. The end of the play has now changed too: we are playing the grace notes much more intimately and that also works better. The Lyttleton is a dog of a theatre to play in; that space is huge and we need a sense of intimacy which is impossible to achieve on such an open stage. I found a much better approach to the humour at the beginning of the play, incorporating Deborah's idea but making Lear more mercurial and unpredictably dangerous with a stronger undercurrent of melancholia. I think this has given it greater depth. Deborah, as a director, is young and reactionary, working against received notions of the play – which isn't always helpful. She is in danger of being contrary for contrary's sake and has to be more detailed and specific. Playing the role I've discovered a lyricism which I had undervalued because of my tendency to play off the wall and look for the humour, which Deborah encourages.

So, we're now in Tokyo, which is a sprawling chaotic Los Angeles, bathed at the moment in smog and pollution. It's incredibly hot and the swimming pool – desperately needed by the company – isn't open. We've got a party this evening given by Tamura-san, Senior Managing Director of the property company which owns the Tokyo Globe: the Tokyo Globe is his passion. It's now, I don't know, 1 o'clock in the afternoon, 1.40. I'm still keeping my English time. I'm going to have a sleep.

Tamura-san is a Jekyll and Hyde; during the day he works and is very retiring and then at night he lets his hair down. The party, given for the whole company out of his own pocket, was arranged at a little restaurant near the Tokyo Globe. I found my old friends Ko Shioya and Yozo Nishimura, two gentlemen from the Shinchosa Publishing Company. Earlier in the year I had made a series of recordings of an adaptation of *Hijack* by Brian Freemantle for distribution in Japan as a teaching-English aid. They knew I was coming to Japan and tracked me down. They had a photographer with them who took a series of photographs of me drinking sake and eating sushi. Apparently I am to appear on the backcover of the Shinchosa weekly magazine, which is a great honour as the Japanese read from the back to the front. I was asked to make a speech of thanks to Tamura-san for his generosity, something we're not likely to experience again.

Looking round when I arrived in the city, I was depressed by the turmoil of the buildings and roadways – great pylons planted in the middle of riverbeds to support yet another flyover – but the people are extraordinary: there's a sense of common goodness around, quietness, very young children travel unparented and unchaperoned on the subway, you don't feel hassled though life is fast and the Japanese are perpetually mobile.

By the bed at the hotel, the Metropolitan – quite nice, fairly normal standard hotel – they give you readings from the teachings of Buddha. Tonight I opened at the passage about dependent origination:

The world is full of suffering. Birth is suffering, old age is suffering, sickness and death are sufferings. To meet a man whom one hates is suffering. To be separated from a beloved one is suffering. To be vainly struggling to satisfy one's needs is suffering. In fact a life that is not free from desire and passion is involved with distress. This is called the truth of suffering. The cause of human suffering is undoubtedly found in the thirst of the physical body and illusions of worldly passion. If these thirsts and illusions are traced to their source they are found to be rooted in the intense desires of physical instinct. Thus desire, having a strong will to live as its basis, seeks that which feels desirable even if it is sometimes death. That is called the truth of the cause of suffering.

And then a little further on:

What is the source of human grief? Lamentation, pain and agony. Is it not to be found in the fact that people are generally desirous? They cling obstinately to lives of wealth and honour, comfort and pleasure, excitement and self-indulgence, ignorant of the fact that desire for these very things is the source of human suffering. But if one carefully considers all the facts, one must be convinced that at the base of all suffering lies the principle of craving desire. If avarice can be removed, human suffering will come to an end. Ignorance is manifested in greed that fills the human mind. It comes from the fact that men are unaware of the true reason for the succession of things.

That's the end of my entry for today, September 11, first day in Tokyo. Tomorrow we go to the Globe.

Wednesday, September 12

We went to the Meiji shrine in the morning, the shrine of the Emperor at the time of the Restoration in 1868. We wandered round and looked at the offerings and prayers written on little slats of wood. It's such a pleasant contrast to the surrounding city: suddenly this shrine, and to walk down to the little lake and tea house, the Empress's tea house. There are turtles swimming in the lake and the carp are so tame they come and feed out of your hand. It's very beautiful.

We went back to the Globe on the subway and Ian, Clare Higgins, Richard O'Callaghan and I had lunch on the way at a soba bar I remembered from my trip before, a little bar dedicated to soba, the Japanese noodle. All I could remember were soba and tempura, so I ordered some.

The rehearsal began at two o'clock and there was the usual hiatus, wasting time because nobody takes a decision to actually start and then Deborah complains that we haven't started. We did start and things went fairly smoothly.

The Globe is a mishmash. It's based on Shakespeare's Globe but it's very much a Japanese idea of an Elizabethan stage. Apparently, halfway through its construction Tamura-san made a visit to the Swan Theatre at Stratford and arriving back in Tokyo promptly redesigned the seating in the upper galleries. The staff are greatly helpful and very, very concerned about the work. All over the theatre there are signs in English saying 'All cigarettes must be distinguished.' The only problem is that the space isn't quite right. We've abandoned sets and are performing with no decor, partly on account of travel expense but chiefly because this is an Elizabethan stage and the sets have been designed for a proscenium stage. We're having to work in a very basic way. Fine for *Lear*, not so fine for *Richard*, which has become so locked into its production demands that it will suffer from the openness of the Globe stage. A perfect rough setting, but not for *Richard* at this point in the tour. Even a rough setting has to be

92

prepared for. I tried to get the measure of the house, which was fairly easy, but the atmosphere has to be created purely by the text.

I came off and crashed for about two hours, hit by jet-lag.

In the evening we returned to *Richard*. It's a very linear and frontal production, placed in a setting which isn't designed for it. Ian, I think, feels very naked and slightly vulnerable, mourning the lack of the Lyttleton stage. Richard Eyre is more pragmatic. Deborah enjoys the space and feels it will liberate us. The one advantage is that we can be very intimate, we can play it very quietly. But the floor is another problem: the most exposed element, and it looks a bit like a village hall stage. It needs some texture.

So far the morale of the company is very good. I took most of them back to the soba bar after the show and settled them down and then went off and had some sushi at a tiny sushi bar opposite the Globe Tavern, the Japanese nod to an English pub.

Ian was saying he likes to be part of a group. I think he likes touring because he feels he is part of a family. I don't feel that. I can muck in but I need my home, I need to be surrounded by people I love, things I love – not that I've been very good at it in the past. I suspect that I'm a theatre animal but not the sort of theatre animal Ian is. I don't think I'll ever be.

Readings from Buddha:

> Reality of human life. People in this road are prone to be selfish and unsympathetic. They do not know how to love and respect one another. They argue and quarrel over trifling affairs, only to their own harm and suffering, and life becomes but a dreary round of unhappiness. Regardless of whether they are rich or poor, they worry about money. They suffer from poverty and they suffer from wealth because their lives are controlled by greed. They are never contented, never satisfied.

Tomorrow we have our first performance of *Richard*.

Stephen Marchant's wife rang me in the middle of the night, 2.30, to try and get hold of Stephen. I'm a social centre now as well as everything else. I panicked, knowing Stephen. He was probably out with the lads. He was expecting her arrival and was so looking forward to it. The front desk couldn't understand her, couldn't give his room number, put her through to me. I ran out onto the landing, wearing only a dressing gown, to use the landing phone since she was on mine, trying to get his number from the front desk, running backwards and forwards between the two phones. I'm reading an extraordinary book called *The Strange Life of Ivan Osokin* which is all about repetition . . . I've just had a brainstorm: now I'm convinced that everybody's wives are going to ring me trying to get hold of their husbands or vice versa. It's going to be crazy.

The demands of eight performances a week, the separation from loved ones have taken their toll. A lot of relationships, particularly among the young members of the company, are under a great deal of strain. You are a constant hostage to it in the theatre. I've already sacrificed one home, one family. I don't think I'm prepared to sacrifice another, though it may be too late. When I see these young actors travelling . . . coming home with them on the subway from the Globe to the hotel, there they all were, several of them married, feeling this sense of separation, feeling how difficult it is to be without their loved ones, trying to hold on, to find ways of diverting themselves. They don't have the compensations that I have – I'm playing King Lear and Buckingham, I have something on which to focus, something to fill my hours. It's more difficult for these young men and women and my heart goes out to them. Freedom is the essence of an actor's life; freedom in terms of experience, not necessarily in their relationships.

Thursday, September 13

The first night of *Richard* in Tokyo. Performances are almost sold out apart from one for Princess Anne, a gala of *Richard III*, for which they want everyone to wear dinner jackets, and of course people in Japan don't like going around in dinner jackets, they feel embarrassed. So we're trying to get some Japanese actors to turn up in monkey suits.

We had a long day, technicals. If I have to tech *Richard* one more time I shall go mad, it drives me crazy. I feel so strait-jacketed, there's no room to breathe in the production, no room for manoeuvre.

There was an air of hysteria about the performance, most of the cast were jet-lagged, the soldiers had to stand through the long 'Greenham Common' scene, the scene where the queens confront Richard. They were all practically asleep on their feet. Minutes before her first entrance, Joyce Redman, who I have to walk on with at the beginning of the play in the scene with King Edward, suddenly said to me, 'I don't think I know my words,' and I said, 'Well, darling, it doesn't matter because nobody will understand what you're saying anyway,' and immediately she went on and dried, and in her second line she said, 'Well, the King may be or something or something,' at which everyone on stage fell about in laughter. The audience were extremely quiet as they always are in Japan; they were more quiet off stage than on stage, the noises backstage were extraordinary. I have to act against a fork-lift truck, which is preparing for Richard's entrance, and during one of my speeches there was suddenly a great 'beebeebee' sound, like a huge buzzing. I have a line, 'When holy men are at their beads, 'tis much to draw them thence,' and I imagined Richard making royal jelly and said 'When holy men are at their bees' because of this buzzing. There was also a horn on the truck which suddenly sounded in the middle of one of the scenes. At one point Ian came into my dressing room and said, 'Am I being over the top tonight?' and I looked at him and said, 'Just a little.' People were in quite good spirits, actually it turned out to be rather an enjoyable performance.

I had an incident in the afternoon with one of the actors which got rather out of hand. For the first time in many years I wanted to hit somebody, namely him. I think he felt the same about me. It was partly to do with tiredness and partly to do, I think, with the difficulty he has had with everybody, which boiled up today. I nearly slugged him. Richard Eyre walked into my dressing room and said, 'I know he's a bit difficult at times but fighting won't help,' and I suddenly found myself saying 'Why not?' – for a man of forty-four it seemed rather silly, and it was, extremely silly.

What else in the day? I went to my little sushi bar, which was very

95

quiet which I enjoy, before the show. They're very sweet. I don't understand a word they say, they don't understand a word I say and I sit in a sublime blanket of non-communication. We sent most of the cast there last night and they've put up menu signs for us in English – a very thoughtful thing to do.

I'm trying to get two seats for Harué Momoyama, Toshi Tsuchi-tori's wife, who speaks no English, only French, and I speak no French or Japanese. (Toshi, among other things, is the percussionist for most of Peter Brook's productions.) She's going to come on Saturday night, I think. They say they're sold out, but I can't believe we can't find two seats.

I think the Japanese audiences are very odd. They're very undemonstrative – the sound of one hand clapping. This may be just the Globe. We were a bit thin, because of torrential rain. We were suddenly hit by it, rain like you have never seen, it fell like a waterfall. The typhoon season is about to begin and may affect us for a fortnight. Tokyo's a paradox, all the hurry and burry, all the people scurrying round you and yet at the same time a great generosity of spirit and sense of honesty – it's rather overwhelming. The setting leaves a lot to be desired, especially when it's thick and muggy as it has been today. I bought an umbrella and got my watch fixed, which was a ceremony in itself. Umbrellas are very fashionable, particularly at this time of year.

It looks as though Cairo will be out because Saddam Hussein has now signed a treaty with Iran. There'll probably be war in the Middle East and Mubarak will find himself in the thick of it. I'd like the Cairo date to be cancelled so I can return to London and spend some time at home. Though at this point it's difficult to know where my home will be.

Tomorrow is the first night of *King Lear* and we have rehearsals all day. The company are fed up with endlessly rehearsing these shows, but of course when you get into a new space you have to.

I'm finding it impossible to sleep. I went to bed at about 2.30 last night, had a glass of champagne and tried to knock myself out, read for a bit, finally fell fast asleep and then woke up.

I began the day talking to Martin Naylor who suggested coming to work in Japan, something which doesn't exactly draw me at the moment. I met Martin when I was last in Japan. He's an entrepreneur who specialises in bringing the current crop of English-speaking theatre to Japan, a great rival of Tamura-san. He was quite interesting about property in Tokyo. Property is at a premium here: in the area near the Globe a 73-square-metre flat four or five years ago cost in the region of 29 million yen and is now closer to 225 million yen. The realtor company which owns the Tokyo Globe is having a bit of financial difficulty and as from this year it's going to be called the Panasonic Globe because Panasonic are bailing them out.

I went to the theatre and we continued the technical rehearsal of *Lear*, doing the storm scenes and making a few cuts. There was a sequence David and I had put in, a montage sequence struggling with the wheelchair which we cut out, going straight into 'Blow winds'. Deborah has decided to have the house-lights in the auditorium up, which I wasn't sure about but actually worked quite well. It did show up the fact in the evening that a number of seats had not been filled, which was extremely exasperating. The seats at the Globe cost something like £40 each but most of them are bought up by companies or given away to patrons and, if they don't use them, of course there are empty seats. Also, apparently Tamura-san will not sell restricted view seats. If you haven't got the actual bums on the seats and there are gaps in the audience it means performances are not quite as dynamic as they might be.

In fact, contrary to expectation, it went extremely well. It was fast and had a flow about it and all the new things worked.

Afterwards there was a drink at the Globe Tavern and the ceremonial breaking open of a barrel of sake which Ian performed. I had a word with Richard Eyre, who, I must say, is an extraordinarily kind man and very considerate. I have enormous respect for him and feel very guilty that I cannot stand doing *Richard III*. He asked me if

I would be going to America with *Lear* and I told him that at this stage I couldn't possibly consider it. I think the play has a history of affecting the actor playing Lear. It's the questions the play asks about life and the values of life. I find it more and more devastating, I keep breaking into tears. On the whole it has to be said I've gained a lot from doing *Lear* and ironically, on occasions, have enjoyed it but I don't enjoy doing both plays and I can't face the idea of going on beyond March to America, it just is inconceivable. Maybe my mind will change. I don't think so.

Deborah came round in the interval, excited by the way it had gone and full of new faith in the play having seen it in this space. She said we must think about doing it at the Majestic at BAM in New York. It seems impossible to break the package. What can I do?

People are going to Kyoto for the weekend, to see the shrines and the older parts of Japan. I'd quite like to go to Fuji but I'm not up to moving about much. I haven't slept for the last four nights and God knows I'd love to be able to.

Teachings of Buddha:

> On the way of practical attainment. The four points to be considered are: first, to consider the body impure, seeking to remove all attachment to it. Second, to consider the senses as a source of suffering, whatever their feelings of pain or pleasure may be. Third, to consider the mind to be in a constant state of flux, and fourth, to consider everything in the world to be a consequence of causes and conditions and that nothing remains unchanged for ever.

Saturday, September 15

We did a matinée of *Richard* and an evening performance of *Lear*. Ian and I had a talk between the shows about why I didn't want to go on to America. I said I don't feel work can be my whole life any more. I didn't explain about *Richard*. He said that he thought *Richard* would go on irrespective of *Lear* though there might have to be cast

98

changes. Some of the cast will be disappointed but what can I do? I simply cannot go on with the work. We talked a little about how he became involved in the gay movement, his year off after coming back from America and how it had really changed his life. He was very generous, a little guarded.

The performance was a bit of a sham. The audiences are very strange, there isn't much comeback, they're not really proper audiences, and then there were the empty seats though they say the thing is sold out. It was the same when I was here two years ago. It's as though we are here for a private performance.

Poor Clare Higgins has got very bad bronchitis and went to the doctor. He thought she might have pneumonia which alarmed the poor girl considerably. Nick Blane collapsed too. No air conditioning onstage, and during the dreaded Greenham Common scene where the guys have to stand around for twenty minutes he thought he was going to have a heart attack. I made him lie down on my bed in between shows and have a bit of a nap. Physically people are very frail at the moment though their spirits are high. Being away from home makes them vulnerable.

In the scene with Cordelia, the waking scene, I broke down and came off stage and couldn't stop crying. I was crying and crying and crying uncontrollably. It was very difficult. I do find the part very demanding.

After the show we all went off – Deborah and Richard O'Callaghan and Ian and David Bradley and Cordelia Monsey – and had a fairly jolly meal. Everybody's off to Kyoto for the weekend. I've been asked to go but I don't feel I can.

I had a visitor tonight, Harué Momoyama, Toshi's wife, who sang in *The Tempest* absolutely beautifully. She came to see *Lear* and was obviously affected by it and tomorrow I'm going to meet her after the show. We have one performance tomorrow, *Richard*, which was scheduled for the evening but we've suddenly been told it will be in the afternoon. I think I'll have a lazy day on Monday doing nothing. I hope to speak to Irina this weekend. Whether she'll ring or not I don't know.

I'd better stop now as my voice is wearing out, talking into this machine.

Although the nature of Buddha is possessed by all people, it is buried so deeply in the defilements of worldly passion that it long remains unknown. That is why suffering is so universal and why there is endless recurrence of miserable lives. But just as by yielding to greed, anger and foolishness evil deeds are accumulated, so by following the Buddhist teaching the evil sources will be cleared away and rebirth in the world of suffering will be ended.

Sunday, September 16

Quite an eventful matinée. Clare Higgins was off. We're going to take her, poor girl, to the hospital tomorrow to be X-rayed for pneumonia. Most people are going away so I've volunteered to take her. She wanted to go on but it was impossible; it would have been crazy. Eve Matheson swopped parts and played Queen Elizabeth and Helene Kvale played Lady Anne. Just as Helene was about to go on, Eve came rushing through into the Green Room, having dropped her dress down the toilet, a clean toilet, I'm glad to say, but the dress needed drying out. Two hairdriers were brought and the second hairdrier managed to fuse the sound system with the result that Helene's performance of Lady Anne could not be relayed back to the dressing rooms. There was a certain build-up of nerves on everybody's part, especially poor Eve's. They both gave a very good rendering, though, and appeared surprisingly confident. It actually gave the afternoon a lift – at this stage in the proceedings it is probably precisely what we're needing.

I spent the evening with Harué Momoyama. It was fascinating to hear her criticism of *Lear* and the storm, which she felt was relatively ineffectual because, she said, western drummers do not breathe from their centre and the music doesn't therefore come from the pit, only from the top half of the chest.

I've just spent the morning at the hospital with Clare. It's been raining in Tokyo all day and I couldn't get a cab and the cab we did get tried to drop us in the middle of nowhere because we have no Japanese. I was extremely impressed by the efficiency of the hospital. When we arrived it all seemed very difficult because there was nobody around who spoke English. We understood that we had to wait for an hour, and in fact we were there for two hours but the first part which was meant to take an hour was over in two minutes. We sailed through, Clare had her X-ray and then we got the various medicines for her. Fascinating to watch Japanese bureaucracy at work – very swift, very super-efficient. The suspected pneumonia hasn't materialised but she has extremely bad bronchitis. She's very tired and may not be able to make the performance tomorrow night.

I had an extraordinary evening. I was talking to my two friends from the Shinchosa Publishing Company – about the whole nature of Japanese culture and how difficult it has been for Japan since the war, a society that's had to reinvent itself, though reinventing itself is a skill which they obviously have. The Japanese strive so hard to be good and honourable and of course to save face. Ko was saying, before they talk about business they talk about everything else. I don't think this is about saving face – it's a very Western concept – I think it's intended to put people at their ease and try and keep them in a state in which the deal can be done to the best advantage. In war it's a different thing, because in war they regard defeat as ignoble and to be treated with contempt. We talked about the Japanese philosophy of life, how they were still caught in Shintoism, about Hirohito's influence on life in Japan till his death in 1988, the fact that they had been trapped in a tradition which was only overthrown by the war, by the bombs dropped on Hiroshima and Nagasaki. After the war came a new kind of energy. Seven years of American occupation and dominance in world technology made them ask, 'How do we beat these people?' It wasn't really a question of beating them, it was a question of adapting and developing, of becoming viable and economically sound. In the use of the abacus in a Japanese market you can see the kernel of their phenomenal business acumen. Their gifts are to a certain extent a neurosis, the neurosis of a pioneering spirit in search of something quite spiritual and profound, a neurosis that Portugal and Spain felt in the fifteenth century with the expeditions of Columbus, Cabot, Vasco de Gama.

It was the best evening I've had in Tokyo. We talked about the war. Ko told me about his brother who died in the war when Ko was only four and how being the youngest son was the most disadvantageous position. The one thing that came out of tonight's conversation is that the place I have to see is Hiroshima, it's the crossroads, the crossroads of ancient and modern Japan.

> It is true that everything in this life is transitory and filled with uncertainty but it is lamentable that anyone should ignore this fact and keep on trying to seek enjoyment and satisfaction of his desires.

Tuesday, September 18

A good day. Mainly sightseeing with Ko and Mr N. They took me to the downtown district, the fishmarket and a restaurant and to the pearl and kimono-trade district. Then we went back to Shinchosa and were shown round the publishing company which is quite an extensive enterprise with its own television studio and sound mix facilities. I arrived back late to find that the drugs Clare had been given had made her quite woozy and she wasn't up to doing the shows. The understudies went on and it was an extraordinary evening. Helene Kvale did an excellent Cordelia, statuesque and centred. Eve Matheson came into her own as Regan, very dangerous, very unpredictable, very sexy in a way and quite surprising. It was an exciting show and we all felt so good afterwards we went to the Globe Tavern and celebrated. The Crown Prince came to the show and apparently enjoyed it very much.

Ian is unhappy about the way the Globe is run – still these empty seats and still we're told it's sold out – and the fact that there seems to be no publicity. There are these great gaps in the audience and there's also something about the seating arrangements – people sit back, separated from each other, they're too comfortable in that auditorium. I'm reminded of Yefremov, Director of the Moscow Art Theatre, and his dislike of the new MXAT, his wish to get back to a more intimate and more tactile space where the audience sat elbow to elbow.

Wednesday, September 19–Thursday, September 20

Yesterday I did some sightseeing. We went to Kamakura to the Buddhist temple there which has one of the largest bronze statues of Buddha in the world. It's amazing, this huge thing that dominates the temple – well, the temple isn't there any more, it was blown down by a great tidal wave in the sixteenth century. We had travelled to Kamakura through suburban Tokyo past Yokohama and I was with two of the younger actors, Pete Sullivan and Phil McKee, and the Assistant Director, Cordelia Monsey. I happened to be talking to Cordelia about various things and children, and mentioned that my ex-wife had conceived stillborn twin boys. We were walking up the hill to the temple and as we approached the great Buddha, Peter Sullivan noticed that there was a shrine off to the left. So we went off to the left and were met at the top of the hill by the most extraordinary sight: hundreds of little statues, all covered in baby clothes. I discovered that this was in fact a shrine dedicated to stillborn children and children of abortion, children who had died at birth. The statues had bibs and rattles and little toy windmills and Coca-Cola cans; it was partly obscene but incredibly moving and, given our conversation only five minutes before, the synchronism made the hairs on the back of my neck stand up. I remembered my children and bought some flowers and laid them before a group of these statues.

The performance last night was *Richard III*. Clare Higgins was still ill and Ms Kvale and Ms Matheson did more sterling work. We've had a typhoon warning. Tomorrow, apparently, a typhoon will hit Tokyo. It's already started this evening. The wind is quite ferocious and the rain is beating very, very hard. We've been told we'll get a message at 2 o'clock as to whether we're on because apparently everything stops in Tokyo if there's a typhoon. Yesterday there was a humidity factor of 92 per cent.

I'm going to Hiroshima at the weekend. My friend Ko, who has been extraordinarily kind to me, has arranged for me to go by plane on Sunday night, stay in a hotel and fly back on Monday in time to pack, leaving for London on Tuesday. In Japanese social life there is a tradition of *giri*, when one person is indebted to another. I have built up a strong *giri* factor to Ko and Yozo Nishimura.

The typhoon didn't materialise or rather it came in the night, blew a few trees down and didn't seem to make too much disturbance.

Today was a day for sight-seeing and going round Tokyo. I went to the Asakusa district with its huge temple dominating the market. We went to see the Japanese puppet show, the Bunraku, at the National Theatre. I didn't have a translating headset, just a copy of the text in English which I consulted, but the narration was a *tour de force*, the different voices, the concentration, things sung and spoken, accompanied by a guitar instrument. The puppeteers were on the whole very good, some remarkably so. You couldn't see the puppeteers' faces. In Bunraku, one man controls the legs, one man controls the left arm and the main puppeteer controls the right arm and head. The programme was in three sections, starting at 11.30 and finishing at 3.30. We saw the second section. Towards the end a character appeared; this puppet made an entrance and the weight, the displacement of air as the puppet moved was astoundingly precise. Eventually you could see the face of an old gentleman who must have been in his seventies. This was Tamao Yoshida, the greatest puppeteer in Japan. He barely moved the puppet at all, he just breathed life into it, pulsed life. The story is roughly that the protagonist is summoned to appear before the Shogun Yoshi and is given a high place at table. He's seeking to avenge his father's death, a theme that goes through all the plays. The puppeteer had such concentration that the puppet seemed independent of him, and there was a moment when the puppet exits, when he does a particular expression, which leaves you up in the air for the next ballet – he did this in a way that spoke volumes, just moved the face very, very lightly and then he made a very quick exit.

After that we did the moat walk round the Imperial Palace to the square where Emperor Hirohito's famous surrender speech on the last day of the war was heard by a kneeling crowd, some of whom did not get up because they committed hara-kiri on the spot.

Then I went to the bath house which was the high point of the day – basically municipal baths, but there is something about abluting in the style of a country. I've done it before on my travels, I did it in Turkey, but not in Russia though it was something I wanted to do. You go into really, really hot baths like huge ordinary tubs and then come out and scrub yourself down and soap yourself and repeat the process. It's very invigorating.

I was a bit late for the show as the bath house was quite a way from the theatre and I didn't time it properly. I gave David Bradley a headache. He'd been to a karaoke club where they sing till the early hours of the morning accompanied by a backing track and hadn't got in until 6.30 in the morning. By the time I arrived at the theatre he was a little jittery – he's my understudy – and I said, 'Well, Bradley, I'm just trying to keep you on your toes.'

During the performance of *Lear*, which went quite well, there was an odd mishap. I couldn't turn the wheelchair over, it took me three goes before I could do it.

I did a link-up with 'Kaleidoscope' in London who were asking about the typhoon and the effect it had had on the performance – none, in the event.

Tomorrow is the Royal Gala performance of *Richard III* in the presence of HRH Princess Anne. Ko is going to come and pick me up for a last shopping spree. The trouble with shopping in Japan is that you see something and immediately think it's a bargain. Richard O'Callaghan kept talking about a camera that Martin, one of the drummers, was going to buy and saying, 'It's £300, it's only £300. And back home it would be £900.' I said, 'There's this wonderful video camera for £25,000 but here you can buy it for £15,000.' A lot of money is a lot of money.

We've just had an extremely glowing notice in *The Times*, *The Japan Times*. My performance is a masterpiece of power, perception, delicacy and humour . . .'With more than a little help from his friends, Cox delivers a kind of Lear that makes us want to travel in time to compare it with the great Lears going all the way back to Burbage. Cox is that good .' Oh dear, oh dear.

Today was our performance of *Richard III* on behalf of the UK 90 Exposition in front of HRH Princess Anne, the black tie affair. Unfortunately most of the house had to be papered and the black ties really couldn't be mustered. There is a black tie tradition but a very small tradition, and there were last-minute panics. Anyway there was a house, more or less, and Tamura-san laid on a very good reception afterwards. Her Royal Highness seemed to enjoy herself, the Crown Prince of Japan was there also and I spoke to him briefly. He'd seen *King Lear* three nights ago and was very impressed by the production. As if from nowhere loomed Peter Hall, like the ghost of Christmas past. Apparently he was on his honeymoon.

Earlier in the day I'd bought myself a Japanese suit, which I changed into in the shop and continued my shopping and sightseeing down to the electric district, Akihabara, a sort of computer city. I bought Irina a first-night present as she's about to open in Nottingham in *The Importance of Being Earnest*. We had a fairly late night and I drank whisky for the first time in years. Tiredness is creeping up again and the whole claustrophobia of company life, though I think the company on the whole are marvellous and this week, particularly with the understudies going on, there's been a great sense of pulling together. That and the fact that we've all been dressing in close proximity. I think it does matter, it is important where people dress when they're working together. At the Lyttleton we were all in our separate cubicles; here at the Globe there's a greater sense of community between the actors.

On Saturday we did a matinée of *Lear* and an evening performance of *Richard*. Pamela Edwardes, my editor, came to the matinée with her husband Peter who is working in Tokyo at the moment. She was well and heavily pregnant and I thought about her and the 92 per cent humidity. I got a letter from the lady who is typing the transcripts, Caroline Keely, saying she hopes the next lot of tapes are slightly cheerier than the last fourteen. God, I do too.

I'm now halfway through the Sunday performance of *Lear* and I had a sort of turn in the middle of the performance, in the 'reason not the need' scene. I became aware of someone sitting in the audience who obviously found the play too distressing. She was flapping her hand as if to push the experience away. The effect it had on me was to shift my performance into a wholly different area of, I suppose, pain. When I came off I was so upset I was shaking. I looked at David in the wings and thought, 'Why don't you do it? Why don't you do it? Why don't you finish it? I've had enough.' This is the second or third attack I've had of this kind. David suggested that I should get out of doing the Duke of Buckingham.

Lear had a great energy yesterday, I think it has touched a new level since we've been in Japan but I was so tired in the evening, so tired, and I had to go out to dinner with Tamura-san whom I have hardly seen since I have been here; Ian's been doing most of the socialising, I haven't been up to it. We had to drive for thirty minutes with Mr Oni, the production manager, and myself both fast asleep on the way there. We had our meal in a very nice restaurant with Tamura-san who asked me if I'd like to run a drama school in Tokyo and how much money I'd need. The idea of running a drama school couldn't be further from my mind. Then we drove back and I fell asleep again and got into bed.

Tonight I'm off to Hiroshima.

Sunday, September 23, evening

I've just arrived in Hiroshima. It's a very eerie feeling. As you arrive you are shown a video of your landing: to fly over the city at night and see it just before you and the plane come down beside the river is quite haunting. So far my one taxi driver in Hiroshima doesn't seem to be wearing the gloves that I've begun to get used to in Tokyo but they have a method of opening and closing the door automatically which makes me nervous, it's like the invisible man getting out of the cab.

A long conversation with Ko last night about Japanese history – the chaining of the islands, the Shogun, the revolution of 1868, the need to reassert the Emperor's power because in the feudal structure of the Japanese hierarchy the Emperor was the weakest link; he had the smallest army, the smallest amount of land, he was merely the spiritual head. The clan chiefs wanted to take power away from the Shogun and give it back to the Emperor, under their control – very complex, very sophisticated. They talked about the effect of Christianity; the forming of the Japanese character.

Monday, September 24

It's 8.00 a.m. and we've just caught the ferry to Miyajima, an island just off the coast of Hiroshima . . . you can hear the noise of the engines in the background . . . We've just moved from the Red Gate which rises fifty feet up out of the sea . . . We've climbed to a shrine up in the hills, incredibly peaceful. It's extraordinary here, the deer come up to you; Miyajima is known as the deer island and the deer are so gentle. GONG. That was the bell being sounded to carry our prayers. I am just about to sound it. GONG.

I've just visited the peace museum in Hiroshima. It's almost imposs-ible to know what to say. It's quite devastating. I've always avoided this kind of museum in the past, but I think it's very important to begin to understand something about Japan and how certain things came about. It's a strange city, Hiroshima, it's particularly empty at the moment. People usually come in August, not September. But walking round this museum which is mainly devoted to the day of the bomb – August 6, my son's birthday – seeing the stopped watches, the shadows cast by the heat intensity, human shadows burnt into the ground, the effects of black rain, the keloids growing after twenty-four hours, a month or so, on the victims, such a scale of devastation is quite unbelievable. It seems to me that everyone should see this. The most moving sight is the statue of a little girl who died of leukaemia. She had asked for paper cranes to be constructed in memory of the children who died in Hiroshima and there are literally millions surrounding her.

My reading from the Buddha has been irregular. This is the last one. The way of purification.

Purification of the mind. People have worldly passions which lead them into delusions and sufferings. There are five ways to emancipate themselves from the bond of worldly passions. First, they should have the right idea of things, ideas that are based on careful observation, and understand causes and effects and their significance correctly. Since the cause of suffering is rooted in the mind's desires and attachments and desire and attachment are related to mistaken observations by an ego neglecting the significance of the law of cause and effect, there can be peace only if the mind can be rid of these worldly passions.

Second, people can get rid of these mistaken observations and resulting worldly passions by careful and patient mind control. With efficient mind control they can avoid desires arising from the stimulation of the eyes, ears, tongue, nose, skin, and by doing so cut off the very root of all worldly passions.

Third, people should have correct ideas with regard to the proper use of things; that is, with regard to articles of clothing and food. They should not think of them in relation to comfort or pleasure but only in relation to the body's needs; clothing is necessary to protect the body against the extremes of heat and cold and to conceal the shame of the body; food is necessary for the nourishment of the body and enlightenment. Worldly passions cannot arise through such thinking.

Fourth, people should learn endurance; they should learn to endure the discomforts of heat, cold, hunger, thirst; they should learn to be patient when receiving abuse and scorn: for it is the practice of endurance that quenches the fire of all worldly passions which is burning up their bodies.

Fifth, people should learn to see and so avoid all danger: just as a wise man keeps away from wild horses and mad dogs, one should not make friends with evil men nor should one go to places that wise men avoid. If one practises caution and prudence, the fire of worldly passions which is burning in one's vitals will die down.

London

Wednesday, September 26

I'm back in England. It's midday Japanese time, 3 a.m. English time. I can't sleep. The Japanese experience has been pretty overwhelming, finished off by the long flight from Tokyo, Virgin Atlantic Airways, with no less a personage than Mr Richard Branson as in-flight host. The video system wasn't working and he kept us entertained, like a flying crêche, asking the NT if they'd care to perform – God forbid. He substituted the Senators, a pop duo he had in tow, accompanying them with a group of body-builders doing a kind of muscle display.

The journey gave me a chance to reflect. The feeling of Hiroshima will never quite leave me – or perhaps it will. The ghost-like quality of the city keeps coming back to me. When I got back from Hiroshima I discovered I'd left one of my shoes there and they say when you leave something behind you always mean to return. But I can't see myself going back there.

Our last do in Tokyo was a British Council party given by Joe Barnett, who had been to see *Lear* two or three times and was very affected by it, a nice man, sensitive, has spent seven years in Japan and still finds the Japanese very, very difficult to understand. There was also a man from the Embassy with a scar on his face, very

English, who was angry about the way Hiroshima had been used as propaganda for Japanese nationalism and said that we had to see it in context, I had to see it in context. No context could ever excuse such a barbarous, brutal, inhumane act. It's no good being tit for tat and quoting what the Japanese did in Manchuria. I found I couldn't talk to him any longer, he made me so angry, so I left and went to the other side of the room where I spoke to Deborah.

She asked me about my little collapse during the matinée of *Lear*. I told her I'd seen a woman in the audience, either bored or not able to cope during 'the reason not the need', and just at that point I began to touch other areas; it was distressing given my general state and when I came off I couldn't move. Deborah asked what could be done and I told her I didn't know, David Bradley had suggested perhaps I should come out of *Richard*. I don't know how to remove myself from the production, though I feel more and more it's the sort of theatre I find myself at odds with. I find it difficult to tell Richard Eyre what I feel because it's something so fundamental. I feel I am being a negative force in the company and that my judgement isn't all that accurate, perhaps erratic. I'm sure Ian feels I'm having this effect though he is wonderfully discreet. My problem is that I always show my feelings, my negative emotions hang on me like so much washing on the line. Deborah said she would back me whatever way I wanted to move. I also told her some of what I felt were problems arising in *Lear* and she said perhaps I wasn't being clear, which perhaps I wasn't. I'm in no position to be clear at the moment, I'm just overwhelmed by feelings and emotions which seem to be beyond my control.

When I got back to the hotel in Tokyo I greeted Natasha Parry, Irina's mother, who had come to do *Hamlet* with Cheek by Jowl. I went up to bed and started to pack and packed until about 3.30 in the morning. At 6.45 a.m. Ko rang me from Hiroshima to say that he was still there. We'd gone to the airport early when we'd decided I'd seen enough. It was raining quite heavily and they'd made a 50-50 decision to close the airport: there were no more flights coming in from Tokyo. There was one plane on the ground and I was booked on the next. Ko, by showing my picture from the Shinchosa magazine, was able to get me a seat on the plane that was in and I took off, leaving him behind. When he rang me he told me all the later flights had been cancelled and the bullet train was full so I would have been stuck in Hiroshima unable to catch my flight back to London.

At Tokyo airport there was the usual hanging around. Stephen Marchant had no passport, it was back at the hotel with his American wife. I think this might have been a subconscious act on his part as he didn't want to leave his young lady behind. David Bradley spent the time doing his magic act for a group of Cambodian orphans. The plane took off minus Mr Marchant.

Towards the end of the flight, when we stopped off at Moscow, I took great delight in saying I wanted to get off and buy some Camel cigarettes for Irina, but they wouldn't let me off. Branson offered to go and get some for me, but unfortunately they wouldn't let him off either. I arrived back in England and decided to forgo the coach and to make for the train. Hearing the English voices, looking at the dismal English houses as I sat in the train with all my baggage, I felt extremely depressed to be back. I rang my friend Beth Patrick who kindly picked me up at Clapham Junction.

The house is empty, Irina is in Nottingham. I couldn't sleep. I posted a card for my daughter Margaret's birthday which is on Thursday. Then I slept for about an hour. I got up and unpacked and started to wrap her present, the present I bought for Irina and also my son Alan's. Today I'm going up to Nottingham to see my darling Irina. I miss her terribly and long to see her.

Nottingham

Sunday, September 30–Friday, October 5

I drove up – for the second time – having spent the week recovering from Japan, a fairly hectic week: up here to visit Irina on Wednesday, then down to my daughter in Cheltenham because it was her birthday, then back to London for a long chat with my agent. These attacks I've been having during *Lear* – the pressure of the part and of the work is getting too much, so I asked him to call Richard Eyre and see if it would be possible to drop Buckingham. That was on

Friday. I then went to see Otto Plashkes about a possible film next year and spent the weekend trying to rest – with great difficulty because my mind is severely troubled at the moment and I feel very raw.

On Sunday, yesterday, morning I drove back up to Nottingham and spent a lovely day with Irina. We went to Belvoir Castle. We're living in Southwell, just outside Nottingham, and it has a beautiful little minster. Irina is staying here this week, opening in *The Importance* at the Playhouse. It's ironic that we're here at the same time. She's naturally very nervous about playing Cicely so I have to be careful not upstaging with my problems.

Today, Monday, I went in to the Theatre Royal which I remember from playing here with *Strange Interlude*. We did a technical rehearsal, rough bits of *Lear*. I was slightly nervous about *Lear* having had such a *crise* in the middle last time. So, with two of my fellow actors before the performance I drank a bottle of champagne. It's not something I recommend and it's not something I regularly do either. The performance went well, though the Nottingham audience are great coughers; we'd forgotten about the coughing English, we're now so used to the polite Japanese, the coughing English, the bronchial English, it's quite damp up here at the moment. The biggest problem was the acoustic which is dead. The *Lear* set has so much canvas and so much covered stuff that it has no reverb. Anyway, it went well and I returned home quickly to Southwell to say goodnight to Irina. The poor girl had to be up early the following morning to do her dress parade and work on *The Importance*.

On Tuesday I drove to Newstead Abbey, Byron's home, with Deborah and on the way I got a telephone call in my car. I'd forgotten I had to see a journalist back in Nottingham, I'd arranged it with Methuen, my publishers. She was very sweet, the journalist, and waited for me and I came back, dropped Deborah and had a long chat with her.

In the afternoon, Deborah told me that Jeremy Conway, my agent, had rung Richard and Richard was naturally very hurt. It was a complete aberration on my part because I had every intention of speaking to him first. I was going to speak to him when I got back from Tokyo but I just couldn't face it, couldn't face going into the

National Theatre. Richard was arriving that evening for the performance of *Richard III*. Jeremy did his job but I was angry with myself for not having realised he was going to move so fast.

We did the technical of *Richard III* in the afternoon and the acoustic, because of the wood in the *Richard* set, was so much better than for *Lear*. The performance went very well. Ian was on form and even I was on form. Just before the performance Richard Eyre arrived and I told him about what had happened in Tokyo and asked him if he would release me from Buckingham when we returned to London in January. I told him I was no longer sure whether I could get through a performance. Richard has had this experience before, with the demands that parts make. He directed Daniel Day Lewis in *Hamlet* and Dan was in the same state apparently and told him he wanted to be released, and then had this *crise* when in the ghost scene he saw the ghost of his own father, the Poet Laureate. In Ian Charleson's case, I believe playing the part of *Hamlet* had the effect of prolonging his life, and clearly, from Richard's account, his performance had a remarkable insight into Hamlet's deliberations on death. Ironic how the same role can have such a contrasting effect on two actors. Richard was very understanding.

As I say, the performance went well and afterwards I went and had some fish and chips with a couple of the girls from the company, as Irina was going to be back late from a post mortem with her fellow actors on the work they'd done. It's funny this business of people working in companies and their allegiance; they're like families but the bonding lasts for such a short time. Of course the work unites but it is so transitory; ultimately there has to be more. Work and life must balance; life isn't work – though it needs work. I say that now in my position of strength, receiving a lot of work, but for actors who don't, work and touring are very important. At my age I feel a hostage. Ian McKellen, who has sacrificed absolutely all private life for his work, is a monk of the theatre. I can't be, and yet if my private life collapsed, as it could very easily do, would I embrace the theatre again as I did in the past? Would I make it the centre of my world as Ian does? On our walk round Newstead Abbey, Deborah was describing the business of coming home to a hotel at 1 a.m. to be greeted by a load of drunken actors and stage managers, and this is the pathetic part of touring, this world we're forced to inhabit

. . . choose to inhabit. It's why a philosophical basis to what one does and the need to work on oneself is more and more important. I thought I had a philosophy but it seems to me now an excuse of the moment. It must be possible to have a continuum in life, something to sustain you, not merely to live from event to event. There are people who have purpose, real shape to their lives. At the moment I can't see how the theatre can give you that. I feel I'm a victim of my own career and I must shift. But I don't know what the next shift will be. The future seems more uncertain than at any time in my life.

One of the pleasanter aspects of the past week was coming back and visiting my son, spending the morning with him and talking to him in a way I've never done before. He told me about a young man whom he had helped on his first day at drama school. He didn't say it in any self-congratulatory way, he was slightly embarrassed, thinking it might be taken in the wrong way as patronising. I was very proud of him, of that effort and caring. And going to see my daughter in Cheltenham I told the school authorities not to let her know I was coming, so when I arrived it was a complete surprise and the look on her face was so delightful and moving. She was taken completely off-guard. My poor daughter, she tries not to be involved in the theatre but she's been asked to audition for *Fiddler on the Roof* at school. I hope there's a greater consistency in what my children do with their lives.

It's Wednesday morning. Irina is still asleep upstairs. I'm looking at Thornton Wilder's *Bridge of San Luis Rey*, about fate and why five people come to the same end at the same time. Makes me shudder, the notion of fate. There's a line which is interesting, I don't know if I can make any sense of it, it just struck me as being pertinent. The brother of one victim decides to investigate the relationship of the five people killed; they didn't know one another, though they had passed over the bridge many times before the bridge snapped and the five were hurled into the ravine. The brother asks, 'Why did it happen to these five?' If there was any plan in the universe, if there was any pattern in a human life, surely it could be discovered in those five lives so suddenly cut off. 'Either we live by accident and die by accident, or we live by plan and die by plan.'

This morning I read in the paper that Jill Bennett, who I knew quite well, though I hadn't seen her for some time – I played Lovborg to her Hedda – has died, suspected suicide. It adds to my despair.

I'm sitting at the Royal Moat House Hotel in Nottingham. I've just missed two performances, one of *Lear* and one of *Richard*, and I think probably a third this afternoon. I strained my voice on, it must have been, Wednesday. The performance was very good but it meant that I couldn't play yesterday or the day before. David Bradley has finally been thrown in the deep end.

Things have come to a head, really, in my private life as well as my professional life. Irina feels crowded by my presence in Nottingham and I've come here to give her breathing space. I feel very confused. I can't wait for *Lear* to stop. *Richard* I think I've escaped, though I have to talk to Ian and I feel very guilty not to have done so.

It's extraordinary to be here. Nottingham has a strange history for me. I first came here in 1966, when John Neville had just opened the Playhouse and we were doing a production from the Royal Lyceum, my first job. I was touring with Fulton Mackay and Duncan Macrae, one of the great Scots eccentric performers and philosophers, and I remember sitting outside the new Playhouse which at that period represented a spirit of renaissance – the fact that a famous actor like Neville had given up a lucrative life in London to go to the provinces to do something original. Sitting out there on a warm August day talking to these actors, I remember Duncan Macrae saying, 'The trouble with everyone is we live in balloons – you're in your balloon and I'm in my balloon, but my job is to burst your balloon.'

A few years later I came back to Nottingham for a season, which was the first time I worked with my then wife. The season had been extremely difficult and ironically I lost my voice. I thought I wouldn't get through the repertoire. I asked David William, the Artistic Director, if he'd release me from the company. My wife, Caroline, was supposed to have played opposite me in *The Three Musketeers* but David wanted one person to play two parts and it was decided that Caroline would be dropped. I decided to honour my contract and

11. Joyce Redman (Duchess of York) (background left), Richard Eyre (Director) and Clare Higgins (Queen Elizabeth) rehearsing the 'Greenham Common' scene where the queens confront Richard. Act 4, scene 4. (Photo: John Haynes)

12. Richard O'Callaghan as Ratcliffe (left), Phil McKee as a soldier (right). Ian McKellen as Richard: 'Come, bustle, bustle; caparison my horse.' Act 5, scene 3. (Photo: John Haynes)

13. Ian McKellen as Richard: 'I do the wrong, and first begin to brawl.'
Act 1, scene 3. (Photo: John Haynes)

14. Sam Beazley as body of King Henry VI (foreground).
Eve Matheson as Lady Anne: 'Set down, set down your honorable load.'
Act I, scene 2. (Photo: John Haynes)

15. Ian McKellen as Richard (right) to Brian Cox as Buckingham:
'My other self, my counsel's consistory, my oracle, my prophet!
my dear cousin.' Act 2, scene 2. (Photo: John Haynes)

16. Brian Cox as Buckingham in Act 1, scene 3. (Photo: John Haynes)

17. The army. (Photo: John Haynes)

18. In the rehearsal room: Brian Cox as Lear with David Bradley as the Fool in the background.

19. Brian eating sushi in Tokyo. (Photo: Courtesy of Shinchosa Publishing)

20. Brian as
Lawrence of
Arabia in Egypt.
(Photo: Helene
Kvale)

21. Brian leading a
masterclass in Paris.
(Photo: Caroline Rose)

22. Members of the company for King Lear and Richard III:

Back row (left to right):
Richard Simpson, Sam Beazley, Jane Suffling, Nicholas Blane,
Hakeem Kae-Kazim, Fiona Bardsley, Ian McKellen, John Caulfield

Third row:
David Collings, Bruce Purchase, Peter Sullivan, Susan Engel, Peter Jeffrey,
Deborah Warner, David Bradley, Mark Strong, Richard Bremmer,
David Milling

Second row:
Richard O'Callaghan, Phil McKee, Joyce Redman, Clare Higgins,
Brian Cox, Richard Eyre, Eve Matheson, Hildegard Bechtler

Front row:
Colin Hurley, Helene Kvale, Derek Hutchinson, Cordelia Monsey,
Stephen Marchant, Bob Crowley, Wendy Fitt
(Photo: John Haynes)

stayed. It put an enormous strain on us, the first crack in our relationship. With my wife back in London I moved to a hotel and it was there that one morning two policemen came to my door to tell me my mother had died in California.

Another thing I remember about Nottingham – I had a close friend at the time, an actor called Dudley Foster, and one day I came to the theatre to be told that Dudley had hanged himself, aged forty-four – exactly the age I am now – because of domestic trouble. I don't know why I'm saying all this but it seems to have some kind of connection – and to read this morning about Jill was quite a shock.

Irina – it's a curious coincidence that she should be working up here when it looks as though that relationship is coming to an end. It's so difficult to make any sense of it. The need to balance my life and my work. I can't go on sacrificing one for the other, there must be a co-existence, a balance. But this balance is so difficult to achieve: I'm not alone, I look at every member of the company and see the same. I look at Ian and see the sacrifices he has made for his work. I can't do that, I won't do that. God, it's so very, very hard.

Cardiff

Tuesday, October 9

I spoke to Ian at the weekend and told him I wanted to be released from *Richard III* in the New Year, to which he was very sympathetic. He was worried about how people would react – not necessarily in the company – to my leaving the production, how it would look and how I'd feel about that. I told him that was something I could deal with.

Cordelia Monsey recommended a very good, good isn't quite the word, an extraordinary woman who came round on Sunday, called Rosa Pamelzhoffer, an Austrian lady, who does acupuncture and deep massage, shiatsu I think, and went to work on me for three hours just before Ian arrived. I wished she'd come after Ian, not before. She really went to town and picked up all my defences, my physical defences, particularly in the area of my liver, the seat of

117

emotion. It's very difficult to describe, because if you describe it, it sounds rather pretentious and I'll leave it to the imagination rather than going into any great depth, but I certainly feel much calmer and better able to cope.

Irina and I are going to be separated for the next two weeks, a trial separation. By mistake, she has taken my car keys so I couldn't drive down to Cardiff and was late arriving here. The weather is rather beautiful and the country around here, though I won't be able to see it without a car, is beautiful. I spent the morning in my hotel room. Camilla Mayer, our tour organiser – Roger Chapman's assistant – and I talked at length about the nature of touring and what value there is in it, and the only value seems to be for the audience. Some actors do enjoy it but the whole business of saving on per diems – daily expense allowances – and . . . Ian was amazed that people were trying to save on their per diems, being away from home you eat more, you tend to comfort yourself one way or another. I find hotel rooms on the whole rather comforting, I don't know why, I always have done. I think it's because of all the ancillary things. Anyway, I'm going out now to see if I can catch a bit of the day as it's quite pleasant.

Wednesday, October 10

Our first performance of *Richard* last night went extremely well, better than *Lear* the night before. I'm convinced that provincial audiences are not ready for the length of *Lear* – last buses etc. – though the Welsh National Opera have a major following and a lot of their operas are longer. But then that's an opera audience who are a dedicated minority. We've had a lot of restless sixth-formers being brought to *Lear* who disturb the concentration of the audience. I'm urging Deborah to examine ways of re-doing the curtain call and generally re-working and keeping the interval down to a minimum if we don't cut the play – which she obviously will not do.

We had the Welsh Electricity Board last night, they are one of the main sponsors. The Chairman, Wilfred Evans, gave us a very good spread and we have another do tonight with Digital, the first of the occasions when we have to wear our PR hats. There isn't the same touring subsidy for Cardiff as Nottingham which has quite a good subsidy from the main Arts Council who deal with England; Cardiff is funded by the Welsh Arts Council and can't afford nearly as much. Though we are playing to capacity in Cardiff the manager of the theatre said that even charging top whack, £17, they're still not going to make any profit. It shows one of the anomalies in the touring policy and a part of arts funding which should be looked into.

A group of us went to Richard Bremmer's house today. Richard lives quite near Cardiff on the road to Abergavenny in the Hereford and Worcestershire part of what used to be Wales, at a place called Longtown. He moved there with his family five or six years ago and – an incredible labour of love – converted a Norman church into a house, single-handedly put in floors, took out beams, put on a new roof. I was amazed at his industry, but it seems so sad that this poor man who has worked so hard cannot enjoy the place because he spends all his time as an actor travelling around and rarely gets back. We had a very pleasant day. I drove up with Eve and Joyce and Helene and we all took bits of food and cheese and sat and everybody was quite speechless. Behind the house is a Norman castle which we walked up to and climbed over and for the first time I felt a real company spirit.

I'm liking Cardiff, it's a nice town, and also very progressive; touristy, but even so I do get a feeling of blight. Britain is very depressing. It's as though we have travelled no further than the fifties and sixties.

I got a call last night from Misha Kokosowski who has asked me to do a masterclass in France at the Odéon. It's going to be a big festival for young directors and will be just after my last performance of *Lear* in Paris. I've said I'll do it on Shakespeare but I don't feel particularly well disposed towards Shakespeare at the moment.

Today we did Welsh castles, two of them, Castle Coch and Caerphilly, site of many a downfall and where Edward II took refuge at some point. I was with Derek Hutchinson and Sam Beazley. Sam loves drawing and did some drawings of various aspects of both castles. Coch was built in the nineteenth century by William Burges for the Marquess of Bute. He moved the village which had grown up against the old castle walls and spent twenty years building this fantastic gothic edifice.

The overall effect of Wales is one of melancholy and depression. I now know what Richard Burton was up against.

Friday, October 12

I think I've made a discovery. I had another of these attacks last night, again the 'reason not the need' scene, which is the most difficult scene for me. I thought I was going to have a heart attack. I wonder if I induce this state, perhaps because of Lear's desperation for sympathy which transfers into my desperation to get sympathy for playing the role and all the role entails. I think because I'm playing an old man, though it's the greatest of parts, at some level I resent it, because my vanity says that I'm relatively young, why am I playing this old man? And the state of my personal life at the moment exacerbates the situation and I use everything to seek some kind of attention or sympathy. I thought I'd lost vanity, but I think vanity is so deep in me that I haven't lost it at all.

Afterwards last night I went dancing. This is the fella who, two or three weeks ago, could hardly get through an evening. I had an enormous amount of energy and I went dancing and danced till about 2.30 in the morning.

Today, Friday, I went to the Welsh School of Speech and Drama at the behest of my friend Andrew Neil, an ex-actor now teaching there. He was at drama school with David Bradley who hadn't heard from him for a good fifteen or sixteen years. He's a very fine teacher who I first met at LAMDA when he was working there. I went to talk to some of the students. One young boy from Dundee asked with great trepidation about the whole business of RP, Received Pronunciation, to which I made a lengthy answer, talking about the heart and head language, immediacy and modification, and the difference between an accent which imprisons the voice like a suburban London accent, and those which release – the Celtic accent. Then a girl asked how I could justify the expense of the tour. I told her I couldn't, it wasn't for me to justify, but if the quality of the work was up to the mark the expense was worth it. Then I talked of the nature of sponsorship and the funding being provided, or not provided, by the Arts Council, which of course she wasn't aware of and why should she be? An Irish lad asked me about nepotism in the theatre particularly in London, and I realised that this was quite a pithy question from a student in a regional drama school. There seems to be a great deal of nepotism, though I think the main problem is not nepotism so much as that more actors' children are going into the theatre as if it were a family business and there are fewer people from the outlying districts coming in. There's less infusion than there was in the sixties when I started, owing to the lack of grants, which limits the access of a whole stratum of society to arts education. It was a fairly lively session.

It was a lovely afternoon and I decided to go for a walk. After the performance I came back to the hotel and started talking to Peter Radmore, who is in charge of the lighting boys, about the age-old problem of the National Theatre, director-dominated, and the need to re-think strategy, why has the National Theatre gone wrong and the usual old guff which went on till 4.00 a.m. when finally I retired.

This morning I rose after four hours' sleep, I'm not sleeping at all at the moment, and am about to get packed and meet Guy Demeure, a journalist from *Le Nouvel Observateur*, who's flown to Cardiff to see the shows and do a piece for our opening in Paris.

Leeds

Tuesday, October 16

We've opened in Leeds. I drove back from Cardiff with Derek Hutchinson, and McKellen administering food in the back of the car like a demented nanny. Arrived in the morning about 2.00 a.m., picked up a cab, went to my house, discovered my car keys hadn't arrived, Irina was going to be sending them down; at 9.30 rang the friend who was supposed to be getting them and they finally arrived with a note from Irina virtually terminating our relationship. Such are the spoils of war.

I then drove to Shropshire to see my friends John and Pauline Phillips. John is an actor, now retired, who recently had a stroke and temporarily lost his sight. I didn't know what to expect when I arrived. We had had an elaborate series of conversations about how he would have to be going to the twenty-first birthday party of his nephew, Mark, and he gave me instructions about how to get to this schoolhouse restaurant. I arrived at about 1.30, didn't know what the party would be like and imagined that if Pauline was sitting away from me John wouldn't be able to see me and all kinds of embarrassment. I was met with two shocks: the first was that when I came in I heard John say 'Brian, hello' and there he was as right as rain – he can see in the distance quite well, he just has trouble close to. The second was that the celebrant of the birthday, Mark, was in a wheelchair, paralysed as the result of a car crash. He was extremely tired from a hectic session the night before and it was a curious lunch, to say the least, with two lady godparents, his mother, his father Barry Jones, who was a retired orthopaedic surgeon, Pauline (Barry's sister) and John. At the end of the table was Mark in his wheelchair and his young girlfriend. I found it rather moving. After lunch we retired to John's house, Allt-y-rhiw, a farmhouse which overlooks Montgomeryshire and Shropshire, by the side of Offa's Dyke, with the most extraordinary view, from time to time like a Japanese landscape. It was a very sane and peaceful day.

I gathered myself together and the following morning bade my farewells and drove through the slashing rain to the grim city of Leeds. It really is a grim, northern, dour place. I'd never been to Leeds before and drove round and was amazed that I was able to find the hotel and the theatre, a real old-fashioned opera house, the Grand; an extraordinary auditorium but the backstage facilities are less than admirable. I then went to my hotel – from which I had been moved. The company manager, John Caulfield, had stayed there and discovered it was too bad for words and moved us into the Metropole, which was equally dreary. Susan Engel and I are going to see if we can find somewhere else in the country because I don't think I can take a week of this.

There have been a few technical problems: the young lighting man, Paul McLeish, is not getting enough support from London. He needs another operator. Peter Radmore, Head of Technical, came up to check everything out and told him to economise, which means cutting back on standards – as they've warned Richard Eyre.

Ian, I think, is very tormented at the moment by John Caulfield's lack of involvement. Each week we seem to have to do a dinner to meet some of the sponsors but John Caulfield, instead of giving us proper forewarning and organisation, is very 'there's another one of these do's tomorrow, can you go' sort of thing. The last one in Cardiff was particularly disastrous because we never spoke to anybody and it seems to me that we must have a strategy to deal with these evenings.

Leeds is possibly the low point as far as Britain is concerned. I can't sleep, I'm losing about three hours a night, I've also got an infection I can't get to the bottom of, I seem to have terrible sweats in the night. I was given some penicillin but I keep forgetting to take it. I don't know where I'm going to be living when I get back to London, whether I'm going to be living in the house Irina and I bought and put so much into or whether it'll have to be sold. It looms like a nightmare. I had asked to come home at weekends but now there's no point trying to get back from Europe.

Tonight is *King Lear* and I go into automatic pilot to get me through the evening. I start in that frame of mind but as the play begins it always takes over and I'm 100 per cent present – but it's the cost.

I've also had some fairly comic problems. A student of mine in the early seventies – he wasn't actually a student of mine but I did take a class he was in – Nigel Planer, is doing a programme, a spoof 'I am an actor, Nicholas Craig', a send-up of all these acting biographies which come out. He's doing a television version in which he wants to include some extracts from my acting programme. I totally refused to allow any excerpts to be used, simply because taken out of context anything can look silly – even in context it can look silly. I was angry at the time because certain things were included that I didn't want to be included, in particular an excerpt from *Titus* which I asked them not to do as it was a teaching programme; I hate demonstrating, it's not what teaching is about, but they thought from the televisual point of view it was good television. Again, one of the many compromises you have to make and I let it pass, but of course Planer wanted to pick up on one of these pieces to demonstrate a point.

123

Maybe I'm being a bit humourless but at the same time I haven't got the wherewithal to deal with it . . .

I expect I shall have to spend one more night in this gothic hotel. I keep thinking I'm in the set of *The Shining* and any minute a hatchet will come through the door.

Thursday, October 18

I've moved to the Harewood Arms Hotel. On Tuesday Susie Engel and I drove round, it was a lovely day and we found a wonderful bed and breakfast place that we're going to stay at in Pool in Wharfedale, run by a very nice couple called Bryan and Ann Stead. So I'm going to move in there. They couldn't take us at once but I decided definitely to get out of the hotel as quickly as possible.

Lear on Tuesday went very well, particularly the first half. I found a greater reserve of energy at the beginning of the play and was much harder, particularly in dealing with the daughters, much more self-righteous. It was good. The second half was dreadful. The Dover scene's gone to pot a bit, I don't quite know what's happening with that; I think I'm playing too many details and not enough overall line.

We had another of these Digital do's. The whole thing is a complete farce but there was a rather nice man who is the head of Digital North-East, David Somebody, kindly, slightly nervous. We were all sitting at tables, unlike Cardiff, and there was a man from the International Leisure Group and another from British Telecom and they talked about the recession in the computer industry which David was obviously feeling acutely. They talked about servicing and I said in my innocence, 'Is it cost effective?' which brought the table to a standstill. Little did they think that an actor would ask such a direct question and the short answer was that it wasn't cost effective because the cost of servicing is great and of course rival servicing companies can spring up which are really very competitive. But I was fascinated by the fact that everything is based on avarice and greed and capitalism and no one realises or understands that there will always be recession. The history of industry from ship-building through to software and hardware is a history of boom and then recession and they don't seem to measure for it, it doesn't seem to be built into the system. There they were complaining that they weren't having it as good as they have had. I think one of the great things about actors is that we live with constant insecurity. We live in permanent recession. It's something I've got to remember, I tend to take things for granted and in all my emotional turmoil at the moment I tend to think of it as all too much, but I could be out of work which might be even worse.

I was appalled at the lack of imagination, at the lack of vision that seemed to be prevalent: all these fellows from Digital, they'd either worked with IBM or Wang or other companies before and all they knew was computers. I suppose all we know is the theatre world. The man from British Telecom talked about the new theatre in York as the place 'to be seen'. Not the place to go and see a play, he actually said it was the place 'to be seen'. At that point Clare Higgins, who was sitting next to me, grasped my arm. The ignorance of the theatre is quite astounding. Maybe it's fostered by people in the theatre but I don't know how you cross that barrier. They didn't seem to be interested in the play though they had had a good evening out.

Yesterday was my last night in the ghastly Shining Hotel and first thing this morning I got up, drove to the Harewood Arms and put my bags in. Then I went with Helene Kvale and some of the others to Fountains Abbey, had a lovely day. Fountains Abbey is extraordinary, it's the largest monastic ruin in Europe – beautiful setting, Studley Royal, geese and exquisite watergardens. We walked round there for a couple of hours, then drove to Pateley Bridge, a pretty little country town, and had some lunch. It's the most beautiful scenery, the difference between town and country in Yorkshire is quite marked. Leeds is so forbidding.

I've had three very quiet days, playing *Richard III* mainly. I moved to this wonderful B&B in Pool – Fairfield House. It's the first time I've stayed at a bed and breakfast for I don't know how many years and I'm sorry I haven't done it before because the atmosphere is so nice and pleasant and the people lovely. This place puts a completely different picture on being in Leeds.

I had to go and talk to the students at Bretton Hall, near Wakefield. The course is run by John Hodgson, a quite remarkable man, an expert on Laban, who's been at Bretton Hall for the last thirty years. He was the first person to organise an MA in the performing arts for actors, which is tied in to Leeds University. The conversation was a bit bleak because I was talking about Russia and the problems of theatre in England. Leeds sums up for me lack of connection between theatre and environment: the fact that the new West Yorkshire Playhouse is built inaccessibly on a roundabout at the end of Hedgerow, the main street in Leeds, and that Leeds itself is built in the middle of a roundabout surrounded by motorways, described by Paul Bond, who drove me to Bretton Hall, as being designed for the car but not necessarily for the motorist, is an indictment of unimaginative urban planning.

They were a bright bunch of kids at Bretton Hall, as at Cardiff, but I despair of the sort of world they're going into, the work they will do, the compromises they will have to make. We constantly came back to the question of theatre within the context of its society and environment. What that context is becomes more and more important. When you haven't got a context the theatre just seems a meaningless activity and so much of what goes on in England, the problem with touring, is trying to put square pegs into round holes. Somebody like Peter Brook creates his own context; his productions have such an organic power that they overcome the physical drawbacks of different venues. Brook carries his environment with him; if you carry your environment with you, then it's powerful; like a magnet, it draws the people. But you can't do that with the *Lear* and *Richard* package, it's monolithic and inflexible and the theatres themselves are equally so. When we tour we're merely servicing the houses, the huge touring gigs, filling a date in a theatre with a compromised piece of work.

I've just been brought a cup of tea and a mince pie by Ann Stead to remind me of Christmas. She said 'But for God's sake, don't send a card because I'll have to send one back.' They really are lovely here. It's so easy and comfortable. Bryan was a cinema manager and Ann was a nurse, then they went into fabrics, retailing, got fed up with that, moved out of Leeds and found this beautiful Georgian house and started the bed and breakfast.

Last night at the end of the performance of *Richard* for some reason I started to sing, just as we were giving the curtain call. I didn't think anyone could hear but apparently they could and I created a distraction. I didn't mean to. I was singing 'Don't fence me in', don't know what that means.

It's amazing, the huge audiences and their response; obviously it's working despite my reservations. Susie Engel told me something which is contrary to everything I've been saying and makes it worthwhile: there was a young boy who hung around outside the stage door after the performance of *Lear* while we were doing the Digital do; he was waiting for us and saw Susie. He was absolutely gob-smacked by the whole experience and had missed his last train back to York. He had to spend the night in the station but felt it was worth it. That is something. You realise there are people who do get an enormous amount out of it; there *is* a need, but we have to tap it and adapt in some way to meet it.

I sit here before this roaring fire – it's so relaxing. I've just been for a walk along the Chevin, which is quite beautiful, with Susie Engel. We went mushrooming. She kept saying mushrooming is competitive and I said if it's competitive I'm not sure I'm into it, and eventually, after finding lots of the wrong kind of mushrooms, we found the mushroom that was the one she'd been looking for.

Postscript on Leeds: Richard Simpson, who has been suffering from chronic arthritis, has discovered a wonderful acupuncturist in Leeds, a Chinaman, who seems to be the answer to all his prayers – but he'll have to live in Leeds to be cured.

Belfast

Tuesday, October 23

If this is Tuesday it must be Belfast. After a fairly gruelling weekend during which my personal life seems to have been turned upside down, I flew to Belfast yesterday, my third visit. The previous times have been in connection with jobs: *Hidden Agenda* which I made at exactly the same time last year and *Rat in the Skull* five years ago, when I came to meet some of the bravest, most extraordinary people who helped me research the business of working for the Royal Ulster Constabulary.

It's strange to be back. The depression that hangs over this city is more intense than it's ever been. People say, 'Oh I'll take you to places which are really exciting and interesting, you'll have a great time,' and of course the social life is very good, but everything stops at ten to ten. People don't like to be around late at night. I think that's one of the things we're suffering from, as our plays will finish at 11.00 p.m. Ian is very alarmed about the booking, it hasn't been too good. We met the front-of-house manager, Michael Barnes, described by the Opera House crew as the Shroud – after the Shroud of Turin. He seemed a perfectly pleasant man, an ex-history don from Edinburgh University in the sixties, who apparently runs a wonderful Festival – which hasn't quite started yet. I remember meeting Michael Palin here last year who had come to do his show: he only ever does it at the Belfast Festival because the attendance and response are so terrific.

We booked into the Quality Plaza Hotel. Last time I stayed at the Europa. I noticed a few changes. There's virtually no security, which is amazing to me. They are the only two large hotels in the centre of Belfast. The Europa has been bombed endlessly; God knows how this new one will fare. The National are virtually its first customers. Rumour has it that in the past the Europa paid an extortionate amount in protection fees. Probably this hotel is similarly covered. It seems to be run by a group of Belfast Indians. My room is fairly pleasant for now but that's because it's new – within four or five weeks it will probably look like shit – polystyrene tiles on the ceiling: anyway, a hotel room is a hotel room is a hotel room. Views of the hills around. I'd like to get out of Belfast for a day and really see some of the country, but we've got a bit of promoting to do first to fill the empty houses. The truth of the matter is, they don't know the National Theatre. The RSC, yes, they've heard of that, the RSC is a big star. *Les Liaisons Dangereuses* with the sixth cast is about to open next week to a full house. *Lear* at the moment is 70 per cent and the matinée on Saturday of *Richard* has only sold 200 seats in a 1,000-seater house, so naturally Ian is a bit concerned.

I've just returned from a press conference arranged by the publicity people at the Europa, where I met a few of the local characters. A large gentleman from one paper announced that he'd started his career with Agnew McMaster doing the fit-ups round Southern Ireland for 2/6d per week. Of course, everyone has a story to tell, that's the thing in Ireland . . . the freebies that were going, the gin-and-tonics, the bars, the perks of the trade which are eagerly sought after, I found it all vaguely depressing. The same gentleman was saying that 80 per cent of the population of the North still live in little farming towns and communities. And the people of Belfast are horrified at all these buildings going up round Blackstaff Square where our new hotel is situated. They're horrified because there are offices going up and they don't know what they're going to put in them. They put a brave face on it but it is the problem of a country in a state of war. Looking out from my hotel window over the town, the wreckage below is 70 per cent unemployment, young people hovering round in the evening. They're trying desperately to smarten up the façades of all these buildings, but the so-called picturesque square is a human midden and refuse tip . . . the broken bottles of cheap wine – I can see a man in the pouring rain sweeping up all the broken glass – and across from here I can see the buildings being built. The biggest is the new Inland Revenue office.

Belfast is a lively city and there is quite a strong sub-culture. The people are among the funniest in the world, with their own brand of wit, something I certainly remember from my first visit when I met the Belfastians in their own homes, the one way to meet them. Living in a hotel room your whole view is narrowed, as it was when I stayed here last year for *Hidden Agenda*. Even so you can get the aura of a city, and the aura of Belfast is depression. People try to ignore it and say 'No, no,' but it's there: the sectarian violence, the RUC patrols; but I haven't seen any soldiers yet.

We didn't get our promised pictures because there was a shooting in the Falls Road and the photographers were on a different priority.

Wednesday, October 24

We've just done our first performance of *Lear*. It was heartening, the reaction of the audience at the end of the play. Suddenly for the first time I felt I understood what I was doing, what it was all about. Maybe because it was a Celtic audience – but so was Cardiff.

Funny old day. Last night after *Richard* I got drunk on whiskey. I haven't drunk whiskey for ages – I think I may have said this in Japan. Then I went to a restaurant and bought a bottle of Dom Perignon champagne which cost me an arm and a leg. As my world seems to be coming to an end in every shape and form I just thought, why bother, let's go out with a bang.

I did a couple of interviews on the radio with Ian during the day on Tuesday, one for Sean Rafferty, who was intelligent and enlightened and talked to Ian about his Aids Helpline. Ian is going to devote a whole morning to his work for the gay movement and of course for Aids in particular, Northern Ireland being one of the last places, really, within the UK to reform its homosexual laws; it's still very repressive here.

Today we went to the downtown radio and talked to someone called Lynda Jane. Ian gave his views on the theatre and how he felt the theatre should be free, his concern that the Opera House was far too expensive. They asked me about *Hidden Agenda* and I tried to talk about how I see Northern Ireland, the war that nobody on the mainland acknowledges. Yesterday one of our dressers was taking her small son to the children's hospital and witnessed a taxi driver being shot as a result of a sectarian feud. Life goes on in Northern Ireland in its usual fashion.

The news yesterday was of an explosion in Derry at a checkpoint: the IRA have stooped to new tactics. They trussed a man up in his lorry, held his family hostage and made him drive to the checkpoint.

The lorry was detonated on arrival and killed six British soldiers plus the driver who was blown to bits. There doesn't seem to be any sense in the brutality up here, it seems to be habit, habit picked up from generation to generation, no longer with any political meaning whatever.

When you look out at our audiences, and they're not as full as they might be, it tells you somehow that theatre isn't exactly a priority in Northern Ireland at the moment, especially theatre for which you pay such exorbitant prices. The gap between that and the real needs of the people here is immense. Belfast would have been the perfect opportunity for us to play our productions in a much rougher way – go into one of the community centres of, say, west Belfast and perform our work to people who would be too inhibited to go the Opera House. If there is any point in taking a work on tour it is to go into the heart of a community.

Thursday, October 25

We had two performances today, a matinée of *Lear* with a load of schoolchildren, who were a magnificent audience, and *Richard* tonight which was a very corpsy show, to say the least. There was a sort of hysteria about us. I think Ian has reacted badly to the thinness of the audiences, has taken it personally. We had some corpsing today as well, I couldn't remember whether I was going to divorce Regan's mother's womb or tomb and she was *sepulcher-ulchering* an adulteress.

We're not quite halfway through the tour but I know what purgatory is like. When you die, instead of purgatory you actually go on tour. The repetition, the smallness of the world and the way one is driven into oneself is the state of play for the moment anyway.

Friday, October 26

We went to the Giant's Causeway, twenty-four of us, in a small minibus organised wonderfully well by Richard O'Callaghan, who, as our tour leader, showed great distinction. The weather was appalling when we left but by the time we got there it was a beautiful day. We went to Bushmills, the whiskey distillery. They received their grant to distil whiskey at the same time as Shakespeare was writing *King Lear*. We were all shown up by Sam Beazley who can move faster and lighter and walk most of the younger members, myself included, off their feet. He gives me thirty years and was skipping along the steep pathways down by the Causeway. At one point I attempted to take a photograph of our little band on the Causeway. They were gesticulating madly, ruining the shot, trying desperately to tell me that the Irish Sea was lapping my knees.

It was a good day, a happy day, all together, and tonight *Richard III*. Belfast looks lovely now, 6.00 in the evening, the light on the hills round the city.

Saturday, October 27

The last day of Belfast and I'm getting a bit chesty, which is the effect of the river, the sea and the estuary. There hasn't been much time on this visit to take in the city, but it's been interesting to see how the young actors have all been hiring taxis to go and look at the Falls Road, no-man's-land, the Divis Flats and the Shankhill and the White Bear Estate. Deborah typically, when she arrived, said, 'Oh, I must see these wonderful murals.' The actor's curiosity is always extraordinary and it reminds me of touring in India. It's questionable, the voyeurism. Yevtushenko describes it in a poem called 'Safari in Northern Ireland' – travelling through the city and watching the animals in their local habitat. The violence that surrounds you – there is a vicarious pleasure to be got from it, it's almost a tourist attraction and part of the black economy round here. There is money to be made from revolution. I've eschewed the sightseeing this visit because I've seen it before.

I had dinner last night with Mr and Mrs Hawthorne and Mr and Mrs Higgins. James Hawthorne is ex-Head of BBC Belfast. One was a Catholic family and the other was Protestant. Mrs Higgins told me a story about one of these new integrated schools that have sprung up, a nursery school. The nursery teacher asked each of the children what they'd done that day. She asked the first little boy whose name was William. 'Well, miss, I played in the sandpit with John,' and she said, 'Sandpit, did you, William? Right, William, spell "sand".' And William spelt it, S-A-N-D. 'That's very good, William. Now, John, what did you do today?' 'Well, miss, I was playing in the sandpit with William.' 'You were playing in the sandpit too, John?' 'Yes, miss.' 'That's good, sandpit, spell "pit", John.' 'P-I-T,' and she turned to the third little boy and said, 'Now, Seamus, what were you doing today?' and Seamus said, 'Well, miss, I wanted to play in the sandpit with William and John but the two wouldn't let me.' 'No, they wouldn't let you Seamus, no, that's terrible, that's discrimination.' 'Yes, miss.' 'Spell "discrimination", Seamus.' I think that story sums up a lot. The real pay-off would be for the little Catholic boy to spell discrimination flawlessly but that's not how it ends.

I got caught out again in *Lear* tonight on 'Is there any cause in nature that make these hard hearts?' I just started to stream. I hit something, I'm hitting the whole business of rejection, it's the most painful thing about this play, his rejection; he's abandoned, completely abandoned by his family, and his girls mean so much to him. It's been more of a revelation to me than anything else that the girls really mean a lot to him. In previous productions the girls don't seem to mean so much but they do have to mean something to him: they are his future, his security in his old age; he has invested so much in them and when he loses it it's devastating. That's why it's so overwhelming when Regan, the last daughter to go, turns on him; he can't believe that she can be the most wicked and of course it is all his fault. I think Shakespeare's sense of the burden of his own responsibility must have been acute, he must have had a real sense of pain and the fact that he was responsible for so much in relation to his own children and his wife. You can't write a play like this unless you're in touch with something quite profound about being a father and being rejected and marginalised and isolated. I must go, it's my call.

*

Had dinner with Pam Brighton who directs for BBC Radio Drama here. She is someone I've known for years in various guises and different parts of the world and who's now found a home here in Belfast and an opportunity to be at the genesis of a new group of young Irish playwrights. The health of Irish playwriting, north and south of the border, is far greater than its English counterpart.

Back to London, a fairly hectic weekend for me. I see my daughter before she goes back to school and then pack up ready to go off to Hamburg and various parts of the world.

Postscript: We've had a few injuries this week. Ian has a suspected hiatus hernia and David Bradley fell over in *Richard* because of these wretched smoke guns which spew oil all over the place.

The World Tour, II

Hamburg

Wednesday, October 31–Saturday, November 3

Arrived in Hamburg yesterday, after a weekend of double packing, packing for the seven weeks I'll be away and all the stuff I'll leave behind. I saw my agent to discuss what I should do next year when the tour is over, the various things in the fire, films, all of which have no money and all of which are possible, fliers in the night.

I left my passport in the dressing room in Leeds, but they picked it up for me and brought it back with my ticket. I got into the car with Sam Beazley who was giving me a lift to the bus at the National Theatre and I said, 'I'll just check my passport is in my filofax.' No passport – to my horror. Well, not to my horror, I couldn't have cared less. I don't know why, it was a wonderful feeling of 'well, if I have no passport they're going to have to get me there'. So we arrived at the theatre and I met the stage manager, Jane Suffling, and I told her of my predicament and immediately Roger Chapman, the tour manager, came down and went into action. There was all this business about whether I had a birth certificate, which I hadn't, but I had my driving licence and in a matter of minutes we were able to get a British visitor's passport. That got the day off to a nice exciting start. Then we made the flight and I had time to buy myself lots of underwear and socks which seem to have all been eaten up by my washing machine at home.

We arrived at Hamburg at about six o'clock in the evening. There was an invitation from Michael Bogdanov who is Artistic Director of the Schauspielhaus in Hamburg, one of the oldest theatres in Germany. In fact it's where the German National Theatre started

135

250 years ago, but the present building is only about ninety years old. Bogdanov has been a man under siege, apparently. On Friday he had had a vote of no confidence from his company – they accused him of being an absentee landlord. He seems quite unpeturbed, though what is going on underneath God knows. I think he'd had a good day because he'd managed to win some more money for the theatre. Ian was supposed to come to the meeting but he was changing hotels because Helene Kvale's parents are coming over from Norway for her birthday this week and he very generously offered to change hotels to make room for them.

I talked to Michael at length. Hamburg is a state, a separate republic in Germany, with a population about the size of Birmingham. The arts subsidy is quite out of this world, enough for a small country. For his theatre, Michael gets 31 million marks, which is in the region of £9 million. Theatre subsidy goes back a long way in Germany and theatre to the Germans is as important as health, housing or any other major factors. In England we have no grasp of this. A leading actor in Germany will earn on average £65,000 a year, middle-range actors around £30,000 a year. Life is relatively comfortable for the actor and perhaps it shows in the performances. We were amazed by the lack of audibility in the, I thought rather good, production of Pirandello's *Henry IV*. At the beginning of the second half the audience started to call out 'Louder'. The production was by an Argentinian director and it was very, very well staged. The leading actor lacked charisma and missed out on a lot of the play's humour but the German audience while praising the actors gave the director the bird, which I thought was unfair. The tradition in Germany is that the audience dictate the number of curtain calls, not the players. After the barracking of the director Ian leaned forward and whispered in my ear, 'No individual calls, I think.'

Afterwards there was a party to which all of our group were invited and, led by Mr Beazley aged seventy-four, we bopped into the night – which was great, I hadn't done that for such a long time and it was fun. I crashed out at 2 a.m. with my new discovery to help me sleep, valerian.

I got up early and went for a walk along the Elbe. Hamburg is really very beautiful, a Venice of the North, a bit like Leningrad which I believe is its twin city. I decided it was time to get some glasses because my sight has been getting perceptibly worse over the last five or six months and I'm now really short-sighted. I went to what turned out to be a very expensive optician and they'll be ready on Friday.

We then had a press conference, run by Guinness, and were all encouraged to drink Guinness at 11 a.m. with the Guinness representative here and the British Council people, an unholy alliance.

We got ready for the first night of *Lear*. Having witnessed the director being given the bird yesterday we were full of trepidation about how we would be treated, but the calls went on for at least ten minutes. A young critic came up afterwards and said he found the English acting style surprising and shocking because of the way we used the audience, which had seemed very full-frontal and threatening but then he found it embracing.

Richard Eyre and I had a long talk, going back to when I first met him twenty-five years ago when he was Assistant Director in Leicester, and he tried to persuade me again to continue as Buckingham, but I just can't.

Ian, Clare Higgins and a platoon of the lads and lasses went off to the Reeperbahn to experience the joys of a sex show. It's something I can't bring myself to do, the whole notion is anathema, but Ian said it was interesting purely in terms of theatricality. He said it was a very small theatre with a performance that he neither loathed nor felt threatened by, but he found the whole experience jaw-dropping. Clare Higgins was rather upset and actually should never have gone. She pushed herself to see it as an experience. I don't know about this business of forcing yourself, but actors do it all the time. They love these kinds of experience and pitting themselves against them. David Bradley thought it was a good laugh and Richard Bremmer wouldn't judge it but thought it was interesting.

I got up to have a final fitting for my glasses and on the way back discovered an Ecuadorean band playing their pipes and drums outside the station. Then I gathered a small group together and we went for a drive round the city with Bogdanov's driver, passing over the docklands of Hamburg on a beautiful bridge way above the city and through the very expensive part of the town. We stopped and had some lunch. Clare still hadn't recovered from the Reeperbahn excursion, it was still on her mind.

The theatre is slap bang in the centre of Hamburg and there's a heavy drug community in the centre of the city, you're constantly seeing people out of their minds; like yesterday at the waffle stand a poor girl drugged to the eyes, tottering around on a pair of high heels and ordering a waffle which she had comic difficulty in eating. And it's very alive, very rich, full of people like the Ecuadorean band or Polish accordion players. You can take part in whatever it is, and what I enjoy is just wandering around.

After our trip round Hamburg we retired to the hotel where there's a waterchute which goes down four floors and Ian and Clare and I rode this thing. It was quite hysterical. As all three of us were slaloming our way down the chute, I started to panic because I was losing my breath and at the bottom there's eight feet of water and I thought I would drown. As I shot down Ian was roaring with laughter at the human bullet coming through. We had a lovely afternoon and a sauna, Clare still having great difficulty about German men wandering round in the nude. One of them turned out to be Oliver Tobias, doing a European mini-series.

I've just read something by Maurice Nicoll on force of personality and happiness and the hypocrisy of man. I wonder if my judgement on the travellers to the Reeperbahn was slightly self-congratulatory and therefore slightly dubious.

We did our second *Lear* in the evening. It's such a pleasure to play that theatre. I've been more inspired than I've been for weeks and I've actually enjoyed playing the part for the first time, I think, ever: I've actually enjoyed playing Lear. The audience's reaction was phenomenal, they went wild; the idea of the Germans being so cold and reserved – with the theatre public it's quite the opposite. Bogdanov was particularly pleased with our reception. After the rough time he's been having he was happy that we were in such good form.

Friday morning I spent reading Shaw. I've been reading *The Philanderer* and *Widower's Houses* all week. I'd mentioned to Howard

Panter a couple of months ago my desire to direct some more Shaw and we're going to meet in Paris and I hope we'll discuss it.

I went to see Ralph Nagel who is Principal of the drama school here. It's a state drama school and over a period of four years he has a total of twenty-eight students, about five or six students a year, working beside the opera school. He told me about his problems in Leningrad with a German-Russian production of *A Midsummer Night's Dream*. I then walked along the water straight into the city and collected my first pair of specs. Life is suddenly clearer – for how long? Two things I noticed on my walk: a helicopter hovering overhead, nose-diving the lake and apparently fishing two, three or four people out of the water . . . God knows why. Perhaps they were testing themselves or perhaps they were police divers looking for something; and a young German man dressed in hiking gear with long shorts, doing knee squats to such an extent that he had a nose bleed. When a passer-by stopped in concern he shrugged it off and glared as if the nose bleed was the desired effect of all this physical effort. Perhaps this is a trait in the German character.

We opened *Richard*, again to absolutely rapturous applause. The audience didn't seem upset by the fascist element. We had no time to do any technical work on *Richard* because things were so behind and mucked about by the fact that they had the *Henry IV* first night on Tuesday so *Richard* couldn't get in. The show was a little underlit but that wasn't anybody's fault. Poor Laurie Clayton, who has taken over from Paul McLeish, had enormous difficulties and all the flying had to be put on the computer which took an enormous amount of time.

On Saturday I just played the tourist. I went for a long run which I haven't done for ages, round the lake, the Aussenalster. Then in the afternoon it was raining and I decided to take one of the bus tours. I went to see St Michael's church where Brahms was baptised and some little shops which were built for the widows of shopkeepers.

Sunday, November 4

We've just finished the last performance of *Lear* in Hamburg. The reception was astonishing, they went on for a full fifteen minutes. David Bradley was quite tearful. He said he'd never witnessed anything like it before in his life and I must confess I felt the same.

Tomorrow we go to Milan but we've got time to kill so I've whipped round the company and I'm going to do a reading of *The Philanderer*. I want to hear the play. And I want people to come along and ask questions.

All in all, Hamburg has been a huge success. We weren't allowed into the Actors' Club tonight. The people at the Schauspielhaus were extremely ashamed at the lack of grace on their fellow-countrymen's part; there's no doubt about it, they tend to be a bit brusque and rude – in contrast to the audiences. Bogdanov has been away, I haven't seen him lately; he comes back tomorrow.

Monday, November 5, Guy Fawkes night

The reading of *The Philanderer* went well and showed me what a marvellous play it is. We have a hell of a journey, to Düsseldorf and then to Milan.

Milan

Tuesday, November 6

Arrived in Milan late last night after a dreadful journey which took five hours, mainly sitting in Düsseldorf airport. The sets had not arrived because of snow and trouble at the border. They finally turned up very late and the actors worked with the techies till early morning unloading the vans. I was whacked and went to bed quite early so I missed out on what was clearly a milestone in company relations.

The company has been split into a series of little hotels which I don't think is a very good idea. I'm staying at a very small pokey little example, but that seems to be the style of the hotels here and it's quite pleasant apart from the double beds, which are two single beds pushed together so you tend to roll down into the gap.

Today I had intended to drive up to the lakes but they suddenly announced a press conference which was supposed to be tomorrow. We went to the Piccolo Theatre for it, Giorgio Strehler's theatre. We are playing at the Lirico which is a big ugly Fascist 1930s building. The Piccolo is absolutely delightful, tiny and intimate, and we did the press conference in the main foyer. I met Strehler, the famous or infamous maestro, our host in Milan, who is an extremely charismatic and rather beautiful man. He must be in his late sixties but has the carriage of a thirty-five-year-old. During the war the Piccolo was the headquarters of the Italian secret police – the dressing rooms were interrogation rooms. Strehler started this theatre in 1947 and it has flourished with his reputation. His best known production, which has been in the repertoire since the theatre's inception, is Goldoni's *Arlecchino, The Servant of Two Masters*. It's shameful that we haven't seen more of Strehler's work in England. At the Piccolo there are videos of his latest work in and around Milan, notably his *Faust* in which he himself plays the title role. Ian saw it in the studio theatre in May. The studio theatre is Strehler's *pièce de résistance*. It's a beautiful horseshoe shape with wooden trapped floors. Nearby is the site of the Grande Theatre, a new building abandoned four or five years ago in the middle of a political row and which will probably never be completed because of the tangle of municipal politics and Strehler's political position – an Italian state senator, he has changed parties at least once. Not an overly modest man, he wants to complete the circle of his career playing Prospero in a revival of an early triumph.

I went to see Leonardo's 'Last Supper', newly un-restored, in the morning. It was rather disappointing, so much had been done to it there wasn't much left. More impressive was a painting of a battle on the opposite wall which hadn't been so messed about.

As the sets had to get in and we couldn't do the technical we went to see *The Servant of Two Masters* performed by Strehler's students. Strehler's drama school has only one intake of thirty students every

141

three years – selected from all over and outside Italy. It was a wonderful production because Strehler had used the doubling which is inevitable with students to theatrical effect and the play was mirrored in dumbshow in the pit by the actors who weren't on the stage. It became *The Servant of Many Masters* as one student took up from another. It was a sort of theatrical relay race.

Wednesday, November 7

I went to talk to Strehler's students who had asked if Ian or I would go and speak to them. They had done some Shakespeare but it was very much a matter of having to behave in the manner the director wanted. I asked them individually about their difficulties with it, read a piece or two for them and then we did some work on Angelo in *Measure for Measure*.

The first night of *Richard III* was rapturously received. The Lirico was like playing in an aircraft hangar, the theatre seats 17,000. The backstage conditions were appalling. The dressing rooms were a cross between nuns' cells and men's lavatories, dripping with water. The boys' dressing room opened out about fifteen feet above the stage and every whisper could be heard. Also there seemed to be as many people offstage as there were in the auditorium, firemen and their relatives, dressers and their relatives, impossible to make an entrance, picking your way through half the population of Milan. Thanks to the unpunctuality of Milanese audiences, the performance started an hour late. Strehler turned up, escorted by his very beautiful German wife, having only seen half of the play. His hair was bright blue.

Thursday, November 8

I decided to escape to Lugano and see a bit of the lakes – fairly spectacular but fairly boring apart from one extraordinary sight – in a park in Lugano a statue of Socrates looking as though he's asleep. In fact he's sitting there dead. Why on earth there should be a statue of a dead Socrates by a Swiss lake God alone knows.

Friday, November 9

I was taken by one of Strehler's students, Mace Perlman, a young American lad, to the secret wholesale stores of old designer models on the outskirts of Milan and kitted myself out.

The first half of the performance seemed to go fairly well, but in the interval Strehler's secretary arrived weeping copiously and full of apologies. She said, 'I am so sorry, so very sorry.' I said, 'What about?' 'The riot.' 'What riot?' There had been a riot, apparently, throughout the first half but the acoustics were so appalling that we'd been quite unaware of it: there was a faint buzzing noise but that was all. Some kids who spoke no English had been creating a disturbance, people in the posher seats had finally had enough and a fight had broken out with the teachers muscling in to protect their flock from being lynched by the rest of the audience. Eventually some of them had been thrown out and then allowed back in. The second half was quieter. Strehler's students had tried to come and were very upset because they couldn't get in. All in all, not a very good evening. It's a shame because Milan has been lovely in many ways but the theatre experience has been less than lovely.

Saturday, November 10

Yesterday I went off to interview Ferruccio Soleri. For the last thirty years he has played Arlecchino in *The Servant of Two Masters*. Probably no other actor, apart from maybe a Kabuki actor – no other European actor – has played a part for such a long time.

Maretti [the previous great Arlecchino] saw my Arlecchino at the school and he said to Strehler, this could be a future Arlecchino. At first Strehler would make me rehearse with Maretti but Maretti was very protective. With all the little things he said you have to find your own way. For instance the trunk scene: Arlecchino is shut in a small trunk and after a few minutes emerges in a complete change of clothes. Maretti refused to tell me the secret of the trunk. At first I wasn't able to do it and then when I was, Maretti wanted to know how I did it. I just told him I did it a different way. On the other hand I've always taught all the tricks to my students. I taught two Arlecchinos the trunk scene. I couldn't teach it with the trunk closed, but when the trunk was open I couldn't do it because it was dark in the trunk, so I had to close my eyes in order to teach them. Now that it's straw not wood [the trunk] and the light comes in, I close my eyes.

Arlecchino is what gave me fame, gave me so many satisfactions and I fell in love with him and I love him like my brother. I think if I had done Hamlet and I had had a lot of success, I don't think I would have been able to do 1,200 times that. A complex character like that, you can dig down and find it up to a certain point, beyond which you risk madness and in fact no actor goes beyond that certain point. Having arrived at that limit, the actor can't grow in doing Hamlet, so when he's done 100 or 200 times he can't do any more. On the other hand, Arlecchino is different because every day I can make it deeper because it's a very primitive psychology, very infantile and so I can always in that simple psychology find a way of improving. If I tried to find this in a complex psychology, you can lose your mind. The other thing is that I have, every day, such a strong, even violent, contact with the public. What other role permits that for you?

144

Sunday, November 11

Last night we did *Lear* again. To prevent the evening being ruined a second time it was decided that there should be a speech to the audience before the performance – which I thought it would be best if I made. Some of the company weren't keen on the idea, but we couldn't have people's enjoyment upset again so I took the law into my own hands. There was much greater quiet throughout the evening as a result and we had a very good performance. We stayed out very late afterwards, till 4 o'clock, and now I'm off to the theatre to do the last two performances.

Monday, November 12

We had two good shows yesterday. I made my little speech beforehand and the last *Richard* went very well, but ... because of the lateness of the performance – we've been finishing later and later – at 12.40 a.m. after a 9 p.m. start we still hadn't got to the battle scenes.

We had an affectionate farewell from the students in the wee small hours of the morning. They all met and applauded us. I was sad to say goodbye, they're a remarkable and talented bunch.

I came home for the dreadful business of packing. I've got packing to a fine art, in fact it's something I actually look forward to. I'm now off to see the top of the Duomo before we go.

The northern Italian farmers are up in arms about the EEC. There was a demo in the square and the roof of the Duomo was closed. Ian's comment on the Duomo was that it must have been built by the same bunch of Fascists as built Milan railway station.

Madrid

Tuesday, November 13

We arrived in Madrid yesterday night at about 7.00 in the evening. Last time in Madrid I stayed at a wonderful hotel up in the old town; this time we're at the worst hotel I think I've ever been in, the Convention. It's dirty and filthy and the touring department have surpassed themselves as far as grubby hotels are concerned. This morning I was woken by a mechanical digger outside my room, digging a hole.

There was a rumour last night that a strike of the Spanish state theatre technicians was imminent. Today I got up late to be greeted by a note from Ian saying a strike was indeed imminent and that he would meet me later on. There was also a row on our arrival because we had no per diems and nobody had any Spanish pesetas. The poor company manager, John Caulfield, got it in the neck, though it wasn't his fault but the Accounts Department, refusing to release the money. There should be somebody at every venue to give us money whenever we get off the plane. Anyway, we finally got the money today.

I arrived at the theatre, the Centro Dramatico, the Spanish National Theatre, which is a beautiful old theatre, to discover that the strike was on and we wouldn't be playing. Apparently the strike is only in those theatres run by the Ministry of Culture. We were offered another theatre but it looked as if we would be strike-breaking if we went to it and our crew wasn't particularly happy about doing that. There was a meeting of our heads of department, Wardrobe, Wigs etc., who had been hanging around all day. Also we discovered that the schedules given to our set drivers were ten hours out and when they arrived at the theatre they were told they couldn't park; they were dismissed and sent off to a car park.

Anyway, the long and the short of it was that Ian and the British Council representative went to look at a possible venue at a school but it wasn't really good enough. So we are somewhat stuck. But the decision as at 6 o'clock tonight is that we will not be playing at the Centro Dramatico and we will try and find a venue maybe at the university tomorrow morning. We have a press conference tomorrow and a gala for Guinness at 7 o'clock on Thursday evening.

Apparently the strike is about pay, the usual problem all over. People are a bit depressed both by the hotel and by the fact that we can't play. The company are on standby and have to remain on call. The note that Ian sent me read as follows:

> To all members of the National Theatre Company. There is an official theatre technicians strike throughout Spain, therefore there is no question of us playing either show in any theatre in Spain. We are investigating the possibility of some sort of performance during the week. To discuss this and other related matters there will be a full company meeting on Wednesday 14th November at 10 o'clock in the hotel. Venue and updates. In the meantime, love Ian.

So Spain is shut. It's a shame. My last appearance in Madrid was in *Titus* and I was really looking forward to returning here to play *Lear*. If we're lucky we may get one performance.

Wednesday, November 14

After breakfast there was the meeting of the acting company about what was going to happen. Ian was frustrated that we weren't going to be able to perform our work to the people of Madrid and suggested that we look at venues with the aid of the British Council. There was tacit agreement but no one considered the ramifications. So we went off and with the excellent John England spent the whole day examining various spaces: the university space, the two universities; Deborah and I also looked at an abattoir. Then there was a place called Les Belles Arts, a club for artists a bit like the ICA in London, with a theatre space, but for safety reasons – it didn't have a safety curtain – it couldn't be used. Again it was a bit of a political football. We all thought it was the best space, though it wasn't the rough setting I've always wanted for *Lear*, and then Ian thought it might be possible for *Richard III*.

147

We returned to the hotel very exhausted and reconvened the meeting. Meanwhile people had obviously spent the day thinking and were very unhappy about our doing the shows. We have got to watch our position *vis-à-vis* strike-breaking, something Ian has been most circumspect about. Then we got into the business of casting votes. The whole company was involved: 22 voted no shows, 21 voted to do both, 3 to do *Richard* and 3 to do *Lear* – which meant there was a narrow majority in favour. Then it was decided that the crew couldn't take part because they couldn't unload the wagons and the trucks, that *would* be strike-breaking. So the first vote was nullified and there was a vote without the crew at which 11 said no, 3 abstained and 16 said they would do something, again a majority in favour. I then made a speech urging people to think hard because there was a lot of rancour around. A couple of actors expressed real unhappiness, not just about the strike but about the fact that when we arrived there were no per diems, a general balls-up and the National should have arranged for the Centro Dramatico to pay us, the Centro Dramatico didn't have the money for us and didn't warn us about the strike in advance.

Thursday, November 15

We've been talking well into the night, it's 5 in the morning. I've just heard the news about Geoffrey Howe's speech and his attack on Mrs Thatcher and I've come back from talking to Ian. He is extremely depressed because he's worked very, very hard and feels there's a lack of commitment and morale isn't too good. The crew have expressed a willingness to help but they cannot touch the wagons. I've urged Ian to put an embargo on the wagons and I will urge Deborah tomorrow the same: we must just beg, borrow and steal things from Madrid if we do these shows. I've also urged that we should do the shows on one day only, on Sunday, and do them in a workshop situation. Ian has just suggested we should send two small groups to recce because Les Belles Arts, the space we found yesterday, we aren't very happy with – it was the last space of the day – and it was a theatre when ideally we want a much rougher setting.

He feels we should send groups that neither he nor I are in, consisting of the heads of department, Ken Petterson, the head crewman, Laurie Clayton for lights, Deborah Warner, Cordelia Monsey and five or six actors, and that they should decide what we should do and the form in which we should do it.

I am going to urge the company to think really carefully about going ahead because the most important thing is for us to redefine and rebind ourselves. We've been under a lot of pressure and emotional upheaval . . . I'm more to blame than most; it has reflected right through the company, my feelings about *Richard III*, and I'm not necessarily in the right about it. I have to say, I'm not necessarily right but it may have permeated through. There is a destructive element, an element of real discontent, not tiredness as Clare Higgins suggested this afternoon, they're not tired, they're frustrated; the crew are tired, they work jolly hard as Ian said, but not the actors, they're only tired because they stay up till 5 in the morning, drinking and partying – but that's symptomatic of something else, a deeper frustration, which was expressed clearly by someone at the meeting yesterday evening, Mark Strong, who is an extremely sensitive lad, about his lack of voice in the company, his general unhappiness about, for instance, standing at attention for fifteen minutes in the Greenham Common scene. It came home to me how dissatisfied people are and how little they are getting out of it: they feel they had no part in the decisions about how things were done because it was all preconceived. That might not be true: Richard Eyre might argue that they all had a hand in it and that they are shirking their responsibility. It's so difficult to talk about these things because we all seem to be treading on each other's toes and really the thing to do is to avoid being judgemental, a huge trap I find myself desperately trying not to fall into and not always succeeding. The irony of living such a family existence and in such close proximity is that in other circumstances we probably wouldn't even invite each other to dinner. Anyway it's 5 a.m., I have to get some sleep, we reconvene tomorrow to see how we're going to go on.

Well, the saga continues. This morning I woke early to go and see Ian and discuss how we were going to handle the meeting and we agreed that what we had to do was retrace our steps and find out where we'd gone wrong in presuming the company would want to do the shows.

We had a very good meeting at which the fundamental differences were aired quite strongly and people were able to speak about their unhappinesses for the first time. People like young Stephen Marchant who said he didn't see any point any more in doing a performance on Sunday, it would be better to cut our losses and have a holiday before going to Paris – which I think was a general feeling. Stephen felt so clearly yesterday that we were professional and should act professionally but was so frustrated by the outcome of the evening, these close votes and no confidence, that I think he was demoralised.

There is, as I speak now at 7.50 in the evening on Thursday, there is the possibility of the strike being over, but we don't know. Anyway, in the end a group was constituted, of Deborah, Cordelia, actors like Phil McKee, Eve, Clare, Mark Strong, Kae-Kazim, who all very much wanted to play. They will decide our fate. It seems important that anything we do should be on a carpet in a space with an audience we invite, but the main thing is for the company to rebond itself through the work.

Deborah, Cordelia, Ian and I also had a discussion about how we would do *Richard III* and Ian was very concerned about how we represent this or that, because he is locked, understandably, into the conception of the production. Deborah very gently and persuasively said we have to throw that away and start again.

The group have returned and apparently they've decided we will use the space I wasn't keen on; there doesn't seem to be another, Les Belles Arts. It's been agreed we will stick by their decision.

Now I'm getting ready to go to a reception for Princess Alexandra at the British Council. She was supposed to be coming to a gala performance of *Richard III*, which of course she can't.

Cordelia Monsey was to have arranged a workshop at the British Council school for today, but she's been under a lot of pressure what with trying to find a possible space for a possible performance and it seemed to me that she was being bullied. I told her she must drop it and went to the head of the British Council at the party and said I didn't think we could do it. Then I met a nice Irishman, the headmaster of the British Council school, who said there would be so many people disappointed. So, being the soft touch that I am, I decided to step into the breach and organise it – with Cordelia's consent. We have ten actors who will take the kids for individual sessions today: I managed to rope in Richard Simpson, Nicholas Blane, Bruce Purchase, Richard Bremmer, Cordelia, Helene, Peter Sullivan, and Ian. We're off to the school in about an hour or so and I'm waiting for a phone call to find out what pieces we're doing. My room is a mess, I've reached the degenerate stage on this tour.

We did the class, we cannot do the performance. Les Belles Arts will not give us the space. They were all Spanish bluff and we can't do the Sunday thing. We can use the National Theatre but only as a rehearsal space. So that's what we're going to do. I'm very sad and I think many of the others are too.

The workshop was a success, very intelligent kids at the British Council school. Founded just after the war as a liberal school in quiet opposition to Franco, it's the only non-Catholic school, though it has a Catholic headmaster. For someone who poohpoohs himself as a drama teacher, Ian excelled himself.

Monday, November 19

This is Monday morning, we're just about to go to Paris. It's been an amazing two days. Saturday was lazy, sleeping late and taking in the Giacometti exhibition. My passion in Spain, the thing I love most, is flamenco, the real theatre of Spain. I took Helene to a place called the Casa Patas, off the Plaza Santana, to see a group with an old master, Isidro Elno, aged about seventy. It was quite amazing, two hours of this extraordinary man; he didn't do very much himself but he obviously choreographed the whole event and when he did do something it was quite electric, the hands, the arms, the precision, the line – a clean line – sensuality. It was astounding in someone of that age. Pencil-thin he was. And his two girls were equally magnificent, Virginia Moreno and Celia del Palacio.

The sultriness and the warmth of the evenings in Madrid and the sense of enforced leisure made us realise how overwrought we were. Watching this flamenco it was as though the group were dancing away all our frustrations.

We took up our rehearsal space at the National Theatre on Sunday. We did *Richard III*, in a circle, and Ian rose magnificently to the occasion; his work is so simple, so direct, and for the first time I saw the real intellectual force of his performance which is sometimes inhibited by the production. We did half of *Lear* afterwards. It was a day of unification, how long it will last nobody knows, but everyone got high on it, and very excited by the work.

Two people had been hanging around all week and came to the hotel determined to see something of our group; finally they were rewarded. They arrived at the Centro Dramatico because they read our notices on the board outside the theatre and we held our last meeting about whether we could invite them in or not. We did invite them in and they were extremely touched. They were the only people in Madrid who saw a performance.

Paris

Saturday, November 24

I haven't made an entry for a week partly because I've just been too busy. I decided I'd keep a low profile in Paris and ended up doing the opposite. We arrived on Monday – 19th – after the débâcle in Madrid. That ended with chaos at the airport check-in desks. John Caulfield has resigned – it's sad. We were sent from pillar to post at the airport and the airport authorities tried to charge massive overage on our luggage. Then there was a row about whether we were a group or individuals. The final straw was when we reached Paris. We were all herded into coaches bound for the hotel and arrived to find that Martin Allen, the drummer, had been left behind at the airport.

This has been an infamous week because on Thursday morning, Thanksgiving Day, Mrs Thatcher resigned. It was a cause for great celebration by the company. After the performance champagne was brought and we are all feeling a backlash because of it. In a way I think her resignation is a good thing but I'm not so sure how good yet, it's early to say. From the point of view of a change of government, I think it would have been better if she had held on a bit longer and then we could have definitely got rid of the Tories. I also think there is a feeling that she was stabbed in the back.

On Monday when we arrived Ian suddenly alarmed me with news of a potential strike here too from the theatre technicians. The actual details I'm not quite clear about at this stage. Nonetheless I think he was greatly relieved to be in Paris. Madrid was an ordeal for him but he can take comfort from the fact that he exercised brilliant company leadership. His fairness and egalitarianism showed remarkable statesmanship.

Tuesday was a free day. I saw my friend Ariel Goldenburg, the Director of the Madrid Festival and the Bobigny Theatre, who has invited us to go back to Madrid if we want next year to complete our commitment there. On Wednesday we continued the work we did at the Centro Dramatico on the second half of *Lear*. Most of it this time was self-indulgent and over the top and bad and didn't have the poignancy of Sunday. (Colin Hurley who stepped in for a sick Derek Hutchinson was particularly good on Sunday.) I think the exercise had already completed itself, but there were certain things we discovered and it was good to warm up the play again.

In the light of what happened last week in Madrid, asking people to examine truthfully why they committed themselves to this tour, I felt it would be hypocritical of me not to go on with *Richard III*. So I told Ian and Richard Eyre that I would continue with Buckingham to the end of the run – also I do seem to have gained a second wind from somewhere.

153

They were very behind getting ready at the Odéon because it took ages to get in. It's surprisingly small and compact as a theatre, which I love, but there's no room for anything; in fact, it's impossible for me to get on stage at the end of *Richard*: I have a quick change and I can't get on for the battle scenes – so I can't play my soldier, which is a great relief to me as I detest it. Interestingly enough, we had a huge standing ovation; *Lear* on Wednesday evening was a great success too.

We've had a lot of pre-publicity, which has been good. Good articles, both for Ian and myself, in *Libération*. Thursday was the fatal news of Mrs T. which occupied our day and we were rung up by various French newspapers to ask what we thought and I told them what I thought. I don't know what McKellen said. Deborah was over the moon by the way *Lear* had gone; for us it was another triumph matching *Titus*. I was a bit shocked on Friday because I thought I was only going to be doing a matinée of *Lear* but it turned out that I was actually doing *Richard* as well.

I met Koko, Michelle Kokosowski, an extraordinary woman with a bass baritone voice, for whom I'm doing the masterclass at the Odéon on Sunday December 2. She is one of those people who take you over completely, 'Daling, everything zwill be all rrright. Koko will fix it.' And she does. And it usually is. I need four actors. Unfortunately I can't use any actors from the company as they're flying on to Cork. I have Ciaran Hinds and Helene Patarot. I'm doing work on *The Changeling, Hamlet, Taming of the Shrew, Macbeth* – in both languages. On Friday I spent the morning going round the little bars of the Marais with Bruce Myers whose wife Corinne has just had a baby and I wondered if she would like to do my masterclass, but I think motherhood is her priority for the moment. A stroke of luck, I got a phone call from a young actress, Caline Carr, a French girl I'd taught in London about three years ago, who might be the answer to my problems. Now all I need is a French actor. I met Koko's partner, Georges Banu, and talked about the possibility of going to Avignon to do some work with young French actors, something I'd very much like to do – an interesting contrast to my experience with the young Russian actors at MXAT.

I had lunch with Peter Brook and arranged for most of the company to see his production of *The Tempest* – to which they gave favourable reviews, one or two dissenters but on the whole the company were excited by it. We talked about possible future plans. He's the one director that, as an actor, I really want to work with. He has a joint project for his company and the NT in 1993 which is truly ambitious, a history of twentieth-century European theatre. This will be centred round the great innovators – Brecht, Stanislavski, Meyerhold, Gordon Craig and Artaud. I have said I would very much like to be involved, though 1993 is a long way off and I really want to try and do some more directing, concentrate less on acting in the theatre and more on directing in the theatre and acting on the screen. I've been reading a lot more Shaw and I'm very keen on the idea of trying to do a production. I'd like to do some more readings now, though it's difficult to arrange them at the moment because people are busy enjoying Paris.

I spent today, Saturday, with my friend Ariel at the Bobigny. We talked about the possibility of doing *Mrs Warren's Profession* in English and French in 1992 to celebrate the creation of the single European market, and he's very keen on it. The Bobigny is a strange place right out at the far end of Paris, one of the last bastions of Communism, with Lenin Boulevard and Place de Karl Marx. It had been described to me and was just as I imagined, full of utilitarian high-rise apartment blocks reminiscent of Truffaut's film *Fahrenheit 451*; the Maison de Culture itself, a breeze-block bunker, has an idiosyncratic atmosphere which is quite exciting. It's a mass of problems but it has a very, very good small space on the top, reminiscent of the Studio theatre at the MXAT, and this is where we'd do *Mrs Warren's Profession* if it came off.

We had a wonderful lunch with Patrick Sommier, Ariel's partner, and Edgardo Lusi, an Argentinian actor/director working in Paris who asked me why the red nose in Cordelia's death scene? After explaining through Patrick and Ariel in great detail and in several languages, there was a long pause and then he said: 'Why did you put the nose on Cordelia in her death scene?' We went to a very good restaurant called La Maison du Coq Blanc, House of the White Cock, a very old family restaurant, twenties-style, traditional French food, and then I went off replete to the theatre to do my second performance of *Lear*.

The performance went well and afterwards I had a meeting with

Howard Panter who very much wants me to do the Shaw project. We talked about the possibility of getting a theatre in London.

I managed to get another actor for my masterclass: David Benent, who plays Caliban for Brook in *The Tempest*, a young actor who at the age of twelve had a huge success in *The Tin Drum*; I'm really looking forward to working with him. I met him yesterday and he's a strange young man, a gimlet-eyed embryo. He's twenty-four and has already played the Fool in *Lear* in Germany as well as Caliban. He comes from an acting family and the breadth of his experience is astonishing. Bruce Myers tells a story of being in a tent in Iran when a little animal crawled in . . . a small child, the baby Benent.

Monday, November 26

I've been ringing round all morning trying to get hold of scripts of *The Changeling* for the masterclass. I'm having lunch with Vernon Dobtcheff who I bumped into at the Odéon metro. Vernon is one of those characters who keeps popping up in everybody's history. He's quite notorious and there is a theory that there are several hundred versions of Vernon spread throughout Europe.

Tuesday, November 27

Tonight we did a Guinness special of *Richard III* and the wife of the Chairman of the European division of Guinness asked the fatal question, why are we going to Cork and not Dublin? To which I answered: because Guinness are sponsoring us, so we're going into Murphy's backyard. It's all so ludicrous, the whole thing. One of the nobs was saying how much she enjoyed *Richard* – as opposed to *Lear* which she didn't really enjoy because of the flowers in my crutch and all that. Oh God, save us from these bloody philistines.

We had a British Council lunch today which was quite sweet –
sitting by Guy Demeure. I'm rapidly running out of patience again
with the sheer idiocy of the Brits. I don't know why I fucking bother.
It was a very dull house and a very dull performance of *Richard III*.
Ian's landed on his feet, he's got the most beautiful flat right in the
area in which *Thérèse Raquin* was set; the flat is owned by Tony
Richardson, so he's quids in. I did my washing today, eight pairs of
socks and four underpants, a major achievement. Also I'm reading
John Bull's Other Island. My God, what a good writer Shaw is, he
makes most contemporary playwrights seem so woolly-minded and
insignificant.

Friday, November 30

Yesterday we were given a magnificent lunch by the Ambassador,
Ewen Fergusson, and shown all over the Embassy, which is the most
beautiful house, once owned by Napoleon's sister, Pauline, with the
addition now of a Henry Moore at the end of the garden. We were
very lucky and really treated well. Peter Jeffrey made a very good
speech and the Ambassador told us how he'd been entertaining
Margaret Thatcher the week she'd lost her first ballot. Coincidence
at such times is intriguing. I was in America, out of the country
again, when Wilson resigned; Ewen Fergusson was PPS to Jim
Callaghan when Callaghan took over from Wilson and this time he
had Thatcher staying with him for the big European conference
when that drama blew up. Apparently she rushed from the dinner
table to confront the journalists on the Embassy steps for the nine
o'clock news. The contrast to the other evening and the stuffy thing
at the theatre couldn't have been greater.

One of the little boys, young Alex who plays one of the Princes,
held his own with the Ambassador. They've behaved in an exemplary
way, all four of them, throughout this whole trip. I'm amazed at their
stamina and how they've looked after themselves, I couldn't have
done it at that age. I think little Alex now can't wait to get back to

England, apparently he's beginning to feel homesick; he's the only one who hasn't seen his parents and he's the youngest. Mrs Clark keeps them in check but I'm very impressed.

We have a new PM, John Major, which is a shock for me; I thought Hurd would have got it to hold the party together. He's the youngest PM this century, the son of a failed trapeze artist, couldn't get a job as a bus conductor, it's extraordinary.

I've finished *John Bull's Other Island* which is a magnificent play and I'd love to do it. It needs a little judicious cutting and shaping but it's astonishingly accurate about Ireland. Ariel and I are going to meet this afternoon to fix up and finalise the 1992 production of *Mrs Warren* at the Bobigny. I think it would be a very good move. The work with David Benent and Caline and Helene proceeds. We finally found a script of *The Changeling* through an American who did a translation of it, which is fairly rough but workable.

This morning I went to see a bunch of Parisian sixth-formers at Ecole Montagne. The whole class was conducted in flawless English. I walked across the Luxembourg Gardens. I haven't seen very much of Paris at all on this trip, not that I particularly mind. My main worry at the moment is where I'm going to live when I get back to London.

Saturday, December 1–Monday, December 3

Absolutely exhausting stint over the last few days. I did two performances on Saturday. There was an incident at the end of the matinée of *Richard* after the applause had died down when a solitary voice, I think that of a director, shouted: 'Reduction of story, reduction of character, reduction of play.' It was quite a little moment. Later that night there was a further contretemps in the restaurant when a young man accused the production of *Richard III* in its Fascist analogy of being patronising to the French and their awareness of English history. *Lear* went well and in the interval I rang some friends in America and fixed up to stay in their flat for a month in London which will give me some time to find somewhere else.

Sunday I had the nerve-wracking experience of the masterclass, fifty young *régisseurs*, directors, who have been working with such diverse talents as Nuria Espert, Sam Mendes, David Warrilow; how odd to find myself in that circle. Anyway, I spent the day doing that. David Benent had unfortunately developed a nodule in his throat, which is rather serious because he's not a strong young man – strong in spirit and imagination. I was lucky to get Georges Corraface, another Brook actor, to step into the breach, and Ciaran and Helene arrived from England. It had been my intention to do the scenes in both languages, but Helene was appalled at the standard of *The Taming of the Shrew* translation and I decided not to risk Ciaran's French on such a travesty. He was a little disappointed as he'd been preparing all week – actually I think he was a little relieved. Caline Carr did Ophelia with Georges and Ciaran sharing Hamlet, amplifying the schizophrenic nature of the scene. And in turn Helene and Caline played a composite Lady Macbeth. The day went well, it was extremely successful but I kept giving myself notes about the visual realisation of the scene, it's always been my weak point; my strength is in the understanding of the text.

Saturday, I didn't get to bed till 5 o'clock after *Lear* and I had another late night on Sunday, a wonderful farewell at a Vietnamese restaurant with Ariel and Patrick and Ciaran Hinds and Georges Corraface and the amazing Kokosowski. Koko let rip into Georges because he was the one Frenchman there, attacking the stiffness of his body and his defence mechanisms, how could he be so hunch-backed playing Hamlet? I said, 'All actors have defence mechanisms and it takes time to break them down. Of course he was stiff, Georges had two disadvantages: first, he filled in at the last moment; second, he had to appear as a guinea-pig before a bunch of fucking directors.'

They've invited me back for the Homage to Ryszard Cieslak, Jerzy Grotowski's favourite actor, who played the blind king in Brook's *Mahabharata*. I didn't think I'd be able to make it but they want me to come and with a judicious rearrangement of planes I can fly from Cork to London, London to Paris, back to London and then on to Cairo.

I think that just about does Paris. It's given me a whole new lease of life and I'm grateful. Lease of life or no lease of life, I think Paris is definitely the place I'd like to die in.

Cork

Tuesday, December 4–Saturday, December 8

It took me for ever to pack and I was late and had to leave a bag, travelling light to Cork. All the passengers had to get off the plane in Dublin and other passengers got on and then we got back on and my first experience of Ireland was coming through passport control at Cork airport with all these Dublin passengers. One unfortunate woman in front of me decided to skip the queue and get out. The passport officer said, 'What do you think you're doing? Get back.' She said, 'I'm Irish, I have no passport.' 'Never mind, get back,' he said, so she got back in line and then he said, 'All right, you can go.' I knew this must be Ireland.

I arrived in Cork fifteen minutes before the plane from London bringing the rest of the company. We were greeted by the Chairman of the Opera House, who shook hands with the first twenty people to come off the flight – only to realise they were Irish farmers returning from protesting in Brussels about the agricultural subsidies.

We're staying at the Imperial Hotel. The usual changing of rooms went on. I had a room with a bath, quite a pleasant room, not a particularly nice outlook, and poor Clare Higgins had a room without a bath and was rather depressed. She was shown every room in the hotel before it was finally arranged that she should have mine and I took hers with a shower which was perfectly adequate for me.

The first thing to do was find the theatre and Clare and I walked toward it and asked a lady if she knew where the Cork Opera House was. 'I do,' she said. 'Just go down to Patrick Street and ask anybody and they'll show you.' The Cork Opera House is a sixties building that looks like a cross between a bingo hall and a cinema, vaguely reminiscent – God forbid – of the Lirico in Milan. The backstage facilities are equally reminiscent. Perhaps there's a connection between Ireland and Italy both being Catholic countries . . .but then again, so is Spain . . . and France – oh, dear, it must be the Irish in me. The communal men's dressing room is a particular joy – breeze-blocks painted white that haven't been finished; they obviously ran out of paint halfway through the job and couldn't decide between them who should go out and get the extra can.

Ian was depressed again about the lack of booking. 'Ireland has let us down,' he said. Apparently it's only 70 per cent for *Richard*. We met Bob Crowley in the dressing room who said, 'I warned you about it, but no one would be told,' but the performance of *Richard* went so well and the audience rose to their feet *en masse* afterwards. So the whole thing was obviously worthwhile and the people are wonderful, great people, very generous.

I am exhausted, after working so hard in Paris. I don't really feel up to doing anything, though I did do a reading of *Widower's Houses* on the Wednesday morning and then the usual radio stuff, local RTE radio.

World news goes apace – no end to the Gulf crisis. Last week the UN backed the resolution that force should be brought to bear on Saddam Hussein and Iraq on January 15. Cairo looms and the situation is still uncertain. Wherever we go there is CNN or Sky TV in our bedrooms, all giving fairly biased and yellow-press news. But it's all speculation and sabre-rattling. I noticed when we had our information packs for Cairo that the British Embassy, Shepheard's Hotel and the American Embassy all seem to be in one part of Cairo and the Opera House across the river in the other – a toss-up which one Hussein will go for first.

Yesterday we did two performances. One in the afternoon mainly to schoolchildren which I was dreading in fact proved a nice experience, they behaved extraordinarily well. If this had been Leeds or Birming-ham it wouldn't have been the same at all. We had a very comic tea at the *Cork Examiner*, hosted by the Chairman and Lord Mayor and the main critic of the paper. Also in attendance was Cork's favourite prodigy, Fiona Shaw. It was charming and quaint and the speeches were very funny, one of the town burghers getting up and misquot-ing, 'As Lady Bracknell, or whoever it was, or somebody said, "Don't put your daughter on the stage, Mrs Thingumyjig,"' and the Lord Mayor explaining that he was a martyr to Shakespeare because he was fed up with his daughter rehearsing it in the front room.

Last night was *Richard III* and this morning I did a talk to some students at Cork University – nice campus – who were very sweet, very young. They were divided in their opinions. One of the girls thought there was far too much humanity in my performance of Lear and *Richard III* was more emblematic. Some had not been exposed to Shakespeare before and were a bit shocked by the unorthodoxy of the *Lear*. They felt that Deborah was too contentious and too deliberate in her wish to shock. The only time – I never read notices, only when they're good – the only time I did here I happened to walk into a paper shop and looked at the *Irish Times* which described me as a buffoon; a fair comment. I think they misunderstand my playfulness at the beginning of the play for madness and sometimes I do feel that if only I could have really worked on the Howard Hughes idea, his reclusiveness, the distance from his daughters, I could have made something of it – but that seems to be in the far past now and pointless harping on.

I went to lunch with Fiona Shaw's parents, Dr and Mrs Wilson, and walked back into town and spent the afternoon resting. We did a fairly jovial performance of *Richard*. Ian at the news of Edward's death staggers and I say, 'Can I get you anything?' and he said, 'No, I'm just overacting.' I managed to lose a vital word in one of my speeches which goes, 'For God's sake, let not us two stay at home,' and I said, 'For God's sake, let us two stay at home,' which caused a certain amount of mirth. It was very much one of those evenings. Ian was complaining of the unprofessionalism and the noise backstage and came into my dressing room saying what an unprofessional bunch they were, making himself late for his entrance in the second half – which he had the temerity to laugh about afterwards.

The crowning glory of the evening was the dancing, the local Cork dancing. We went to a place like a huge disco, but at the back was a room done up like an Irish cottage, with a little parlour and a dancing floor slung together, run by a man called Timmy the Brit who is the organiser of the Cork Folk Festival. We did some wonderful stuff. I was suddenly back to my roots again, this foot-stamping. He had to keep telling me, 'Just remember you're in a kitchen, in a kitchen,' my movements being somewhat large. By the end of the evening Clare Higgins and I were drippin'.

Our last day there was no matinée so we went off, four of us, in a car towards Killarney, but ended up going to Skibbereen, down the south-west coast and driving up to Bantry Bay. It was marvellous country, like Scotland, God's own country, and the air was cold, snow's come early to England and Ireland as well. Airports have been cut off. In fact the set for *Richard* is now still sitting at Rosslare, it hasn't actually crossed the Irish Channel and has to get to Cairo.

We've had a great week, the audiences have been fantastic and the last night of *Lear* was no exception. I'm quite glad we're leaving because I have redeveloped a taste for whiskey, through a person who'd best be nameless because it's still illegal. We had a little cup of the old potcheen which is divine. I must come back to Ireland again. I don't know whether I will, but I feel a great affection for the place.

The audience, when we met them at the British Council reception last night, were quite stunned and proud and tickled by the fact that we'd come to their city. For the first time ever, the Union Jack flew above the theatre and that hasn't happened before without it being burned. There was a lot of pride all round, civic pride, pride in the theatre, in the work. I noticed it was Cyril Cusack's birthday and there was a great spread about him in the Irish papers.

Interesting note, whether it's true or not, Susan Engel observed throughout the week that the majority of the audiences, unlike at home, were men. Tomorrow morning I'm off to Paris, if the flight takes off. It's all a bit worrying as I hear that Gatwick may be shut. We shall see.

Sunday, December 9

To Paris today to see my friends. Helene Patarot picked me up from the airport. I'm staying at the Trianon in my favourite room, 602, with its wonderful canopied bed. After a little rest I made my way to the Odéon for the Homage to Ryszard Cieslak. What was extraordinary was that the Homage was singularly dull. Dull in the extreme. I don't know what I was expecting, something quite exciting, but it wasn't. Grotowski made the first speech for about an hour and Peter, in his usual manner, got the lie of the land and decided that brevity was best, which it was. The only thing was, I felt sorry for the poor man we were paying homage to. There was no mention of Kantor who died yesterday but it seems Koko was madly trying to organise an *hommage* to him. The French are *hommage*-daft. Ariel kept shifting in his seat and groaning. It was like a *Who's Who of European Theatre*: apart from Grotowski and Brook there was Louis Pascal, Peter Stein, Ion Caramitru from Romania – all that talent and they still produced a boring afternoon.

On the subject of boredom, apparently Judi Dench and Sam Mendes had had rather a hard time in their masterclasses from the young French *régisseurs*, who after a week I think had reached the boredom threshold. I was lucky, I was the first Sunday novelty act; by the end of the week they must have been punch-drunk. The course goes on – to next week.

I finished my visit with a splendid Parisian dinner. God, the French can have a good time, these people have become friends in quite a short time. Here I feel much more relaxed than in England, but I have to get back and into the swing of things. I'm dreading it.

A foretaste of Romania: I met Ion Caramitru, our host in Bucharest, the Director of the Bulandra Theatre, famous for his production of *Hamlet* which has been playing since the early 80s, with something rotten in the state of Denmark very much the metaphor for Ceauşescu's Romania. He's a great friend of Richard Eyre, known him for twenty years. Since the revolution in Romania there have been demonstrations going on night and day, before and after the elections. The new government is feared by some to be a reconstitution of ex-Ceauşescuites in coalition with a group of intelligentsia. Ion was Vice-President of the country between Ceauşescu's fall and the elections until the situation became untenable. He's really saddened by the events in his country. He told me he'd been in Moldavia when the miners had moved into Bucharest in counter-demonstration against the students on June 13/14 after the elections and was horrified by what had gone on and shocked at how the miners acted. They had sat in the square and dug up the grass and when the students protested they bludgeoned them with pickaxe handles. The miners were wearing their helmets and had dirt like coaldust on their faces but the hands of some of them were unbelievably smooth. He said they were obviously members of the Securitate. Caramitru's a man who, I think, is in a dangerous position, though very optimistic, very helpful, extremely charming and warm. There was also a young Romanian director, very beautiful, blonde, mustn't say these things, it's sexist, who had defected, had enough, after the miners' strike. I was absolutely fascinated by her complete concentration. I noticed her at the workshop last week.

I've been sorting out my life, ringing my son; making preparations for my return to England, arranging Christmas presents for my daughter. Alan's off to Moscow to study Chekhov at the Moscow Art Theatre school which I'm very pleased about though the news from there isn't very good at the moment. I think Gorbachev is up against it. I'm so glad I'm not there, but I'm glad Alan's going.

Cairo

Monday, December 10

Shepheard's Hotel, overlooking the Nile, Room 505. I see the Great Mosque, the boats going down the Nile, and across the river I can see the Opera House. What a day. Snowing this morning in Paris, I wasn't quite sure I was going to get here but arrived at the airport and found there were no delays. I said, 'Are you sure?' Yes. Of course I go first to the wrong terminal, I go to BA instead of Air France; then I arrive at the AF terminal. 'Are you sure the planes are going?' 'Yes, yes, get on the plane,' last passenger on, all ready to go: 'There will be a ten-minute delay while we de-ice.' After ten minutes: 'Another delay for ten minutes to clear the runway.' Then a forty-minute delay and they decide to serve lunch. Lunch comes, I still have time on my hands because it's one o'clock Paris time, twelve o'clock English time and the London to Cairo plane doesn't leave till 3.15. Finally we leave and I ask them if they can radio and they say they're not sure but will try. I get into London at ten minutes to three with twenty minutes to get on my plane. They rush me through, nobody knows where I am. Camilla Mayer and David Milling, who's temporarily taken over from John, are going absolutely crazy because they don't know where I am, they're extremely cross with me and have every right to be so. Anyway, I settle down for the trip to Cairo. We arrived at ten o'clock and as we got into the buses were greeted by a deluge of watersellers. Now I'm going to try and find something to eat. It's 1 a.m., Cairo time.

Wednesday, December 12

Two days of quite remarkable sensuous experience. First day we went to the Pyramids, the Great Pyramid of Cheops and the lesser one. So close to the city, right by the town. Five funeral chambers, the sheer size and wonder of it is awe-inspiring. It obliterates the sun as you stand close – hard to photograph or capture anyway; the actual experience of standing there seeing these vast rocks with all kinds of legend attached to them, all kinds of myth; the fact that the stones of the pyramids could build a wall round France. The mathematical calculations that must have been brought into play to construct them are beyond my imagination.

We spent the morning in a group, we drove up and I walked around. Then I broke off from the main group and walked down to the Sphinx which, again, was mystical and full of wonder, facing the rising sun. I kept remembering the scene from *Peer Gynt* which I played when I was very young, my one encounter with the Sphinx in any practical sense. I didn't feel happy when I walked into the tombs because it was very crowded, I wanted silence and it was very hard to get silence, very hard again at the Sphinx.

Egypt is fairly depressed at the moment: it's an international war zone, inflation is very high, there is an eerie lack of tourists and they are suffering from it in Egypt, suffering in Cairo. The town is empty, so naturally we are being doubly assaulted by everyone for baksheesh, to go on camel rides, donkey rides and general begging. They really

166

are desperately short of money and we're the only people ripe for the picking.

I walked back up the hill from the Sphinx to the hotel by the pyramids, ordered a drink and waited for the others to arrive. The most beautiful hotel, looking over green lawns, and I sat drinking my white wine. After lunch we went to the bazaar, the usual trading, the cats, the birds, the various little wall hangings and bottles, basic tourist fare.

Then we came back to the hotel and on to a reception at the Embassy where I was introduced to the Governor of Cairo who happens to be a cancer specialist, a surgeon. Once or twice a week he still does a cancer operation. But Cairo is a huge republic, it's run a bit like the GLC whose demise I was lamenting. He couldn't understand how London could be governed without a proper city council. David Collings and I had been reminiscing about when we had worked together twenty years ago in a Goldoni comedy ridiculously directed by a Dutchman whose name we couldn't remember and as we looked up he materialised – across the room at a Cairo reception. I met the ex-PM of Egypt who was a rather jolly man who said he'd studied Economics at Birmingham University and seen lots of the productions at Stratford. He said Mrs Thatcher had been in the job too long, he himself had been Prime Minister for seven years and it wasn't healthy; after seven years you had to change because it went to your head.

Then I met Dr Tariq Hassan, the Director of the Opera House, a true Renaissance man. An endocrinologist, specialist in psychosomatic diseases, a man who is trying to re-establish the life-line of Egyptian culture which has been broken. Apart from the Ancient Egyptian period, most Egyptian culture is less than 200 years old; there have been great gaps and he feels that too much of what is done is imitative. He understands the popularity of nineteenth-century Italian opera in his society but feels it has taken precedence and he wants to go back to the roots of his culture with experimental theatre and dance. We talked about his work and the nature of art and its therapeutic value, and we talked about *zar*, women who are often accused of being witches – they're sort of shamans – women who take on the role of Mother Earth and use music and rhythm to cure depression. He's seen its true therapeutic value and also the

167

way art is in touch with something mystical and extraordinary, quite powerful, the reverberation of which he believes has been deadened in Egypt in all the arts and he wishes to rediscover it. I'm hoping he may be able to arrange for me to go to a turning ceremony, the whirling dervish ceremony which is part of the healing process. I was very invigorated by our conversation.

When we got back to the hotel we were to dine, which I didn't do because I'm trying to lose weight, and were then to be taken round the theatres by the Deputy Minister of Culture. We waited for an hour but Ian had forgotten to check his messages and sure enough there was a message for him to say that the theatres were closed. So we went to experience Old Cairo, smoking the bubble of tobacco, drinking tea and having our shoes cleaned. It was all very lively, the children, the beggars, the ornaments, the whole thing looked like a set from *Murder on the Nile*.

I arranged to go riding in the early morning. I was told I must see the pyramids at dawn. I got up at 4.30 a.m. and drove out to Giza to be met by Salman, who was illiterate but fluent in English, with a soft spot for Scandinavians. We rode out in the pitch black, listening to the noises of the night. These things are always quite frightening because you never know where they're going to lead: the dogs sleeping, the chickens beginning their dawn chorus; riding up alongside the pyramid which one saw lit up against the lights emerging out behind the Sphinx, awesome, and finally going into the desert with no light except the sky, and watching the sky change as the morning came, through various shades of black, grey, to blue, to purple to grey again, and the haze and eventually the dawn. There was no sunrise because it was misty, but even more exciting was to see the sun appear suddenly in the middle of the sky like a great red ball and to turn and see in the distance because of the mist the tops of the Cheops and the other pyramid appear, like ghostly triangles hovering in the sky. At every turn they looked slightly different with a slightly different texture, sometimes they were sharp, sometimes spectral and, galloping through the desert, there was the smell of the horses' sweat, the babble of the guide: I wanted more silence and he got the message. You could hear in the distance the sound of the mosque calling the early believers to prayer and the army base playing Egyptian folk records. The whole experience was like a huge sensuous bath, the smell, the noises and this taste of the sand in your mouth which made one inevitably dry, and the cold, much colder at that time of day, as I underestimated. I rode for three hours and ended by going to the village and standing before the great Sphinx and having a moment alone, feeling the power of the belief in the journey across the river of life and the river of death.

We rode in the early morning to a small village, Salman's village, to see one of his many cousins and to the perfumeries which distil the smells of Egypt, the pure essences of flowers brought from the various oases around the country, jasmine, rose, lemon, crushed flowers whose essences are exported to Lancôme, Yves St Laurent, Chanel, to provide the smells mixed with alcohol. We sat in the shop of a blue-eyed Egyptian who was known affectionately as Rambo. His real name was Rushman but he wanted to be known as Rambo, which is a sorry sign of the age. Throughout the whole transaction, while he was trying to interest me in these smells, a young boy, an assistant, sat watching, smoking, curious at our manner. We were given the customary tea at the perfumeries and then Salman took me to his house, where he showed me his letters of recommendation and various memorabilia which he kept under the mattress. There was his mother lying on the bed and a brand new baby, one week old, born to his sister. In the middle of the living room was a little rabbit sitting there, cowering. The children were just rising because it was very early; one of the boys had to move so Salman could show me the letters. On the walls were pictures he had taken of various tourists. This was his life, it was important to him and not once did he haggle for money. Even when I gave him the money he merely took it, he didn't look at it. He kept saying money wasn't important and I believe him. What was important was the communication. He helped us with the horses and with the other things but he knew his own value and said, 'You will pay me what I'm worth, no more, no less.'

I hurried back to the hotel in the rush hour, which took for ever. Then took a bus to Saqqara, to the tombs, the great Step Pyramid, the oldest pyramid in the world, and the Pyramid of Unas. There are huge burial chambers at the Temple of Unas where generals and officials were buried and in the distance, because the light was so clear, we could see other pyramids. We had great fun with the hieroglyphics, making up stories: it takes four men several days to carry a three-headed woman across a corrugated iron roof and it would cost them an arm and a leg. The weather was beautifully warm, also there was a great feeling of unity among the company, calmness. It was reflected in the children, young Alex and Matthew. You can always tell with children if there's a kind of hysteria, because they catch it immediately and become the receivers and transmitters of it, but these two boys, while getting quite upset about the camel and donkey rides, behaved in an exemplary way. Sam Beazley took out his sketch book and drew the heads of the camels. I bought an Arab head-dress to keep off the sun, looking like an old Palestinian terrorist.

We then went to Serapeum, to the tombs of the sacred bulls, the Apis bulls, born of virgins believed to be struck by light from the gods. None of these tombs were built under duress, they were built with great celebration. The catacombs stretch for miles and miles under the desert. There's believed to be a long tunnel leading to Memphis, where the bulls are slaughtered. We went to Memphis to see the statues of Rameses II. Again, all this was desert though Memphis was in an arable oasis part, but it looked like nothing on earth, massive excavations and very rough.

Various wives and husbands have joined the group, coming out for a holiday in Cairo. I am sorry I haven't got my daughter – with the threatened crisis in the Gulf we didn't even know if we were going to be here. It was a glorious, harmonious day, ending with a wonderful Egyptian meal of tahini and falafal in a restaurant near the pyramids. I was quite exhausted because I'd been on the go since 4.30 a.m.

Everyone was in their summer garb. Ian in his green shorts, Susie in her flowered dress, Sam, as ever, dressed virtually the same whatever the weather, blue cardigan, blue corduroys, bow tie, Joyce looking like something out of an Agatha Christie film. In the distance I could see what I'd seen in the morning, the tops of the Cheops: again, the light was different from the early morning, one side of the pyramids shown in sharp relief by the shadow, looking like diamonds hovering in the air, this time clear as clear, clear as glass.

Sometimes the reasons for doing what we're doing seem so clear: on days like today; talking with Hassan last night about the therapeutic effect of art, the dancers and the whirling dervishes and art as a pool in which we can see where we are and the material, solid world in which we live. This is art in its cleansing role and it's about the body, about being well, a state of well-being. It creates a reflection of everything in its place and everything as it should be. It links through to Cork and the dances we did there on the night of Joyce's birthday. I can't wait to see the turning ceremony.

I must remember the fantasy that Ian and I had about Laurence Olivier. A postcard seller looked like Laurence Olivier in make-up and we reckoned it *was* Laurence Olivier and he was trying to avoid us.

Thursday, December 13

Tonight was *Lear*, it was a disaster. We're back to a huge stage. I had a row with Deborah, I was very angry at this endless string of inappropriate spaces. The reaction at the end, it was all right, but they were people who aren't interested in theatre, a load of socialites.

Friday, December 14

Today I walked round the market and saw a host of theatre. Every shop you pass is like a small Pollock's Toy Theatre. Women lying in the middle of the street, with their children lying upon them, asleep in the busy thoroughfare. Past five men, Dickens-like, blacker than black, polishing brass, absorbing the black from the surface of the brass, the further you went into the shop, the brighter the brass and the blacker the men.

Tonight was the first night of *Richard III* and it went very well considering we had the same problems, and Ian announced that he would never tour again. The flying back wall was built too heavy and the Opera House flying system couldn't withstand the weight. On its first test it broke and never went again so we had to reblock as we went along, the usual chaos.

We went to the citadel in the morning, the old part, the two mosques, the Blue Mosque which is awe-inspiring, and then to the university to talk to the students; and a lively bunch they were, full of vigour and humour, mainly girls, asking questions about the production – the injustice of Cordelia's death, why was Lear wise, Edmund black; why we present the play at all – father-figures being somewhat sacred to the Muslim sensibility. The girls found it a bit unsettling that the daughters treat Lear in the way they do.

The second performance of *Richard* was a fairly giggly one.

I haven't been able to go to the turning ceremony or get to the *zar*; they tried to arrange it for me but there are no festivals. We went to the Wissa-Wassef school out in Haraneya. It's a unique experiment which was started after the war by two Copts who taught very young children tapestry-making. A tradition began and new generations have carried it on. Sadly, the older the weaver the more conventional the tapestry, but the work of some of the teenagers has a vibrancy which is unsurpassed.

After the performance of *Lear* I had a drink with a playwright called Karim Alrawi. We were talking about censorship and how his play had been censored, the Egyptian attitude to homosexuality, the fact that it doesn't exist or they don't acknowledge it, or they acknowledge it in quite a different way.

Hassan apologised that I couldn't go to a *zar* but the Wissa-Wassef was quite fulfilling enough for me, that and our conversation with the Egyptian playwright about the present state of affairs: actors on strike because they're low-paid at the National Theatre, the quality of work, playwrights who have committed suicide in the last fifteen years. The situation in Egypt is a paradox and all tied up with Islamic fundamentalism – both of the fellaheen and of the urban poor, two strands, encouraged mainly by the Saudis. Now, with the Gulf crisis and Cairo empty and desperate, it's a very fraught and interesting time to be here.

Back to London, a gap of three weeks and then we start on January 5 with *Richard III*.

PART SIX

London Hiatus

Monday, December 17–Sunday, December 23

I arrived back from Cairo on Monday, December 17, having left at the extremely early hour of 4 in the morning after only four hours' sleep. Cairo – the trip was good, the theatre was a disaster. I was met by my son, Alan, with keys for the flat in Maida Vale belonging to my friends, the Cookes, which I'm going to stay in until January 24. The poor boy and my daughter, who wasn't there, had come the previous day to discover that I hadn't arrived. In my note I hadn't said which day, it was my fault, I hadn't made it clear. I had to go and collect a wallet I'd left at Heathrow and asked to be sent to Gatwick. When I got to Gatwick it wasn't there, it was still at Heathrow. I then booked my flights from Heathrow to Paris because I have to return to Paris to do some more work with Ariel on Shaw. We got into the car and drove to London, went to my agent's first, who ironically was in Cairo, and sorted through various bits and pieces. My American agent was there and I talked to her briefly, drove to Maida Vale and settled myself in.

Salem to Moscow is going to be published on January 30, so on Tuesday morning I was picked up and taken to Methuen, my publishers, for an interview with a nice lady called Marian Brace, arranged by super-efficient Briar who runs the publicity. I then scooted to Heathrow, checked in at Terminal 4, went straight to find my wallet and they said no, it was at Gatwick, which I couldn't believe. I begged them to have it sent back and they agreed.

We flew to Paris, Margaret and I, and were met by Ariel who took us straightaway to Bobigny. I hoped there'd be an answer about meeting Jeanne Moreau but there was a fax from Peter Brook to say ring her agent, an original thought. After about twenty minutes we made our way to the Trianon Hotel, to which I've become a regular visitor over the last few weeks. The following morning I rang Ariel and through a contact he managed to fix up a meeting that evening with Jeanne Moreau, which made the trip worthwhile.

Meanwhile Margaret dragged me off to Père Lachaise to see the grave of Jim Morrison. It was snowing and looked as if Morrison's grave was being dug up; they were actually expanding it to make it bigger, would you believe, and so there was nothing there, nothing over the grave at all, it was just bare earth. We wandered around trying to find various others instead – Isadora Duncan, Oscar Wilde, Simone Signoret, Edith Piaf, Modigliani, Chopin, a motley collection.

It was a fruitful three days in Paris. I had asked Ariel if we could get in touch with Michel Lonsdale about playing Sir George Crofts in *Mrs Warren's Profession* and I arranged to call him on Thursday. I met Ms Moreau. She was exceedingly gracious. Her first words to me were, 'Do you know Oldham?' Her mother came from Lancashire. Lonsdale is also half English. I finally spoke to him, and he agreed to look at the script. I saw some old friends, introduced Margaret, and had a good time. We had a lovely two days together; it was nice to be with my daughter again having not seen her for about four months.

On Friday we flew back to London. We went to Bobigny to see Ariel before we left and he was like a Jewish mother-hen, packing me off and making sure I was all right, had I got this and that. After the driver had driven off at the airport, I realised he'd gone off with my filofax and passport and tickets lying on the passenger seat. Travelling . . . I have come to the end of my travelling. So we got the tickets sorted out, I had to book new seats, the rigmarole of ringing Bobigny to try and find where the driver was and discovering he'd gone off to lunch. I had just about given up and we had only thirty minutes to go, Margaret was in despair, I was in despair, when suddenly he turned up – having seen the tickets. We rushed through, got on the plane, the last people on, our reservation had gone, we got the last two seats and were off to London.

I arrived back in London to be met by my son again and came back to Maida Vale. I was going to Methuen that afternoon to join in celebrating the advance copies of my book which had just come in. When I arrived, there it was, in the display in the front office and I couldn't believe it. I was overwhelmed by the fact that I who could hardly spell my own name was suddenly face to face with my book. It has a few errors in it, my son pointed out that some of the actors' names had been misspelt. Anyway they were thrilled, my two children, and so was everyone else; there was a real buzz of excitement, which was nice.

I left the kids and went off into town to meet Howard Panter and Rosemary Squire and Simon Stokes, to discuss the idea of a company to play Shaw in London at the end of the year. We decided to put together a package of *Major Barbara* and *Widower's Houses* but first we've got to try and sort out the rights. I then fell into my bed.

On Saturday I went to see Brian Friel's *Dancing in Lughnasa* which was a marvellous experience. I thought the play was not brilliantly directed but well acted and the set I found a little confusing. The moment when the sisters turn on the radio and dance and this Irish music comes pouring out reminded me of Cork, and when they started I just burst into tears, I was completely overwhelmed by the sheer passion of the piece, the link between everything that's been going on in my life. There was a kind of relief, recognition and a joy and a sadness all intermingled, with these five girls dancing round the stage; it was cathartic. And I kept thinking too of Shaw and his work because I'd been reading Shaw all that week, I'd been reading and thinking about *John Bull's Other Island* and how much I'd like to direct it.

Got up late on Sunday morning, Margaret was staying with me, drove over and had lunch with my son and daughter and came to arrangements with my ex-wife about how to do Christmas. Christmas is such a nightmare time of the year. I used to love it as a child, I loved it until quite recently, but after my wife and I broke up it became a melancholy occasion. I agreed that as it was my ex-wife's birthday, the children would have Christmas lunch with her and I would come over in the morning for a drink. She asked me to stay for Christmas lunch but I couldn't, I find these family get-togethers so fraught. For the kids, I suppose, one should do it, but I can't, it just creates enormous tension and actually I'd rather be with strangers or on my own.

Lear and *Richard* seem a long way off at the moment.

175

This afternoon, Sunday, I met Irina, which was nice, and I felt a curious mixture of feelings, on the one hand sad and on the other hand, well, what has to be has to be and maybe it wouldn't have worked out, a feeling that I am beginning a new phase in my life; I've done it so many times now, it seems I've had a glut of new phases, but I'm a survivor and I come from a line of survivors. God knows how long that will continue but I think I've got more resilience than my mother or father had, they were knocked and knocked and knocked and when they pegged out I don't think they could take any more. I seem to thrive on it. I don't know if that's true but I think that's what the dancing in *Lughnasa* reminded me of, the fact that there was in me a spirit of survival and I feel beholden to survive on behalf of my parents, on behalf of my family.

I rang Albert Finney and asked him if he'd like to play Andrew Undershaft but he's playing in another Ronnie Harwood play. I can't believe it.

Tomorrow's Christmas Eve. I suppose I should be sad, I keep thinking I should be sad and trying to get myself in a sad frame of mind. I think it may hit me but I don't know. I'd like to think that I want to be alone, I don't know if I can bear it but I think I ought to experience that aloneness. I've been very lucky because I've been sustained through this last part of the tour, sustained in a way which is difficult to talk about but it's avoided having to be on my own. I shall be forty-five this year. As I was driving along today, someone shouted at me because I was obviously not concentrating and my car veered. He called me a 'fucking four-eyed git' and I thought, what does he mean? I'm not four-eyed, and I glanced in the mirror and realised that I'm now wearing glasses.

Monday, December 31

It's just been announced that Ian has received a knighthood. I'm delighted, he deserves it, a great leader in the theatre, and the work he's done on the tour and for Aids and particularly for gay rights can only be admired and respected. He is dedicated in a way that puts a lot of people to shame.

It's been a good week, much better than I thought it would be, I thought Christmas might be a bit gloomy but I had a good time: a nice Christmas Day with David Aukin and Nancy Meckler and my friends the Robinsons from the US. Then I spent the evening with the kids. Margaret went off to France with her mother and I went up to Stratford with my son and enjoyed myself for two days. I saw Ciaran and Helene and we went to *Troilus and Cressida* and *Two Shakespearean Actors*. The first half of *Troilus and Cressida* I didn't think was very good but the second half was really rather splendid; the production was, I thought, misconceived, but on the whole I enjoyed it. *Two Shakespearean Actors* was a splendid evening, and we went to see my little house in Stratford which is in a pretty awful state, part of the roof has come off, the telephone wire is down and I succeeded in setting fire to the house, practically burning it down. I left Alan to deal with it. There were some twigs in the fireplace and I set fire to them, and within seconds the house was full of smoke and I walked out and said, 'Alan, you deal with it,' I just couldn't cope. And he did, he dealt with it wonderfully well, poor boy, covered in smoke. Anyway, we saved the day, we had to get the carpet cleaned.

Hidden Agenda has been favourably reviewed in Los Angeles and will open in London any day now. On the whole, things are coasting nicely. I've seen some friends, the Byrnes, Oliver Cotton, and presented him with a copy of the book, in which he's quoted. I spoke to Irina, saw her, she did some shopping for me which was sweet of her, and I spoke to her on the phone yesterday. Our relationship seems quite good at the moment. I've also found somewhere to live for six months, which I hope will be confirmed today, a little studio in Kilburn. Isabella Bywater, the designer, has a house there with her daughter and I'll take the studio up above if it's available. I'm beginning to put things back together again though it's a long haul. It's been an odd Christmas, but not a painful one, in fact a remarkably unpainful one. I'm trying to read bits of Shaw and watch the telly. Done a lot of telly-watching, which has been great. Nice to be able to switch off.

Monday, January 7, 1991

I've had a fairly quiet New Year, enjoyed being here in this flat and had a good time with my son on New Year's Eve. Back into action at the Lyttleton with *Richard III*, which played well the other night and tonight; today we did a line rehearsal of *King Lear*. Ian has received his knighthood.

My financial situation is pretty bleak. I went to see my lawyer and I've got to really work out what I'm going to live off: it isn't very much.

Wednesday, January 9

Our first *Lear* last night since Cairo. It was good to be back at the Lyttleton, the size worked. Some friends were there who were also at the first night and they said it had grown a lot. Ian was excellent and so was Bradley, and everybody really. I'm enjoying *Richard* for the first time, it makes a difference not having to do the battles. There's been a fair amount of agitation about Ian's knighthood. Derek Jarman felt he shouldn't have accepted it because of Clause 28. In the *Guardian* today, several people wrote a letter condemning Derek Jarman's attack and the signatories were people like Jeremy Fry, Ned Sherrin, Tony Sher, fairly well-known gays. I find the whole thing a bit of a storm in a teacup myself, but there it is.

The publicity for the book continues apace. I have a fair number of interviews to do over the next two weeks and a couple of signings. I'm going to start my French lessons on Monday in preparation for next year. I'm trying to get on with the two Shaw projects, I don't know whether they are going to happen, I'm having a helluva difficulty with the rights – Duncan Weldon seems to have bought most of them which is proving awkward and maybe I'll have to try and find two alternative plays to do. I made a very useful contact in Michael Holroyd, the Shaw biographer, who is being extremely helpful. In fact I've discovered something which is quite exciting and I hope I can persuade my producer to do it.

I miss my children. Alan has now gone to Russia. I was asked to take part in a symposium of new plays at the Orange Tree in the summer. Things are fairly hectic.

We've heard that another marriage in the company has broken up, Mark Strong's hasn't survived the tour, casualties of war.

The Gulf crisis looms, it looks like war, Baker's discussions with the Iraqi foreign minister have failed. Javier Perez de Cuellar has failed, one more day to go, January 14. War looks like a reality.

Sunday, January 20

On January 16 the Americans bombed Baghdad. Hussein's bluff was called and we finally moved in with the most extraordinary surgical bombing, pinpointing targets, dropping cruise missiles down ventilator shafts, blowing out defence installations, and this has gone on now for the last four days, it's the 20th and it has not stopped. It's going to be a long war, it's amazing because they never thought it would happen. Actually it wasn't the 16th, it was the 17th. The reporters are behaving obscenely about the whole thing; they're on a hysterical high, really getting a kick from it. As somebody said, for most of them it's their first war, and in the age of satellite television it's the first television war as well. So far in England there haven't been any terrorist attacks as promised by Hussein, but everybody has to be vigilant: extra security at the theatre – we have to use our electronic pass-cards to get into the building, all kinds of tightening up. Talking to Ariel in France where there are two million Algerians, he is severely worried about the state of the theatre there. Apparently the West End of London is doing no business at all, we're the only ones doing any business. It's all quite bleak, an eventful week.

The shows have been going very well, I've been enjoying them, Ian and I have had quite a lot of laughter, light-heartedness. He's had a fairly tough time with the brouhaha about him accepting the knighthood. We had a party for him and the whole company sang 'There ain't nothing like a dame.'

The company are now planning to do a play which will take over from *Lear* and it looks as though it will be an Eduardo de Filippo

179

play so there's a lot of speculation about who is going to be playing what and who is taking over from David Bradley and me. Why they want to go on with *Richard* is beyond me, it seems that *Richard* has had its day, but Ian feels there is life in it yet, a possible American tour which would, quite frankly, drive me demented.

We had a very exciting day. We went to Broadmoor,* the hospital for the criminally insane – an experience I had been extremely sceptical of. A consultant psychologist, Murray Cox, my namesake, came and talked to us. Murray I already knew: he wrote the programme note on *Macbeth* when I played it ten years ago. He's an interesting man, obviously very good at his job. Gives the impression of being a little vague. When he came to talk to us I wasn't quite clear about the purpose of this trip. It's all very well to see what we actors get out of it but I wanted to know what the patients get out of it.

Well, it was a shock. It was extraordinary. They were so excited; they had such intelligence and understanding, particularly of the humour – jokes which had never had a laugh before – and the relationship between Lear and the Fool. They were totally involved; they understood everything in a sort of visceral and intellectual way combined. At the end of the speech 'What! Art mad? A man may see how this world goes with no eyes . . . None does offend, none, I say none,' the audience laughed in a particular way, with a particular quality to it which was quite thrilling. A young schizophrenic said that he sympathised with Lear because he talks a lot of crap and it made him realise that he himself talked a lot of crap. Another young man was very eager to know what we got out of it and whether we had been afraid to come, and we had to confess that we had been apprehensive. He totally empathised with Lear's situation, was deeply moved by his death and said that he felt a sense of loss.

I was amazed at the concentration of that audience. I've never played to such a theatrically intelligent audience in the whole of my life. I felt it was what touring is all about. It was a bare room, the rough setting I've always wanted, and the performance totally

* Because of the deep impression this visit made on me, I've covered it at some length in the Introduction.

depended on the interplay between audience and player, the interplay of text and audience. The audience brought it life, made it easy, gave it meaning and I rode on their understanding.

Afterwards various patients were talking about how the play affected them and one young man was particularly moved by the Fool and his logic. He kept saying, 'There's this wonderful logic about him' – usually the Fool seems quite obscure, but clearly this time the sense had come zooming across.

Another doctor was talking about how three of her patients, who had murdered their parents, quite separately came and said, 'I did so envy the ability of Cordelia and her father to say farewell,' and it made me think about my own parents' deaths. There was also great empathy with the three sisters, and the men particularly felt that the sisters were very hard done by.

One psychologist said, 'It's very hard to assess the effect of the play. I don't know what it will be.' He had a particular patient who was obsessed with knives – most of the people there have murdered someone at some point in their lives – and what was fascinating was that every time a knife came out this doctor said he watched his patient quietly lower his head and then come back to watch the action.

We didn't know what these people had done. It was very hard to tell which were patients and which were nurses and psychologists because the patients were very articulate. The most notorious inmates were absent. Peter Sutcliffe, the Yorkshire Ripper, finds it impossible to deal with something of this sort. He lives a very inward-looking life and can't cope with anything theatrical. Ronnie Kray is described as being socially moronic, keeps wholly to himself and the world of Ronnie Kray and can't relate to anything else. And some people, I can see, *would* find it a bit much.

There was one sad story: a schizophrenic, who wanders round the ward listening to tapes of Shakespeare, didn't put his name down to come. The psychologist asked him afterwards why he hadn't and he said, 'Oh, I would've loved to have gone, but I talk out loud to myself when I am watching things like that,' and he was afraid he would disrupt the performance.

The healing effect of art is the theme that recurs. The same psychologist said, 'We will talk about this experience for weeks to

181

come.' I had worried about the effect of the play and it clearly worried the staff there as well but they felt the risk was worth taking. I am sure that it does heal, move towards healing, perhaps because there is a process of recognition and unburdening going on. I've been invited to go back and conduct workshops with them and I've said I would like to. I would be fascinated to do so.

Monday, January 21–Wednesday, February 6

I had a very fruitful month and really enjoyed *Lear*. The morale of the company seems quite good at the moment. We've given our last performances at the NT. It's been interesting coming back to England after the success of abroad and feeling the reticence of English audiences compared with what we've been experiencing in places like Milan and Paris and Hamburg and Cairo, but we've had a good time and played well.

I've been battling on with these Shaws, working all month to try and set them up, but the Gulf War has thrown everybody into a state of panic, particularly the Americans and some of the Jewish people from whom a lot of our finances come; the West End is very quiet at the moment. People are frightened to come over to Europe because they think we're in the war zone. Hussein's threatened terrorist attacks have still not materialised. It's quite crazy, the atmosphere; driving round London it's absolutely empty, the planes are empty and being cancelled, Concorde is flying half full: Howard Panter got to Kennedy Airport to discover his plane had been cancelled and he was upgraded to Concorde, the only flight going out. There's a phoney feeling about the whole of the war, the reporting in particular is quite unreal. There was a distancing effect right from the start when the CNN reporters reported from their hotel room the first bombing of Baghdad by the allies and it has continued in the same slightly unrealistic vein – this new language of war, which is frightening, dispassionate, unconnected, a description of video games.

I've been incredibly busy. *Salem to Moscow* was published on January 31 and was very well received, I was very pleased with the

182

reaction. It's been fairly hectic. I've been travelling around doing publicity interviews and signing books. On Sunday I got home, had to pack which took me all morning, cleaned out the Maida Vale flat, dropped off my bags, got my son to drive me to the plane to Scotland, picked up Richard Jobson, who was doing an interview for the Scottish arts programme 'Excess', and drove to Dundee for a hysterical party with my sister and brother and Aunty Cathy. There was lots of chat, my family putting me in my place. My niece has just broken up with her young man and is off travelling the world, I believe to America; the wanderlust is obviously in the genes. The BBC was filming all this and asked my Aunty Cath if she watched Shakespeare. She said, 'No. It's boring.' My family are organising a bus party to go and see *Lear* when we do it in Edinburgh.

I got up at 6.00 the next morning for more filming on the Law, the hill overlooking Dundee, then went to a book-signing in the town. And in the afternoon there was filming again – my old primary school, St Mary's, Forebank Road, and the Eastern Cemetery, my parents' grave. During the filming at the graveside, I started to laugh because of the inscription on their gravestone. My father had died some twenty years before my mother and my mother had died while visiting my sister in California. Her ashes had been brought back to Dundee and one night my Aunty Cathy had climbed into the Eastern Cemetery, dug a hole in my father's grave and deposited the ashes, urn and all. Later she organised a new gravestone which ended simply: 'Mary Ann Cox, born Dundee 1906, died in the USA.'

After all this I jumped in a car to Edinburgh, caught the seven o'clock flight to London for a meeting with Simon Stokes and Howard Panter about the Shaw plays. It's been very interesting, Michael Holroyd has shown us the missing fourth act of *The Philanderer* and it would be quite a coup if we could include it in our production. I went back to my agent's flat where I'm staying. Rose early in the morning for my French lesson, went to see Betty Glocester about doing some work with Gurdjieff, on to the NT for a lesson in Alexander technique, on to the Critics' Award lunch to receive an award on behalf of Michael Gambon, then to do a video test for a film.

I'm also trying to pursue an acting career: I got a call the other evening in the interval of *Lear*, when I was dressed in roses, from

Michael Mann in Los Angeles, with whom I made the film *Man-hunter*, to ask me to think about playing Colonel Monroe in his coming epic *The Last of the Mohicans*. This I duly did. He sent me the script and I had to call him when I got back after the video test for the other film. I had to go to Methuen to see Briar and arrange an interview with the *Ham and High* and my timetable in the gap between Leipzig and Bucharest. Then I went to see my son in his Russian scenes. I rang Michael Mann in America, rang my designer Tom Piper who had been to Paris to look at the space for the Shaw plays, went to bed and got up to catch the early flight to Prague.

PART SEVEN

The World Tour, III

Prague

Wednesday, February 6

I arrived in Prague at about one o'clock and we drove to this extraordinary edifice, the Praha Hotel, obviously built to house the Communist Party apparatchiks, so luxurious, quite unlike any Eastern bloc hotel I've ever been in. The thing that always strikes me coming to the Eastern bloc is the smell of cigarettes and pungent tobacco, evoking my trips to Moscow. I bought myself a little short-wave wireless and listened to the news when I arrived. I wanted to know what's happening in Moscow with Gorbachev, and the first thing that greeted me when I tuned in my wireless this morning was to hear him say he's decided to hold a referendum on whether there should be a Federal Socialist Republic or whether the whole thing should break up and devolve into a series of smaller countries. Things are moving fast in Russia – I suspect too fast. Gorbachev obviously doesn't want to let go of communism.

The first signs of prosperity in Prague that I noticed driving in from the airport were satellite dishes on the roofs, ready to receive the dreaded CNN which seems to permeate every household in Europe, certainly every hotel in Europe, with its simplistic news coverage of the Gulf War as it proceeds on its merry course. Apparently the Russians have sent their foreign minister for a second attempt at trying to reason with Hussein but Hussein only ended up lecturing him.

I went downtown with Ian and Clare Higgins and Helene Kvale and Sam and Pete Sullivan and Mark. It's a stunning city. The people are a little surly but perhaps I'll get to know them better as the week goes on. It certainly seems much more opulent than the Soviet Union, not so drab. It's been snowing and is 15 below. We walked round the town into Wenceslas Square and went to a restaurant after a great deal of difficulty getting in. We were told normally you have to book a week in advance but we said we were English visitors here at the request of President Havel and they allowed us in. We then tried to buy hats. Mark tried to buy a hat which he was desperate for in the square. There's a black market here, 30 crowns to the dollar. I'd brought one of my hats from Moscow and gave it to David Bradley. We met him at the theatre. Bradley had brought his new video recorder and looked completely incongruous trying to take film as he walked backwards tripping down the steps. It's not his *métier* at all.

The theatre is in two parts and the old part is really an opera house, a huge theatre and not really for plays. Our first horror was that when we got on the stage there was a yawning thirty-foot gap for the orchestra pit which looked worse from the playing point of view than from the audience's. The whole group was shown over the old theatre and given the history, how the stones were brought from all over Bohemia. There is a strong feeling here of Czech nationalism, though Czechoslovakia is a completely fabricated country.

Thursday, February 7

We did a press conference. The snow lay on the ground quite shallowly and it's quite cold. We started at 10 a.m., a pretty boring day just getting into the theatre. It's a beautiful theatre but acoustically a nightmare with a lot of shouting to do. I disgraced myself at the meeting this morning because I complained about the orchestra pit and my director and fellow actors and Head of Touring gave me dirty looks because we have to be nice to the Czechoslovakians, not unpleasant. I don't know why, but there you go. There seems to be a great deal of the cult of personality around; lots of photographs of the President, obviously superseded Lenin, but also the Pope and George Bush – doesn't augur well.

*

I'm in the middle of the first performance in Prague. The audience seem very remote, mainly because of the huge thirty-foot orchestra pit. There's a dead feeling, the humour is flat. I think it is also the people. Kate Nash, my dresser, says they're a bit insular and she may be right. Not very enjoyable, I haven't even broken sweat.

We were presented with huge bouquets of flowers and the reaction was surprisingly good; they seemed to enjoy it though it is a bit long, I think, for them. We threw some of the flowers into the audience. The orchestra pit was so wide we didn't even make the front row. Ian threw a tulip up to Havel. The President grabbed for it, missed and nearly fell out of his box.

We had another of these functions afterwards. The President didn't stay, his bodyguard thought it wasn't a good idea. This was his first public appearance since the start of the Gulf War and he's a target. I met the Minister of Culture and he had just been to see a dress rehearsal of his own play – it seems every minister in this country is a playwright, I don't know if that's necessarily a good thing. Anyway, he was complaining that his play, which was a very small piece and had been directed by the same man seven years previously, was now being done very over-elaborately with all kinds of effects being added so that his little play was disappearing. I knew how he felt. I also spoke to the actor Josef Vinklar who is currently rehearsing *Lear* with Barry Kyle and was telling me that there is a sad tradition to *Lear* in Czechoslovakia. Most of the Lears seem either to have died during a performance or immediately after. I agreed it wasn't a part that made you feel well. I've rheumatism in my arm and my elbow's a bit painful.

Anyway, this morning I had to get up early and go to the Castle and meet various ministers. We had a very fascinating time. We met Peter Oslzly who is Havel's cultural adviser – in theatre matters particularly – and Dousan Sidow, Oslzly's assistant. Oslzly has a special interest in experimental theatre and runs his own theatre in Moravia. He was talking about how to deal with theatre subsidy and the problems of building a constitution. The Czech National Theatre has a staff of over 2,000 and at the moment comprises opera, ballet and the theatre but they want to devolve and cut back. The acting company is about 80, the opera about 50, there are two choruses and two separate orchestras which play in the modern and the old house. The bureaucracy is the impossible thing to dismantle and it's the thing they don't want to let go of, their jobs – which is the difficulty throughout. His master or the Minister of Finance is Vaclav Klaus, whose master is Milton Friedman, so Friedman's economic policies are what Klaus would like to implement, i.e. he would like to abolish all subsidy, particularly for the arts. There are massive problems what with trying to break up the different regions and the autonomy of these regions. There are thirty-eight theatres in Prague and all of these are subsidised by the City of Prague. Only the National is subsidised by the government. There are two National Theatres, one in Prague and the other in Bratislava. They are looking to cut some of the theatres. What the city wants to do is create its own Arts Council to monitor finances quite stringently. Their plans are good ones but as with all Eastern bloc enterprises they have to take care not to throw the baby out with the bathwater – though I suspect that management is very capable here.

We discussed the itinerant working population with young Dousan at lunchtime. Vietnamese immigrants are employed as labourers. They are paid in hard currency and slightly resented by the native population because they do marginally better than the Czechs. I am trying to remember the other things we were talking about. His views on America; fears about Americanisation. The question 'why?' is never asked, why embrace a capitalist ethic? It is clear he feels that the US lacks a profound philosophical basis. He was quite sharp about that and showed great caution over his government's pro-American stance. We also discovered that there are 250 Czech anti-chemical soldiers in the Gulf, purely a defensive force mainly of chemists and doctors.

Just outside the main entrance to the Castle there is something that looks like a tomb, four bulls exactly like the ones we saw at Serapeum, holding some object. Inside the palace, which was Heydrich's headquarters during the war, are some of the most extraordinary examples of Plecnik's Art Deco work.

Ian: And Brian is looking particularly dashing today in a fur outfit with his Giorgio Armani glasses, a multi-coloured scarf. Ian is doing an article for the *New York Times* – get a copy of the NYT in the next four or five weeks.

We went into the Winter Garden which has a huge, low, charcoal-grey marble table, on closer inspection filled with water, like a vast birdbath, and up a small flight of stairs, the most wonderful cylindrical lift. Off the Winter Garden is an extraordinary narrow corridor, on an ellipse, with a series of columns dominated at the end by a single thin black column right in the middle, so fine you wonder how it can stand, elegant but male. Then we moved on to the Rodolfo Room and could hear something in the distance but we didn't know what. We went through that room and into the Spanish Room and there was the most astonishing sight: the Czech Philharmonic Orchestra rehearsing Dvorak's *Stabat Mater*. We were quite overwhelmed; it was very moving.

Deborah: This is the gothic hall we are in now and it is quite extraordinary. Built in 1360, designed by Peter Parler. If you look at the windows they are exactly the same as those we saw, individual lead lights. The architect must have been delighted with this because it is everything that the gothic movement was trying to do, which was to get a light, dancing form of architecture. I have an idea, Brian, for your next production of *Lear* which is to do 'Blow winds' in an echo chamber like this. 1870–1929 the second part was finished.

We had a fascinating morning.

Richard Bremmer hasn't made the trip because he's gone down with suspected malaria. We're all rather anxious about him. David Collings played Albany last night and tonight was the first performance of *Richard III*, in which Sam Beazley very nervously took Richard Bremmer's parts. Sam, because he was playing these other parts, aged seventy-four, spent the whole evening on stage.

Richard Eyre has got stranded because of snow in London and so can't come out for *R.III* and Deborah ended up having an interesting evening with Havel, much to all our envy. Havel was saying that the business of cutting up the maps was particularly poignant, especially with the possibility of Czechoslovakia being re-divided. He is working on his own version of *King Lear* which is a particular favourite of his.

There seem to be hundreds of English teachers in Prague at the moment. The civic forum, which is the ruling body, has just split. And this man Klaus, the Finance Minister who would like to move things towards a Milton Friedman type of economy, has even proposed a tax on books. Apparently the volumes of poetry that were published pre-revolution have considerably fallen off lately. The state did subsidise poets in quite a big way and that doesn't happen now. Oslzly made an interesting point the other day when he said subsidy was the wrong word and it should be looked upon as an investment. I think we in Britain should abolish the notion of subsidy and use the word investment because that's what the theatre is.

We did our performances of *Richard III* which went extremely well and ended with *Lear* last night which had a great reception. Ian asked if I would make a speech, which I did, along the lines of, We thank our brothers and sisters in Prague and something something something something new democracy, and then when we got outside it was wonderful because it was snowing and we had a great snowball fight which went on for hours.

There was a last-night do in the suite of Mary Soames, the Chairman of the NT, who has been staying with us all week. She reminded me that her father was the MP for my home town in 1922 when he crossed the floor, Winston Churchill – small world.

Ian has been bemoaning the fact that we've not met any actors here and puts it down to Barry Kyle's influence, though his Fool did sneak in to see a whole section of *Lear* and Derek Hutchinson got a rather nice present from the actor playing Edgar, 'For E. from E.' But otherwise we've seen none of Kyle's actors.

Monday, February 11

Today is a free day. I got up late and went with Ian to the Jewish cemetery. We went round a very moving museum dedicated to the children of Terezin, Jewish children who were taken away and exterminated between the months of May and October 1943. This was just the school drawings, incredibly touching, and there was one in particular, just a study in light, which was quite enchanting.

The Hotel Praha is unbelievably empty, there doesn't seem to be anybody staying here apart from us. The sauna situation is excellent, a wonderful cold plunge and showers. Ian and I had a sauna and a very interesting massage in which a lady with a harelip, an extremely ugly woman, covered us in what seemed like winter green; we were burning and continued to burn for the rest of the day.

In the evening we had a formal dinner with the Ambassador and obviously our visit has had a great effect. Apparently the President referred to the play in a press conference and talked again about the poignancy of the play and the thing I've always gone on about that if you don't get your family right you don't get your politics right.

Afterwards I walked across the Charles Bridge, an extraordinarily ornate bridge with statues. Prague is a very idolatrous city. It is extremely beautiful, there's no denying it, but it's all a little over-ornate for my liking. The end of the bridge was all lit up and there was a film crew at work: my friend Oliver Tobias – Clare Higgins' naked German from Hamburg – and Robert Walker still doing their Euro series. It's a beautiful city to walk round at night in the snow.

Now we're off to Bucharest. The company are in very good humour. I disgraced myself the other night by going on stage, well, nearly on stage, without my tie. There had been a certain amount of hysteria in *Richard III* and I had to rush off for my tie leaving poor old Joyce to go on by herself. I tried to make it up to her by buying her a bottle of vodka and after the initial sulking she was all right. She said she'd decided to get drunk at the Ambassador's do.

The Ambassador was telling us that he wanted to write a book called *Laughter in the Streets*. People do seem a bit depressed but there is a sort of pessimism about the Czech character. They aren't exactly outgoing, much more an introvert people, people of the valley. But they undoubtedly have the most charismatic leader in the world today. Quite clearly a man of principle and humanity, putting all our politicians to shame. Helene Kvale bought me a pamphlet about the events at the end of November 1989 when the revolution took place. There's one picture of an old woman holding a stick with a look of ecstasy on her face. Let's hope the Czechs get it right – and there's every possibility they may. It is interesting that there is more opulence here, and always has been, than in the rest of Eastern Europe – food where there is none in Bucharest or for that matter Moscow. And there's also probably a better sense of self-preservation. Let's hope they're survivors.

Bucharest

Wednesday, February 13–Thursday, February 14

Here I am in the city of Sofia in Bulgaria, looking out of my window on the fifth floor of the Hotel Pliska and all round me I can see tenement buildings, new post-war constructions. Why, you may ask, am I in Sofia? Well, yesterday we flew from Prague in the afternoon and because of adverse weather conditions, i.e. a mixture of high winds and fog, which seems an unlikely combination but that's what it was, we were unable to land at Bucharest and we had to come on here to Sofia. We sat in the transit lounge at Sofia airport for about two hours, not knowing our fate, playing Trivial Pursuit. Our companions were three young Ethiopians, itinerant workers trying to get a flight out of the country, who had been in the airport for two days and were being given an extremely rough time by the airport officials. Roger Chapman went off to try and get hold of the Embassy staff. He finally found an excellent man from the British Council who came to our rescue and it was decided that we should spend the night in this hotel.

This morning, with Bucharest airport still closed and the weather conditions not due to lift until this evening, we're going to drive to Bucharest, a six-hour journey cross-country in coaches which have been arranged by Roger. We had a very jolly meal at the hotel last night so at least we've had one day's reasonable food before going to Bucharest, though I'm told the situation in Bulgaria really is just as bad as Romania. I look down from my window and see hundreds of people milling about, obviously going off to work, the post office across the road fairly busy, telephones in use, but there is no food, apparently, except in these hotel establishments. Last night we had fetta cheese and tomatoes, something I'd been dying to get hold of in Prague and saw as I passed closed shop windows on Sunday. And Joyce regaled us with stories of the old days.

She had a wonderful story of some play or other in which Edith Evans was playing the lead. There was an actor, now dead, called David Hutchinson and the director said, 'Oh, David, don't you understand, you're in love with her,' to which he replied, 'In love with her! I wouldn't piss on her if she was on fire.'

Crisis points, again the company always seems to come together remarkably well, with great good spirits. A lot of joviality yesterday, particularly from David Bradley to whom I had lent my red fox hat which he has made great and comic use of over the last week: this figure wandering around with a huge fur head and an RNT bomber jacket and a video camera – the most ridiculous sight to be seen last week in Prague. Another thing, we had all our batteries confiscated flying out of Prague because Prague is the biggest exporter of Cemtex; all it needs is a couple of batteries and you have a bomb. The Czech airport authorities were particularly diligent in their search for batteries.

We are just leaving Sofia: we had a bit of an incident with Stephen Marchant's telephone bill and the rate of lev to the pound. His father was dangerously ill in London and Stephen was calling London at a prearranged rate which was doubled when the time came to pay his bill. Stephen refused to pay. They confiscated his passport and refused to allow him to leave. I went to the hotel manager, a large gentleman who was totally unsympathetic and insisted that Stephen should pay. It was a rather ugly scene. We finally got him onto the coach while Roger Chapman settled the matter.

A mile-long queue for petrol, we don't know what we are going to do ourselves about getting petrol. We had a dapper gentleman from the CSA Airlines looking after us, who met us at the airport when we got off the plane last night and seems to have been with us ever since. He arranged for us to go to the airport and pick up a load of trays and bottles of coke filled with some curious green liquid. He's just bid us a rather sad farewell and his parting remark was, 'It's very good for you to see my country. You can see the mess that it's in as you travel through.'

Skirting the airport we're passing the most unbelievable shanty towns, obviously no sewage or anything, barely any electricity, it's poverty on a scale that I've never seen. Someone's just said that it pulls you up short to see this ... unbelievable houses. There's a kind of snobbery about it, I don't know why it's so much more shocking to look at something like this than the squalor in Egypt ... we're going through rather a nice area now, suddenly the houses look a bit better ... Just left the town of Pleven or Plevna as it was known, which has the last surviving statue of Lenin in Europe – one of the last – the one they overlooked, rather a nice one . . . We've just arrived at the Romanian border, having been through the Bulgarian border, to be greeted by people from the British Council, people from the Romanian Ministry of Culture and a television group who have been waiting for us. McKellen is out doing his stuff, peace and goodwill to all. They've taken the passports again.

We've now reached Bucharest, where there is light, contrary to popular belief; there are cars but there are no people; cobbled streets. On the right you can see the cemetery of the Revolution, it's pretty massive – oh, my God – with lots of foliage on identical tombs with crosses on them, from December 1989 . . . it's very poignant.

We've arrived at the Hotel Ambassador which is like old times back with the Soviets. I have what is probably called the suite, with one light bulb in one room, one light bulb in the other, black-and-white television – so basic it isn't true. Anyway, what else can you expect? I'm going to see Ian's room now . . . It's exactly the same as mine.

Ion Caramitru explained to us that the hotel was right where the revolution started. The troops moved into the centre of Bucharest when the people were beginning to demonstrate. For the whole of that day Ion had not been able to get home and had been trying to ring his wife who was heavily pregnant. When he finally got through she told him the general in charge of the army had been shot and it wasn't clear whether it was suicide or not. Ion went down to tell the soldiers in the tanks who were nervous and edgy, uncertain what to do, their guns pointing at the crowd. He talked to them calmingly till confirmation came through on their headphones and they immediately pulled off their ear-pieces and started to weep. He persuaded one of the tanks to drive to the broadcasting studios which they took over.

Ion took us to the Actors' Union to do a press conference, which went quite well and was mainly about finance, the problems of financing the theatre in these countries – as we'd discussed in Prague. We were shown all over the building, which used to be Nicu Ceauşescu's house. A lot of MFI fittings. It had been owned by an opera singer, became the Communist Party headquarters, and then the Ceauşescus, brother and sister, moved in. The most notable thing about it was the bullet holes in the attic rooms – in the curtain and through the bathroom window. It's reckoned this was where the Securitate bodyguard probably lived. Five Orthodox priests were brought in to exorcise the house after the revolution, but it was decided to leave the bullet holes *in memoriam*.

We're now in the National Theatre canteen. We've just heard that there's a production going on tonight which the techs didn't know about. They're having real difficulty turning things around.

Embassy incident: in the Embassy compound bar some American marines accused our American sound-designer of being pro-Arab because he was wearing an Arab scarf. It got a little bit heavy. No fisticuffs.

The Piata Victoria. I'm standing outside the Communist Party headquarters and on my left I can see the burnt-out museum building which housed the library; next to it is the Securitate headquarters, a tall imposing green building like the Lubyanka, all the windows are at least fifteen to twenty feet from the ground. The Hotel Athénée Palace, made famous by Olivia Manning in her *Balkan Trilogy*, is opposite and we're looking at the balcony from which Ceauşescu made his final speech. He completely misinterpreted the crowd who started to jeer him and quite inexplicably he signalled to them to sit down. The crowd shouted him down and that was the start of the revolution.

We had a very good evening tonight. We went to see a wonderful production of *Medea* directed by Andrei Serban which he'd first done about twenty years ago at the Romanian National Theatre. It was stunning, the Medea was marvellous; her voice production wasn't all that it might have been but her actual playing was remarkable. We also went to the British Embassy where I met a fascinating man, the Vice-President of the Liberal Party, Professor Sorin Botez. Between the ages of nineteen and thirty-four he was in prison. I asked him what had sustained him and he pointed to his wife. When I asked him how he had coped he said, 'Well, I just played the works of Shakespeare over in my head and some wonderful classical

195

music.' A man of great warmth and charm and twinkle. I was very taken by him. He is also a big collector of autographs apparently.

Then Ion Caramitru arrived. He'd been at a meeting earlier and complained that the finance ministry had told him that culture would be given 0.33 per cent of the GNP which is precisely 0.33 per cent of nothing, and he said it was very hard to see how he was going to manage with his company of fifty-three and two 400-seater theatres. There was further discussion at the Embassy do and then at his house about what the GNP actually was. He gave us a wonderful meal, with his wife Micaela – a fairly smart flat, very like the flats I saw in Russia, with video and TV and a wonderful collection of icons and painted eggs – Macedonian pie, a cheese and vegetable pie, hummus and olives and lettuce. I really wanted to find out what the GNP was but they kept going on about Romania being a rich country, that the Romans plundered the Transylvanian hills for gold and that it was the grain basket of Eastern Europe, which is ironic because the bread is the worst I've tasted in my life. There's an enormous pride in being Romanian, but it's hard to see on what premise the new Romania can be built.

Karen Archer, who was there at dinner, has travelled out from England to join her husband David Collings, bringing with her a whole load of supplies, clothes and stuff for the hospitals, but the great fear is that they will get sold on the black market. She's already been to two hospitals with Clare and David Bradley, who did his magic show for some of the kids. She's done a remarkable job to bring all this out here.

Friday, February 15–Sunday, February 17

Friday, February 14 or 13, I'll double-check [15th]. I slept in late this morning because I had a late night last night after Caramitru's dinner. There was a blizzard raging. Caramitru was due to go to Prague and Richard Eyre was due to come from London but we weren't sure whether he was going to make it as he missed his meeting with Havel last week.

I went to the Ambassador's residence for lunch and met the

Ambassador, Mr Atkinson, who was a perfectly pleasant gentleman, and a nice man from Nomura Bank, Mr Prindl, a really charming man who was on his way to Moscow to discuss banking and the possibility of training people in Russia. We talked a lot about Russia and training and investment in training and how to run good training courses. Terrible that the Brits just aren't doing it. I had a talk with Alec Paterson from the British Council who has been here in Romania for three years and who seems to have made quite an impression. He's an old-style missionary type but struck me as being someone concerned with problems of reciprocity in cultural affairs. It was clear that he was worried about what Britain would get out of it and hadn't really cracked the fact that one has to treat these Central European countries as third world countries and it's an investment, a means of helping a nation towards democracy while at the same time acknowledging its great cultural assets.

Ian couldn't understand why Caramitru would not accept the fact that his company would have to be cut now that he has been allotted 0.33 per cent of the GNP. They are going to have to face up to it here. The companies will have to go but they don't want to give up the privileges they've achieved: the one thing that the Eastern bloc has really taken care of is theatre, though in the last few years Ceauşescu did ignore the theatre, I think.

We met the Minister of Culture, Pleschu, who seemed a very nice, erudite man. He's in a difficult position, not a Communist though the government is still largely ex-Communists, a member of the government but not a member of parliament: not all members of the government are necessarily members of parliament but they have been voted onto the government by parliament and they have to answer to parliament. Pleschu was Head of English at Bucharest University and fell into disgrace under Ceauşescu. He was sent off to work on the farms and when Ceauşescu fell the peasants summoned him into the large farmhouse and asked him to explain what had happened. Some of them were crying, tearing their hair and being very emotional, they didn't understand what had happened and Pleschu had to explain very carefully what had been going on and what Ceauşescu really represented. He was made Minister of Culture but has had a rough ride from the press. There's a sort of neo-Fascist paper, *Vatra*, Home of Romania or Hearth of

Romania, which has accused him of stealing two gold pens from Ceauşescu and other nonsense. The press have become very free and very *Sun*-like in their simplification because most of their readers are extremely ill-educated. Apparently there are something like 130 newspapers in Romania, I must check that, there do seem to be an awful lot on sale. One of the views the press has promulgated is that Timisoara is where the whole revolution really began – it's in the south and received much more information from the outside world via television than they did in Bucharest so they knew what was going on.

Halfway through lunch came the announcement that Saddam Hussein was prepared to talk about leaving Kuwait. The Ambassador was naturally sceptical. He told us about what had happened to him during the revolution. We were actually lunching in his new residence, the old residence had been opposite the TV station, and on the day of the revolution while he was at work in the Embassy – another building – his house had been taken by snipers to fire on the TV station. People fired back and his wife who was in the house at the time had to hide in the basement. They lost quite a lot of their stuff because they'd just arrived and it was all in packing cases up in the roof which caught fire from the tracer bullets. The telephone lines came down and he couldn't communicate at all with his wife, which must have been quite distressing.

After lunch we went to the theatre, Ian and Roger Chapman and I, through fairly thick snow and it was quite hazardous. Bucharest is deep in snow now. We arrived at the theatre to find that our crew had been working all night on the set. Although they'd been told the theatre would be empty in fact the directors of the National Theatre of Romania had put on *Medea*, *Trojan Women* and *Elektra* for a Frenchman who was interested in transferring them to Paris in the summer. It really screwed up our lot. They'd vowed they'd never do all-nighters again and suddenly there they were doing an all-nighter. They were exhausted, poor guys. And there had been a lot of difficulties with the Romanian crew. Ken P. was beside himself with anger at the fact that they'd buggered off a few times during the night and it was much quicker just to do things on their own.

Also, when we got there I blew a fuse because I took one look at the set and was in despair. The stage was vast, huge, they were using its whole depth but the opening of the stage, the proscenium, was quite small. The auditorium itself was raked and there was a forestage which again wasn't being used, so there was an immense gap between the audience and the players. I'd had enough of it, I really had. I'd put up with this production in Cairo and in Prague. Prague we had the thirty-foot orchestra pit, in Cairo the theatre was dreadful, like a Muslim ladies' loo, a huge cavernous space, and our production which was designed to be on a rake and to look like an expanse of space has to be lit really well which they can never, ever do as it is done at the Lyttleton. It's not the fault of the electricians who work extremely hard, Laurie Clayton who has been with us for most of the tour has worked very, very hard. So I just threw a fit and said I wasn't prepared to play *Lear* again in an endlessly compromised fashion as I have done so many times. The last performance that made any sense was Paris.

We brought up the forestage and tacked down a piece of white cloth and brought the whole stage further down, we moved the set, moved the back wall further down and Laurie was able to light, not brilliantly, but well, as well as could be expected. We don't have an Assistant Director, Cordelia Monsey has now left us, but I must say I was really, really angry because I'd had enough of compromising myself and the work, especially after discovering so much about the intimacy of the play as I had done at Broadmoor.

The performance started fairly shakily; I was a little apprehensive and didn't know if any of things we'd done were going to work, but they seemed to be OK. The flower scene went the best I've ever done it. What was marvellous was that the audience seemed rapt and were most appreciative at the end of each scene. I didn't think it was going particularly well but I did think it was going better than I thought; however at the end the applause was tremendous, they were really excited. Afterwards we had a party and the Romanian actors kept coming up to me and saying how human my Lear was; that's always been what I wanted, to make Lear as human as possible. They said I must be Romanian and not English, probably the best compliment of all.

Also at the party were the crew who were exhausted. Apparently there had been a blackout during a scene which I wasn't involved in. Gerry, one of the electricians, was weeping because he had been so tired he had made a mistake. He said he'd been at the National for ten years as a technician. It was very touching to see how distressed he was. I talked to the crew during the evening; most of them had been working in shifts just to get through the show because they were completely worn out and I just don't think people should be put through this. They say it's theatre but then we should travel in a very, very simple way. The setting isn't what's important, it's being with the audience, accessible to the audience, which is really important. These theatres we've played in we haven't really checked out beforehand. Anyway, the evening was deemed a success.

At the party, Ian was talking about Radu Beligan, who used to be Director of the theatre before the revolution. He had been regarded as a supporter of Ceauşescu and fired and is now living somewhere in Bucharest. Ian is going to see him. Ian was saying he didn't know what he would have done in the same situation; with twenty-five years of living under Ceauşescu he thought he might have behaved in the same way. Given his political history, I think Ian underestimates himself but it's very hard to know what you'd do as an actor. The thing is that in the *Mephisto* situation – the film about the German actor who collaborated with Hitler in order to protect his job – or the Elia Kazan situation, in order to make films, one has to make compromises. I think in the end maybe when I was younger I would have done that myself, but now I couldn't, I couldn't do it, I would have left the country. Maybe not, but I feel that – I don't know – I feel that what I've done I've done by hard work and in a hard way, and even as a leader of this company I find myself compromised and I don't like it. I feel not free and it's not a good feeling.

We're in a model village which is just outside Bucharest and has lots of wonderful houses transplanted from Transylvania and Moldavia. I bought a nice Moldavian rain mask that I liked. The snow is very deep and it's absolutely idyllic, like a winter wonderland.

It's Saturday night and we've just finished a performance of *Richard III* which went very well. Poor Gerry, tonight he fainted while doing the lights and was sent up to bed. It's very sad that people are having to do this and the sound boys are now going to have to take it in turns to mind the equipment because a couple of sets of earphones have been stolen. Tomorrow we have two performances, one at 10.30 which is ridiculously early and then one at 6 p.m.

All the shops are shut. They are shut today which is Sunday so it's understandable, but they were also shut yesterday.

Just done a morning show of *Richard III* and everyone was fairly weary but the audience received it very well. Everyone is getting nervous about what's going to happen when *Lear* finishes and *Richard III* carries on. Ian was quite funny, he had had nothing to eat all day and was given a tin of sardines. He was starting to drool over it and getting frenetic.

The performance of *Lear* has just finished and my voice is shaking because everybody has respiratory infections in this town and my chest is pretty bad. It's been a long day, we've been at it since 10.00 this morning. Here is a note that came with some flowers:

> Nobody can play Sir William Shakespeare plays better than his English people. I've seen with your remarkable help that somewhere in England, Sir William Shakespeare is still alive. Thank you. A simple man, Teodor Hanciu.

Monday, February 18

This has been another eventful day. We did a boring press conference this morning at which somebody asked about the relation between tyrants and said what about the relation between Alexander the Great and Buddha – a young Romanian student being cheeky. I had an interesting afternoon with Andrea, a young director here, who told me about her ideas for setting up – trying to make an honest buck, I suppose – a marriage bureau for marrying young Romanian actresses to northern Italian farmers, a fairly bizarre idea. Amazing discussing the ethics of that in relation to her work as an artist and director – highly dubious, but given the situation she's lived in probably highly understandable.

The show was very successful. It was the last performance of

Richard III and again the reaction was phenomenal. In Prague and even more so in Bucharest I see where Richard Eyre's inspiration lies for his production of *Richard III*. Whatever reservations I have about the production it is quite clear the effect the performance has on audiences in the Eastern bloc and it validates the whole conception. It was a big evening for Richard and he made a wonderful speech at the end of the performance. When he asked for an interpreter the audience almost with one voice cried, 'No interpreter. In English, we understand.' The only blemish on the evening was the notable silence when the name of Ion Caramitru was mentioned. I think poor Ion overstayed as Vice-President and has hurt himself. I hope he will recover. The nice thing is that Helene Kvale will take over Lady Anne; she did an audition for Richard Eyre.

These are the last hours of Bucharest. It's been really strange, like Russia, a formidable experience, seeing how people reconstruct their lives, the traps in their way, the problems of someone like Andrea, and trying to encourage her in the thought that her theatre should reflect the turmoil of her country with a positive face.

Leipzig via London

Tuesday, February 19–Sunday, February 24

This has been an amazingly hectic week back in London, culminating in the news tonight – I've just got back from Manchester after doing a book-signing and I'm off to Stratford tomorrow – that Peter Jeffrey has got septicaemia and is in hospital, which means that Bruce Purchase will have to go on as Gloucester and I will have to take him through it on Monday. So I'm going to need to rest and I'm going to need to rest a lot. I could do without Stratford tomorrow, but that's life.

Collateral bombing, these are the phrases of the war, the land forces have just moved in. This is Sunday, February 24, and the battle for Kuwait has now started. All those young men who are going to die –

collateral bombing means killing all men and boys, body counts. This whole vocabulary of the war is quite revolting.

Monday, February 25–Wednesday, February 27

Tuesday morning, February 26.

We arrived in Leipzig on Sunday after a long journey by bus – three hours from Berlin through the night. The usual hanging about at Gatwick which I'm afraid I've had enough of. How do you plan a holiday after this and avoid an airport? Stay at home.

After Hamburg and the experience of West Germany I wanted to do my research into the background of East Germany. The GDR bore the full brunt of war reparations: in the ten years after the war, while West Germany received 4 billion dollars in Marshall Aid from the US, East Germany had to pay 10 billion in war reparations to the Soviet Union; whole factories and railway lines were dismantled and sent east. The strain became too much and three months after Stalin's death in 1953 East German workers went on strike. As a result, the USSR cancelled all outstanding reparations and the workload was reduced. One fifth of the population left East Germany before 1961.

Because of a dispute yesterday morning between Deborah Warner and the National Theatre, Deborah is no longer with us. She is sitting in Spain without leaving a forwarding address and working on a script of *Electra*. So I was asked if I would take the rehearsal yesterday, which I did. It meant two understudies had to go on as well as Bruce and Sam Beazley, who had to play Bruce's parts. We worked from 11 in the morning through to 5 p.m. with about a twenty-minute break and then the performance. I've been suffering from tennis elbow and I can hardly lift my arm. It's the result of a year of pulling wheelchairs on rakes and all kinds of things. Bruce was, needless to say, very nervous. He's been with the company for a year, a wonderful actor, very distinguished. Ironically, he played my father many years ago in a television series about Henry II.

I was shocked at the lack of detailed work done on the scenes between Gloucester and Edmund. I couldn't believe what had gone on in the rehearsals. Kae-Kazim had my sympathies as Edmund and so did Derek Hutchinson, but I realise that this must have been a lot to do with a breakdown in communication between Peter Jeffrey and Deborah – and whose fault I couldn't say. Sometimes a director and actor just don't click. I've been in that position myself. But the simplest things didn't seem to have been negotiated in these scenes and it meant that one would really have had to start again from scratch, which was impossible to do in the time. I did a patch job as well as I could and told Bruce to use his largeness as a sensualist, that that was what was important, that sensual drive. He used it, I think, to advantage and certainly in the Dover scene his wailing was incredibly moving. With luck he will get another shot in Dresden as Peter is still ill. We had a very good reception; I was very pleased.

Unfortunately I have not been able to see anything of Leipzig yet though I'm intending to see a bit this morning. It seems rather a grey town and a little polluted, it has to be said, but of course it's the Leipzig of Bach. He was *Kapellmeister* at Thomaskirche and I want to go round today and see quite a lot of the sights. I have a few hours before my call. Leipzig's demonstrations were really the start of the East German revolution and it's sad to think that almost a year to the day from the demolition of the Wall there are unemployment marches and the first signs of scepticism about reunification. The city went bust just before the RNT got here, so there was a panic about how our hotels were going to be paid.

Sam Beazley, Stephen Marchant, David Collings, Richard O'Callaghan, David Bradley and I all made a pilgrimage to Colditz yesterday. On our way we passed a couple of Russian military convoys. There is still a very strong Russian presence in East Germany but in the one Russian base we passed there was an aimlessness about the soldiers – all dressed up and nowhere to go. We had a wonderfully enthusiastic guide called Stefan, sporting a Ben Turpin moustache, who showed us all over the castle. We saw the tunnel dug by the French from the top floor down the wall of the stairwell and under the church. It was discovered because the foolish French hadn't thought of a proper way of getting rid of the debris and decided to hide it in the ceiling of their quarters. Of course the weight was too much and the ceiling gave way.

The great thing about Colditz was the theatrical atmosphere, which appealed to us all. There's a little museum dedicated to the efforts of the prisoners, with photographs of every escape attempt and objects like the wooden sewing machine built by a prisoner to make fake uniforms, the skeleton keys, cardboard German hats. On his return home the prisoner who made the sewing machine was accused by his spouse of being undomestic; it was only the fall of the Berlin Wall which allowed him, now in a wheelchair, to drag his wife back to Colditz, be lifted up three flights of stairs, and defiantly display his extremely domestic contribution to the war effort.

Colditz is now a geriatric/mental hospital and has been for some time. In fact it was a hospital before it was a prisoner of war camp.

At lunchtime the restaurants were closed and when we asked why, we were told because it was lunchtime, German logic at work. Outside the castle, up a little side-street, I found a stall selling brotwurst and bits and pieces. David Bradley had to have a Colditzburger.

We had a good evening, the British Ambassador came and Bruce did his Clarence which was very good. I saw it in the afternoon. Ian's voice was a bit dicky so I had to make the speeches of thanks to the Ambassador, the Lord Mayor and the Director of the theatre.

We're off to Dresden this morning. I went to the Thomaskirche to see Bach's tomb and the museum and pay my respects to Leipzig as a city of culture. '

Postscript. The bedsheets tried to strangle me. They're incredibly narrow in these Eastern bloc hotels.

Throughout the tour we've had scenes of haggling about hotel bills. It may be an old African custom to bargain wherever you go but certainly Mr Kae-Kazim follows this custom to the letter.

Dresden

Wednesday, February 27–Saturday, March 2

There was more damage done here by the war than to Hiroshima and Nagasaki put together. It's extraordinary, like a hideous housing estate built in the middle of a bombed-out version of Prague. Some of the buildings are really beautiful, baroque, very, very ornate, and then you come to these long *strasses* which look like the most appalling council developments on the outskirts of Glasgow or Edinburgh.

We've just been to the opera to see Rossini's *Barber of Seville*. It was drab, terrible, I couldn't believe it. I have an ambivalent attitude to opera at the best of times but when it's really bad, I can't stand it.

I want to relate a strange dream I had last night: I was with some of the younger actors at a workshop set up by Deborah to which she had invited the writers William Styron and William S. Burroughs. The workshop was being conducted (funny, my dreams which have left me lately have suddenly come back and I'm beginning to remember them), anyway, the workshop was conducted by Deborah and somehow I wasn't involved, I was supposed to be doing some kind of musical thing which was very odd. I left Deborah to her workshop, came back and was in the playground at school when I saw her again and she greeted me. I'd had a conversation with Burroughs in which he said he was no longer taking drugs, he was off them and would never work and take drugs at the same time, it was impossible. He was wandering around, the worse for wear, in a slightly comatose state. I wasn't too alarmed by this and walked over to greet Deborah and she seemed very pleased. I embraced her and we started walking when suddenly Burroughs turned and smiled at Deborah and said, 'Hello Deborah'. Deborah waved, and then Burroughs threw a lance which looked like a piece of fencing and went straight at her and landed in her thigh, to which she remarked, 'You see what happens when I become so open.' I can't quite work out what this dream means but it was very vivid and strong.

I'm about to go to the theatre and help Bruce with his work because he's feeling a bit neglected.

*

A story about the GDR by a woman who taught English at Leipzig University: she had just been to the British Embassy to try and get on one of the courses in Britain teaching English. She had tried to leave the GDR on several occasions. The first time she was told she couldn't go because her father lived in the West, and then when her father died she was told she was too attractive and might be lured into marriage, and the third time she was told she was too old and they wouldn't waste currency on her. Finally, when she went to the British Embassy and spoke to the cultural attaché, Ian Fraser, he suggested the summer courses but she asked to go earlier because she'd been studying Wordsworth and wanted to go during the daffodil season.

The performances over the week at both Leipzig and Dresden have not been very remarkable. The Leipzig audiences were much more appreciative than the Dresden ones. Dresden is known by the people of the north as lying in the valley of the clueless, the inhabitants seem particularly knocked-off and the people that we met at the theatre functions seemed to be very right-wing. Apparently there was a mild protest the other night at a performance of *Richard III* when Ian and I, who are quite tired and fairly giggly, corpsed in the Lord Mayor scene. The local actors were shocked at our lack of discipline and the sounds of seats being thrown back were heard. If we offend it is with our goodwill.

Talk about a full circle, here we are in the middle of Dresden, surrounded by this terrible mixture of buildings, the over-decorated and the under-designed. I've come to a memorial, a bombed-out church, the Frauenkirche, and in the centre of it are cranes on crosses. These are the cranes I saw in Hiroshima. It's very strange, the sight of these same origami cranes woven into the barrier round the statue of Martin Luther. The Frauenkirche was the largest Protestant church. It is the symbol of what happened to Dresden: 35,000 people killed. The city at the time was packed with refugees from the Eastern front because war was nearly over. The allies were already at the doors of Berlin when this act of revenge took place. The day we arrived in Dresden was the day the Gulf War ended, the day the bombs stopped dropping on Baghdad, and scrawled by the church we see: *Dresden 1945, Phnom Penh 1971, Baghdad 1991*.

Edinburgh

Monday, March 4–Saturday, March 9

It's Wednesday, March 6, we've just done a performance of *Lear* and I'm about to go in and do *Richard III*. I've been ill for the last three days, which is ironic considering I'm coming to the end of this business. But I had to move house and uproot myself at the weekend and finally I collapsed – which is what I did yesterday – out of complete exhaustion. Anyway it's great to be back in Edinburgh, the first time I've played in this city since 1969. The reaction was wonderful last night, considering how ill I was and considering everything else. It was fabulous. Peter Jeffrey's come back – about a stone lighter. I hope he'll last the week. Had a long chat over tea, the great Scots pastime, with my cousin Sheena and her son, Colin Ritchie, who wants to be, would you believe it, an actor.

It's been quite a week one way and another. This is Saturday night. I had the flu for the first three days, I was struck down and from my sick bed I went to do the first night of *Lear*. I spent most of the time in bed, recuperating.

On Thursday morning Ian and I went to see Jack and Jean, Ian Charleson's parents. They're a marvellous couple and I don't think they'll ever get over his death. We had a bowl of soup with them and a toddy and a chat. We went to see the grave, which is only five minutes from the house. It was a lovely morning, very misty as it has been all week. I haven't seen it like this since I was a child.

There were two performances on Thursday and after the last show we went to an extraordinary place run by an Armenian, Petros, in what I believe was a former police station opposite Holyrood Palace. We did some Armenian dancing – well, I didn't do very much but the two Davids certainly kicked up a storm. It was very

208

jolly, Eve, Helene, David Bradley, David Collings, Deborah who has joined us for the last few days, and it went on until very, very late.

The following day I had to get up and do a boring interview with the *Edinburgh Evening News*, which apparently goes out today, and then I did lots of exhausting bits and pieces, Scottish TV etc. I had a lovely lunch with John McGrath and Liz McLennan at their house, talking to them about their work over the years with the 7.84 company. The consistency of principle in their life made me feel very envious.

Then we did *Lear*, the penultimate, to which my family came from Dundee in their hordes. They'd hired a bus and it was amazing, absolutely amazing, because afterwards we went back to my suite at the Caledonian Hotel and didn't have enough glasses and there wasn't enough beer and there wasn't enough this and that and my relatives from Edinburgh turned up plus an old boyhood friend of mine, Frank Charlton, it was all very moving – for me certainly, very touching.

It's been great to come back to Scotland, particularly because it was the first time ever that my brother has seen me on the stage and I was really thrilled to bits about it. We had a splendid evening, which went on until the early hours, and this morning I did a signing session for my book and had tea with my aunty Jean, my Edinburgh aunty. She was my mother's youngest sister who ran away to Edinburgh and married a Protestant. In true convert form, she has been a staunch member of the Kirk for the last sixty years. The theatrical member of the McCann family, Aunty Jean was my landlady during my first job at the Edinburgh Lyceum.

I then had to rush here and do the last performance of *Lear* and it was going well, I thought it was going well, I thought it was going fine until the last scene and as soon as I went on in the last scene I just completely broke down. It was very strange, partly relief, and the reception was wonderful at the end of the performance. I just came into the dressing room and cried like a baby. It was so many many things and, I don't know, I was completely overwhelmed by it. Also I was extremely glad that Jack and Jean Charleson came to see it, I was particularly pleased, and we went to have some tea together. My cousin Sheena's urged me to come back up to Scotland and I really feel I want to make the effort.

A nice fellow, too, from the Scottish Youth Theatre, a nice chap called Robin Peoples, has asked me to become a Patron of the Scottish Youth Theatre, a wonderful organisation networked throughout Scotland, not Glasgow-based which the earlier version was. So I feel really thrilled to be asked and I now feel ready to do something like that. There we are.

I've just been speaking to Nick Blane. His dad died of cancer near the beginning of rehearsals but he was very keen that Nick should do this job. Those first three weeks, Nick knew there wasn't much time for his father. He's just told me how much the collapse of the Berlin Wall meant to his dad. Last Sunday as we flew out of Berlin he just kept saying, 'I want to tell my dad.' Apparently he said to Susie Engel, 'I want to tell my dad about this whole year, I just want to tell my dad,' and then he cried throughout the journey home.

Quotes from the back wall of *Richard III*. There has been a tradition of writing things on the back wall of *Richard*:

> *Is it all right if I don't stay for the whole show?* (Cordelia Monsey). *Oh, they're not here yet* (Nick Blane on arriving in Richard Bremmer's room in Tokyo). *Where's my, my, my, my Guardian?* (Everybody). *Will that lady who eats too many cakes be there?* (Mitch, talking about Clare). *Fuck the baggage, let's build the fire* (Scott, Prague). *If we be conquered, let men conquer us and not the fucking vans* (Richard O'Callaghan in Milan). *What's that? Oh, the floor* (Bremmer, Milan). *I ain't walking up no fucking hills* (George Cunliffe, Prague). *We might spot the Happy Eater on the way* (Nick Blane boarding the bus to Romania). *They're so badly paid, they have to share cigarettes* (Lady Soames talking about the Prague room-parties). *I think I'm lagging* (George). *Welcome to Bulgaria* (British Council in Bucharest). George *I think I'm lagging* was Nottingham, Cardiff, Cork, Cairo, Prague, Leipzig and Edinburgh. Spike, on being offered a fruit pastille, returning from Romania, *No, no, I need vegetables. Anything you say on tour doesn't count* (Clare, Prague). *What, fifty of my followers within a fortnight! What's the matter, sir, in a clap?* (Brian, Milan). That's me and I'm misquoted.

London

Sunday, March 10

It's all over. After the show, I couldn't wait to shave my beard off. I hadn't seen my face for eighteen months. I went to the party forty years younger – but nobody noticed. I left about 3 a.m. I waited for the crew to arrive but after that I was too knackered and went back to the hotel and started to pack.

Next morning I made my way to Glasgow to look at the new Scottish Youth Theatre and do a masterclass at the Royal Scottish Academy of Music and Drama. Flew to London in the evening and went to my agent's to find three scripts based on a Fay Weldon novel waiting for me.

The following day I got up early, moved into my new place, and went to the first rehearsal of *Gitta's Atonement* – a play about psychiatry adapted from the German by Shaw – which I've been arranging over the last week, persuading actors on board; I've got Charlotte Cornwall and Diana Quick and Helene Kvale, Stephen Boxer, Oliver Ford Davies. We rehearsed for a week without anyone for the main protagonist and finally got Robin Ellis. We're doing it at the National Theatre studio.

Here I am in my new flat at Kilburn Priory, filling my diary, thinking, hoping, wondering about a holiday.